IB
AND FORMENTERA

THE MINI ROUGH GUIDE

Forthcoming titles include

Devon & Cornwall • Malta
Tenerife • Vancouver

Forthcoming reference guides include

Cuban Music • Personal Computers
Pregnancy & Birth • Trumpet & Trombone

Rough Guides online

www.roughguides.com

Rough Guide Credits

Text editor: Polly Thomas
Series editor: Mark Ellingham
Production: Mike Hancock
Cartography: Ed Wright, Katie Lloyd-Jones

Publishing Information

This first edition published March 2001
by Rough Guides Ltd,
62–70 Shorts Gardens, London WC2H 9AH

Distributed by the Penguin Group:

Penguin Books Ltd, 27 Wrights Lane, London W8 5TZ
Penguin Putnam, Inc., 375 Hudson Street, New York 10014, USA
Penguin Books Australia Ltd, 487 Maroondah Highway,
PO Box 257, Ringwood, Victoria 3134, Australia
Penguin Books Canada Ltd, 10 Alcorn Avenue,
Toronto, Ontario, Canada M4V 1E4
Penguin Books (NZ) Ltd,
182–190 Wairau Road, Auckland 10, New Zealand

Typeset in Bembo and Helvetica to an original design by Henry Iles.
Printed in Spain by Graphy Cems.

© Iain Stewart 2001. 368pp, includes index
A catalogue record for this book is available from the British Library.

ISBN 1-85828-660-3

IBIZA
AND FORMENTERA

THE MINI ROUGH GUIDE

by Iain Stewart

with additional contributions by
Martin Davies

ROUGH
GUIDES

We set out to do something different when the first Rough Guide was published in 1982. Mark Ellingham, just out of university, was travelling in Greece. He brought along the popular guides of the day, but found they were all lacking in some way. They were either strong on ruins and museums but went on for pages without mentioning a beach or taverna. Or they were so conscious of the need to save money that they lost sight of Greece's cultural and historical significance. Also, none of the books told him anything about Greece's contemporary life – its politics, its culture, its people, and how they lived.

So, with no job in prospect, Mark decided to write his own guidebook, one which aimed to provide practical information that was second to none, detailing the best beaches and the hottest clubs and restaurants, while also giving hard-hitting accounts of every sight, both famous and obscure, and providing up-to-the-minute information on contemporary culture. It was a guide that encouraged independent travellers to find the best of Greece, and was a great success, getting shortlisted for the Thomas Cook travel guide award, and encouraging Mark, along with three friends, to expand the series.

The Rough Guide list grew rapidly and the letters flooded in, indicating a much broader readership than had been anticipated, but one which uniformly appreciated the Rough Guide mix of practical detail and humour, irreverence and enthusiasm. Things haven't changed. The same four friends who began the series are still the caretakers of the Rough Guide mission today: to provide the most reliable, up-to-date and entertaining information to independent-minded travellers of all ages, on all budgets.

We now publish more than 150 titles and have offices in London and New York. The travel guides are written and researched by a dedicated team of more than 100 authors, based in Britain, Europe, the USA and Australia. We have also created a unique series of phrasebooks to accompany the travel series, along with an acclaimed series of music guides, and a best-selling pocket guide to the Internet and World Wide Web. We also publish comprehensive travel information on our Web site: **www.roughguides.com**

Help us update

We've gone to a lot of trouble to ensure that this Rough Guide is as up to date and accurate as possible. However, things do change. All suggestions, comments and corrections are much appreciated, and we'll send a copy of the next edition (or any other Rough Guide if you prefer) for the best letters.

Please mark letters "**Rough Guide Ibiza and Formentera Update**" and send to:

Rough Guides, 62–70 Shorts Gardens, London WC2H 9AH, or Rough Guides, 4th Floor, 345 Hudson St, New York, NY 10014.

Or send email to: mail@roughguides.co.uk
Online updates about this book can be found on
Rough Guides' Web site (see opposite).

The author

Freelance journalist and co-author of the Rough Guides to Guatemala, Maya World and Central America, Iain Stewart first took his bucket and spade to the Balearics as a toddler and has been returning regularly ever since. He currently divides his time between London and Ibiza.

Acknowledgements

Thanks to Mike Hancock for patient typesetting, Ed Wright, Katie Lloyd-Jones and Maxine Repath for brilliant maps and Nikky Twyman for painstaking proofing. The author would like to thank Polly Thomas for her ruthless editing, Martin Davies for considerable historical and cultural input, Senyor Antoni Roselló, Kirk Huffman of C'an Forn, Nacho, Paul Richardson for inspiration, Amics de la Terra, Jazz and Jill, Bas, Andy Wilson, José Saché, Roberta Pachá, Zuka, Base and Chill, Medrano, Marital, Juanjo and Fiona for coming along for the ride.

CONTENTS

CONTENTS

MAP LIST

MAP SYMBOLS

═══	Paved road	▲	Tower
───	Dirt road	▥	Archeological site
······	Path	▣	Fuel station
───	Waterway	P	Parking
⩘	Mountain range	⬚	Beach
▲	Mountain peak	⬚	Salt pan
✈	Airport	▬	Building
♦	Point of interest	✚	Church
◠	Cave	◉	Accommodation
⚓	Lighthouse	▣	Restaurant/bar/café
✗	Windmill	✉	Post office
⚐	Viewpoint	ⓘ	Information office
⚬	Campsite	Ⓗ	Helipad

Introduction

Widely acknowledged to be the world's clubbing capital, **Ibiza** is an island of excess, a unique and almost absurdly hedonistic place where the nights are celebrated with ferocious vitality. Thanks largely to the British tabloid press, the popular perception of Ibiza is of a charmless, high-rise party island, but, while it's true that high-octane techno tourism is central to the local economy, there's much more to the island than the clubbing scene.

> "Pitiuses" is the general term used to refer to Ibiza, Formentera and their outlying islets; in turn, the Pitiuses are part of the Balearic archipelago, which also comprises Mallorca and Menorca.

Dotted around Ibiza's dazzling shoreline are more than fifty **beaches**, which range from expansive sweeps of sand to exquisite, miniature coves nestling beneath soaring cliffs. Many of the best beaches were insensitively transformed into functional holiday resorts in the 1960s, but plenty of pristine places remain if you're inquisitive enough to seek them out. Ibiza's hilly, thickly wooded **interior** is equally beguiling, the countryside peppered with isolated whitewashed villages and terraced fields of almonds, figs and olives. The charismatic capital, **Ibiza Town** harbours most of the island's architectural treats, including the spectacular walled enclave of **Dalt Vila**, and a historic port area replete with hip bars, stylish restaurants and fashionable boutiques. Within easy distance are the small beach resorts of Talamanca and Figueretes, pleasant enough places to spend a day by the sea.

However, for a better selection of beaches, head for the disparate **east coast**, dotted with family resorts such as Cala Llonga and Es Canar as well as beautiful undeveloped coves like Cala Boix and Cala Mastella, and the slender sands of Aigües Blanques, a naturist beach. The east coast's main town, **Santa Eulària** is an agreeable but unremarkable place, though it does boast a decent crop of restaurants and a helping of culture and history on the Puig de Missa hilltop above the town. The isolated, remote **northwest** is Ibiza's least developed region, with a rugged coastline ideal for hiking, the two small resorts of Portinatx and Port de Sant Miquel, and a smattering of spectacular coves including the cliff-backed bays of Cala d'en Serra, Benirràs and Portitxol. Inland, the scenery is equally impressive, dominated by the soaring pine-clad Els Amunts hills; between these peaks lie a succession of diminutive, isolated settlements such as Sant Joan and Sant Miquel, each with its own fortified whitewashed church and a rustic bar or two.

Though you'll often see and hear Castilian Spanish in the Pitiuses, the official language is Catalan, which has replaced Castilian on street signs and official documents in recent years. We've followed suit and used Catalan in this guide, giving Castilian alternatives where useful. For more on language, see p.312 onwards.

On the western coast, Ibiza's second largest town, **Sant Antoni**, is no architectural beauty, but can boast a dynamic bar and club scene, plus a selection of mellower chillout bars on its much-touted **Sunset Strip**, home of the infamous

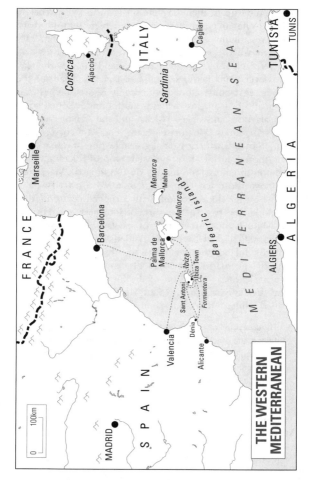

THE WESTERN
MEDITERRANEAN

Café del Mar. Sant Antoni's beaches tend to get packed in high season, but west of the town, Cala Conta and Cala Bassa offer luminous water and fine, gently shelving sands. The wildly beautiful **south** of the island boasts over a dozen beaches, from tiny remote coves like Cala Llentrisca and Cala Molí to the sweeping sands of Salines beach and Es Cavallet on the outskirts of Ibiza Town – two of Ibiza's most fashionable places to pose.

Serene, easygoing **Formentera**, the other main island of the Pitiuses, is just a short ferry ride south of Ibiza. With few historical sights apart from some sombre fortress-churches and a few minor archeological ruins, Formentera's main appeal is its relaxed, unhurried nature and its miles of ravishing, empty sands that shelve into breathtakingly translucent water. Comprised of two flat promontories linked by a narrow central isthmus, the island is very thinly populated; even **Sant Francesc Xavier**, the attractive but drowsy capital, is little more than village-sized. Though Formentera is equally dependent on tourism, it's much less developed than Ibiza; its best **beaches** – Platja Illetes and Platja Migjorn – have barely been touched, and the sole resort, Es Pujols, is a pleasantly small-scale affair.

When to go

Ibiza and Formentera are at their hottest between June and late September, when cloudless skies are virtually guaranteed. The heat can get intense in July and August, but even at this time of year cooling sea breezes usually intervene to prevent things getting too uncomfortable. Winter in the Pitiuses is pleasantly clement, with very little rainfall, and temperatures (even in January) high enough to enable you to sit comfortably outside a café.

As far as crowds go, there's a very clearly defined **tourist season** on both islands that begins slowly in early May, peaks in August, and slowly winds down throughout September. By the end of October, when the last charter flights depart, both Ibiza and Formentera are very quiet, and remain in virtual hibernation until the following year. Winter is a wonderfully peaceful time for a visit, and though you'll find that only a fraction of the bars and restaurants are open – and just one club, *Pacha* – it's an ideal time for an inexpensive break, as hotel and car rental prices plummet.

IBIZA CLIMATE TABLE

	AVERAGE DAILY TEMP (°C)	AVERAGE HOURS OF SUNSHINE PER DAY	AVERAGE NUMBER OF DAYS WITH RAIN
Jan	15	6	5
Feb	15	6	4
March	17	7	3
April	19	8	4
May	22	9	2
June	25	10	2
July	28	11	1
Aug	29	12	1
Sept	27	8	3
Oct	23	6	7
Nov	19	5	6
Dec	16	5	5

BASICS

Getting there from Britain and Ireland

By far the easiest and cheapest way to get to Ibiza and Formentera is to fly to Ibiza airport; if your final destination is Formentera, you'll then have to catch one of the very regular ferries and hydrofoils that shuttle between the two islands.

Most people arrive on **charter flights** from the UK and Ireland, either as part of a package holiday or on a flight-only basis. You could also consider travelling **via mainland Spain**, from where there are plenty of flight and ferry connections, though this may not be that cost-effective and is probably best considered if you want to explore other parts of Spain as well.

For more on getting to Ibiza from the rest of Spain, see p.18 onwards.

CHARTER FLIGHTS

Between Easter and October, you should have no problem

finding an inexpensive, direct **charter flight** from any of the main British airports and from Dublin airport. All the main tour operators fly to Ibiza, and even in August there are usually plenty of spare seats to be had; however, bear in mind that there are no charter flights to Ibiza after October 31. Travel agents, such as those listed on p.6–7, Teletext (ⓦ *www.teletext.com*) and the Internet are the best places to start looking for flights; visit ⓦ *www.thefirstresort.com* or ⓦ *www.cheapflights.co.uk*, or any of the tour operators' Web sites listed on p.8–9. In addition, newspaper travel sections and magazines such as *Time Out* and *TNT* are well worth a browse.

Fares are generally pretty inexpensive. If you book two to three months ahead, a return ticket typically averages £160, while if you leave it to the last minute, rates often drop to around £100. Lack of flexibility is one the most obvious inconveniences of a charter flight; all carriers operate on weekly and fortnightly return schedules, so if you want to visit Ibiza for, say, a long weekend, you'll probably have to start looking at scheduled airlines. Another possible drawback of booking a charter service is timing; most flights arrive in the early hours of the morning – perfect for hitting the clubs, but not so convenient if you're slightly less up-for-it.

SCHEDULED AIRLINES IN BRITAIN AND IRELAND

Aer Lingus ⓣ 0645/737 747 (Northern Ireland); ⓣ 01/886 8888 (central booking line); ⓦ *www.aerlingus.ie*. Twice-weekly direct flights to Madrid from Dublin (May–Sept only).

Air Europa ⓣ 0870/240 1501; ⓦ *www.air-europa.com*. Flights from Gatwick to Ibiza via Madrid, Barcelona and Palma.

British Airways ⓣ 0845/722 2111 (UK); ⓣ 1800/626 747 (Dublin); ⓦ *www.british*

-*airways*.com. Flights from Heathrow and Gatwick to Barcelona, Palma, Alicante, Valencia and Madrid, plus Manchester, Birmingham and Glasgow to Madrid and Birmingham to Barcelona, with the flight to Ibiza with Iberia under the Oneworld partnership.

British Midland ☏0870/607 0555 (UK); ☏01/283 8833 (Ireland); ⓦ*www.britishmidland.com*. Flights from Heathrow to Madrid, Barcelona and Palma all year round.

EasyJet ☏0870/600 0000; ⓦ*www.easyjet.com*. From Luton and Liverpool to Palma, Barcelona and Madrid.

Go ☏0845/605 4321; ⓦ*www.go-fly.com*. Direct flights to Ibiza from Stansted, daily between May and September only.

Iberia ☏0845/601 2854 (UK); ☏01/671 1290 (Dublin); ⓦ*www.iberia.com*. Scheduled flights from Heathrow and Gatwick to Ibiza via Barcelona, Alicante, Palma, Valencia or Madrid, plus flights from Manchester direct to Madrid, from where there are regular flights to Ibiza.

SCHEDULED FLIGHTS

Just three airlines offer **scheduled flights** from Britain, and only no-frills airline Go fly **direct** to the island, from Stansted between May and September only. Iberia and Air Europa fly to the island all year round, usually via Barcelona or Palma, but you may have to change planes in Madrid, Valencia or Alicante. There are no scheduled flights to Ibiza from any Irish airport at any time of year, so it's best to get there via London or Madrid.

It pays to **book well in advance** because, although flights to mainland Spain or Palma are easy to come by, connecting flights to Ibiza are frequently fully booked, particularly in the summer.

Scheduled **fares** vary considerably, and depend mainly on the flexibility of the ticket; you'll have to pay a little more if

GETTING THERE FROM BRITAIN AND IRELAND

you want the freedom to change dates. Iberia usually have some good winter deals with special offers from around £130 return, though £160–£200 return is a more standard price. The cheapest tickets are usually out of one of the London airports, but British Airways also offer also direct flights to Madrid from Glasgow, Birmingham and Manchester, and flights to Barcelona from Birmingham, while Iberia offer direct Manchester to Madrid flights. As Iberia and British Airways are partners in the Oneworld alliance, shuttle connections to Ibiza can be easily arranged between these two airlines.

TRAVEL AGENTS

Avant Garde, 3 Betterton St, London WC2 ⊤ 020/7240 5252. Flight and villa rental packages via Ibiza Trips, plus quality apartments and bespoke Ibizan holidays are also available.

AVRO, Vantage House, 1 Weir Rd, Wimbledon, London SW19 8UX ⊤ 020/8715 4440; ⓦwww.avro-flights.co.uk. Specialists in discounted charter and scheduled flights.

Joe Walsh Tours, 8–11 Lower Baggot St, Dublin 2 ⊤ 01/678 9555. Inexpensive packages and flights.

North South Travel, Moulsham Mill, Parkway, Chelmsford, Essex CM2 7PX ⊤ 01245/608 291; ⓦwww.nstravel.demon .co.uk. Excellent service and competitive scheduled flight prices. Profits aid projects in the developing world.

Spanish Travel Services, 138 Eversholt St, London NW1 ⊤ 020/7387 5337. Spanish flight and package specialists.

STA Travel, 86 Old Brompton Rd, London SW7 3LH ⊤ 0870/160 6070; plus branches across the UK; ⓦwww.statravel.co.uk. Independent travel specialists, plus discounted flights.

Thomas Cook, 45 Berkeley St, London W1X 5AE ⊤ 020/7499 4000; plus branches through-out the UK; 118 Grafton St, Dublin 2 ⊤ 01/677 1721;

Ⓦ *www.thomascook.com*.
Ibiza packages and flights.

Travel Bug, 125 Gloucester Rd,
London SW7 4SF ℡ 020/7835
2000; 587 Cheetham Hill Rd,
Manchester M8 5EJ
℡ 0161/721 4000;
Ⓦ *www.flynow.com*. Large
range of discounted flights.

Usit CAMPUS, 52 Grosvenor
Gardens, London SW1W 0AG
℡ 020/7730 3402; for
branches nationwide call

℡ 0870/240 1010;
Ⓦ *www.usitcampus.com*.
Youth/student specialist.

Usit NOW, 19–21 Aston Quay,
O'Connell Bridge, Dublin 2
℡ 01/602 1600; 66 Oliver
Plunkett's St, Cork ℡ 021/270
900; Fountain Centre, College
St, Belfast BT1 6ET
℡ 02890/324 073;
Ⓦ *www.usitnow.ie*.
Inexpensive flights for
students and young people.

PACKAGES

Most people travel to Ibiza, and to a lesser extent
Formentera, as part of a **package holiday**. All sorts of different deals are available, from simple self-catering apartments to luxury hotels. These package holidays generally
represent very good value for money, though accommodation is usually in somewhat soulless large hotels or apartment blocks in the main resorts. You'll also have far less
flexibility to change your accommodation or resort if you
book a package holiday than if you make your own travel
and hotel arrangements, though if you protest strongly
enough to your holiday rep, alternatives can sometimes be
arranged.

On the plus side, package holidays are very convenient,
with direct flights from all the main UK airports, inclusive
airport transfers, and children's activities often laid on in the
hotels. Package holidays can also represent exceptional
value, with **prices** falling to almost absurd levels, especially
if you travel early or late in the season. In May and October
there are usually deals available through Teletext from as lit-

tle as £120 for a week, or around £150 for two weeks (based on two people sharing). At these prices, you'll almost certainly be allocated basic self-catering accommodation in Sant Antoni, as other resorts tend to be more expensive.

Listings of accommodation in Ibiza and Formentera start on p.205.

Listings of accommodation in Ibiza and Formentera start on p.205.

Numerous tour operators now also promote **clubbers' holidays**, which in most cases are package holidays dressed up with a bit of promotional hype. Check carefully what these deals actually include: many often involve nothing more than a free mix-CD of dubious musical content and accommodation in a noisy hotel. The better operators, like Kiss in Ibiza, include free club entry, while Ibiza Trips can book quality hotels and villas in the hills, as well as providing guest-list club entry to customers.

TOUR OPERATORS

Astbury Formentera
☏01642/210 163;
ⓦ www.formentera.co.uk.
Formentera specialist offering a wide selection of villas, cottages and apartments.

Dancexport ☏0870/907 0099;
ⓦ www.dancexport.com.
Holidays in Sant Antoni and Platja d'en Bossa, and bargain last-minute deals.

Club Freestyle ☏0870/550 2561; ⓦ www.club -freestyle.co.uk. Inexpensive

holidays geared to the youth market, plus flight-only deals.

Clubbers' Guide to Travel
☏0870/513 3833; ⓦ www .ministryofsound.com/travel.
Ministry of Sound's burgeoning travel division has some excellent clubbers' deals with well-selected accommodation all over the island. The Web site is also a good source of cheap charter flights.

First Choice ☏0870/750 0001;
ⓦ www.firstchoice.co.uk.

Package holidays to all the major Ibizan resorts, and plenty of high-season charter flights from airports across the UK.

Ibiza Trips ⓣ020/7240 5252; ⓦ*www.ibizatrips.com*. Clubbers' breaks in conjunction with Manumission, with everything from self-catering apartments in Sant Antoni to luxurious country villas, plus guest passes for club nights.

JMC ⓣ0870/607 5085; ⓦ*www.jmc-holidays.com*. Massive selection of charter flights and holidays in Ibiza, from one of the UK's biggest tour operators.

Kiss in Ibiza ⓣ0870/750 0450; ⓦ*www.kissinibiza.com*. Well-established clubbing holidays, organized in conjunction with 2wenties. Punters are guaranteed free entry to one club every night.

Lincoln Travel ⓣ0870/055 6093; ⓦ*www.partyinthesun .com*. Inexpensive packages and flights.

Panorama ⓣ01/670 7666; ⓦ*www.club25.ie*. Irish-based company offering youth/clubbers' breaks to Ibizan resorts, and direct flights from Dublin.

Portland Holidays ⓣ0870/500 2200; ⓦ*www.portland -direct.co.uk*. Packages to nine Ibizan resorts, including Talamanca.

Thomson ⓣ0990/502 555; ⓦ*www.thomson -holidays.com*. Vast selection of package holidays, plus flight-only deals.

GETTING THERE FROM BRITAIN AND IRELAND

Getting there from North America

With no direct flights and a very limited number of tour operators offering vacations in the Balearics, Ibiza and Formentera are not major destinations from North America.

You're not entirely on you own, however, as plenty of travel agents can arrange flights and many can book accommodation. Getting to Ibiza from North America usually involves changing planes in at least one Spanish airport; Barcelona is the preferable gateway, with the greatest number of connecting flights and ferry services to Ibiza, though there are also air routes via Madrid. However, if you're flying from New York, you might want to take advantage of the relatively inexpensive flights to London, and pick up an onward flight from there (see "Getting there from Britain and Ireland", p.3, for details).

The best **fares** to Ibiza are usually found via the discount travel agents listed on p.13, though you could also contact the airlines direct and see if they have any special promotional offers. The cheapest regular tickets (APEX and special APEX fares) can also be competitive, although you'll generally have to pay in advance and are likely to be penalized if you change your schedule. Regardless of where you buy your ticket, the fare will depend on the **season**: around mid-May to late September is high season, but rates also increase around Easter and Christmas.

AIRLINES IN THE US AND CANADA

Air Europa ☎1-800/327-1225; ⓦ*www.air-europa.com*. Five flights a week from New York to Madrid, with regular, year-round internal shuttle connections on to Ibiza.

American Airlines ☎1-800/433-7300; ⓦ*www .americanair.com*. Daily non-stop flights from Miami and Chicago to Madrid.

British Airways ☎1-800/247-9297 (US); ☎1-800/668-1059 (Canada); ⓦ*www .britishairways.com*. Twice-daily flights from Toronto and daily flights from Montréal and Vancouver, plus 21 gateway cities in the US, to Madrid and Barcelona all via London.

Continental Airlines ☎1-800/231-0856; ⓦ*www .flycontinental.com*. Daily non-stop flights from Newark to Madrid.

Delta Airlines ☎1-800/241-4141; ⓦ*www.delta-air.com*. Daily non-stop flights from New York and Atlanta to Madrid and Barcelona.

Iberia ☎1-800/772-4642; ⓦ*www.iberia.com*. From New York, Miami and Chicago non-stop to Madrid, with frequent shuttle connections on to Ibiza.

United ☎1-800/538-2929; ⓦ*www.ual.com*. Daily non-stop flights from Washington DC to Madrid.

Iberia and Air Europa are the only two companies that fly **from the US** to Ibiza, via connecting flights from a mainland Spanish airport. Both offer very competitive

return fares, at around $595 in low season and $765 in high
season from the East Coast, and $650 in low season, $850
in high season from the West Coast. Alternatively, travel
agents can often get similar rates by flying you from the US
to Spain with one of the other airlines listed on p.20, and
organizing a connecting flight to Ibiza with either Iberia or
Air Europa; from the East Coast, expect to pay around
$625 in the low season, or $800 in the high season; from
the West Coast, reckon on paying around $700 in low sea-
son, $900 in high season.

There are no non-stop flights **from Canada** to Spain, so
you'll have to fly there via the US, or alternatively via a
European capital, and then on to Ibiza. Round-trip fares to
Ibiza start at around CAN$950 in the low season or
CAN$1320 in the high season from Toronto or Montréal
via London or Madrid, and CAN$1295/1740 from
Vancouver.

TOUR OPERATORS IN THE US AND CANADA

Central Holidays, 120 Sullivan Ave, Englewood Cliffs, NJ 07632 ☎1-800/227-5858; ⓦ www.centralh.com. US agents for Iberia, offering good flight deals as well as flight and accommodation packages in three- and four-star Ibiza Town hotels.

European Escapes, 111 Ave del Mar, Suite 220D, San Clemente, CA 92672 ☎1-888/387-6589; ⓦ www.europeanescapes.com. Villa rentals in rural locations.

Odysseus Travel, PO Box 1548, Port Washington, New York, NY 11050 ☎1-800/257-5644; ⓦwww.odyusa.com. Gay vacations company with choice of packages based in Ibiza Town.

Rainbow Travel, c/o Algonquin Travel, 3777 Strandherd Drive, Nepean, ON K2J 4B1 ☎613/825-4275; ⓦ www.rainbowtravelnetwork.com. Gay tour operator with locations throughout Canada, offering good-value two-week packages in Ibiza.

DISCOUNT TRAVEL AGENTS IN THE US AND CANADA

Airtech, 588 Broadway, Suite 204, New York, NY 10017 ☎1-800/575-8324; ⓦ*www .airtech.com*. Standby seat broker; also deals in consolidator fares and courier flights.

Council Travel, Head Office, 205 E 42nd St, New York, NY 10017 ☎ 1-800/226-8624 or ☎ 1-888/COUNCIL; plus branches all over US; ⓦ*www.counciltravel.com*. Nationwide specialists in student travel.

STA Travel, 10 Downing St, New York, NY 10014; ☎1-800/777-0112; plus branches all over the US; ⓦ*www.sta-travel.com*. Worldwide specialists in independent travel.

TFI Tours International, 34 W 32nd St, 12th Floor, New York, NY 10001 ☎1-800/745-8000. Consolidator.

Travac, 989 6th Ave, New York NY 10018 ☎ 1-800/872-8800; ⓦ *www.thetravelsite.com*. Consolidator and charter broker mostly dealing in flights to Europe.

Travel Avenue, 10 S Riverside, Suite 1404, Chicago, IL 60606 ☎ 1-800/333-3335; ⓦ*www.travelavenue.com*. Discount travel company.

Travel CUTS, 187 College St, Toronto, ON M5T 1P7 ☎1-800/667-2887; plus branches all over Canada; ⓦ*www.travelcuts.com*. Canadian student travel organization.

Unitravel, 11737 Administration Drive, St Louis, MO 63146 ☎ 1-800/325-2222; ⓦ*www.flightsforless.com*. Inexpensive flights.

GETTING THERE FROM NORTH AMERICA

Getting there from Australia and New Zealand

There are no direct flights from Australia or New Zealand to Ibiza, so you'll have to change planes two or three times in order to reach the island. It's possible to get to Ibiza within 24 hours if you travel via Asia, or 30 hours via the US – not counting time spent on stopovers – with flights routed through Asia generally being the cheaper option. Virtually all international flights enter Spain via Barcelona or Madrid airports; of the two cities, Barcelona is the better gateway to Ibiza, with more flight connections and regular ferries.

Flying to Ibiza **via London** is the cheapest route, as the city is the main destination for most international flights from Australia and New Zealand. You'll have no problem finding an inexpensive charter flight to Ibiza from London between May and October, though if you're travelling to

Ibiza in winter it's best to book your (scheduled) connecting flight well in advance. For more on getting to Ibiza from London, see p.3.

AIRLINES IN AUSTRALIA AND NEW ZEALAND

Garuda ⊤1300/365 330 (Australia); ⊤09/366 1855 or ⊤1800/128 510 (New Zealand). Several flights weekly from major cities in Australia and New Zealand to London, with either a transfer or an overnight stop in Bali or Jakarta.

Japan Airlines (JAL) ⊤02/9272 1111 (Australia); ⊤09/379 9906 (New Zealand); ⓦwww.japanair.com. Daily flights to Madrid from Brisbane and Sydney, and several flights a week to Madrid from Cairns and Auckland with either a transfer or overnight stop in Tokyo or Osaka. Code-shares with Iberia and Air New Zealand.

Olympic Airways ⊤02/9251 2044 or ⊤1800 221 663 (Australia); ⓦwww.olympic -airways.com. One flight a week to Barcelona and three weekly to Madrid from Melbourne and Sydney with a transfer in Athens, plus three flights weekly to London from Sydney and two weekly from Melbourne.

Qantas ⊤13/1313 (Australia); ⊤09/357 8900 or ⊤0800/808 767 (New Zealand); ⓦwww .qantas.com.au. Daily flights to Madrid from major cities in Australia and New Zealand, with transfers in either Singapore, Bangkok or London.

SriLankan Airlines ⊤02/9244 2234 (Australia); ⊤09/308 3353 (New Zealand); ⓦwww.airlanka.com. Three flights a week to London from Sydney with a transfer and overnight stop in Colombo.

United Airlines ⊤13 1777 (Australia); ⊤09/379 3800 (New Zealand); ⓦwww.ual .com. Several flights weekly to Madrid from Sydney, Melbourne and Auckland, with transfers in LA and Washington.

The best place to start the search for **tickets** are travel agents, such as those listed below, or the Internet; ⓦ *www.travel.com.au* and ⓦ *www.sydneytravel.com* offer discounted fares online. Return **fares** vary according to the season; you'll pay the most during the high season (mid-May to mid-Sept). Regular return economy flights to Ibiza cost around A\$2050 in the low season and A\$3050 in the high season from eastern Australian cities, and around NZ\$2300 and NZ\$3300 respectively from Auckland.

The least expensive return flights to London with Garuda or SriLankan Air are A\$1950/NZ\$2250 in high season, dropping to around A\$1400/NZ\$1700 in the low season, while Olympic Airways and Japan Airlines are usually a little more.

If you're planning to visit Spain as part of a wider global trip, **round-the-world (RTW)** tickets offer greater flexibility and better value than standard return flights. Using a network of airlines, such as Star Alliance (Air New Zealand–Lufthansa) and Oneworld (Qantas–British Airways–Iberia), they are priced according to the number of stopovers you make. RTW tickets from Sydney or Auckland to Singapore, Delhi, Frankfurt, Madrid, Ibiza, Madrid, New York, LA, Honolulu and back home again start at A\$2499/NZ\$2950.

DISCOUNT AGENTS

All the agents listed below offer discounted airfares (including RTW tickets) and most can also arrange car rental.

Budget Travel, 16 Fort St, Auckland, plus branches around the city ☎09/366 0061 or ☎0800/808 040; ⓦ *www.budgettravel.co.nz*.

Destinations Unlimited, 220 Queen St, Auckland ☎09/373 4033.

Flight Centres Australia: 82 Elizabeth St, Sydney (☏ 02/9235 3522), plus branches nationwide (for the nearest branch call ☏ 13 1600). New Zealand: 350 Queen St, Auckland (☏ 09/358 4310 or ☏ 0800/354 448), plus branches nationwide; ⓦ www.flightcentre.com.

Northern Gateway, 22 Cavenagh St, Darwin ☏ 08/8941 1394; ⓔ oztravel@norgate.com.au. Discount flights to the UK from Darwin.

STA Travel, Australia: 855 George St, Sydney; 256 Flinders St, Melbourne; plus other offices in state capitals and major universities – for nearest branch call ☏ 13 1776. New Zealand: 10 High St, Auckland ☏ 09/309 0458; plus other offices in major cities and university campuses – for nearest branch call ☏ 0800/874 773; ⓦ www.statravel.com.

Student Uni Travel, 92 Pitt St, Sydney ☏ 02/9232 8444; plus branches in Brisbane, Cairns, Darwin, Melbourne and Perth; ⓔ sydney@backpackers.net.

Trailfinders, 8 Spring St, Sydney ☏ 02/9247 7666; Elizabeth St, Brisbane ☏ 07/3229 0887; Hides Corner, Shield St, Cairns ☏ 07/4041 1199; ⓦ www.travel.com.au.

Usit Beyond, cnr Shortland Street and Jean Batten Place, Auckland ☏ 09/379 4224 or ☏ 0800/788 336; plus branches in major cities; ⓦ www.usitbeyond.co.nz.

GETTING THERE FROM AUSTRALIA AND NEW ZEALAND

Getting there from the rest of Spain

Getting to Ibiza (and then on to Formentera) by plane or by ferry from mainland Spain or from Mallorca is a fairly simple business. Flying is by far the quickest option, of course: Ibiza is a 45-minute flight from Barcelona or thirty minutes from Valencia.

Fares vary tremendously, depending on the time of year and even the time of day you want to fly, and because availability can be difficult at all times of year it's best to book as far ahead as possible. There also plenty of **ferry** routes to Ibiza from the mainland ports of Barcelona and Dénia, plus a fast hydrofoil from Valencia in the summer months. Prices on the ferry routes are consistent throughout the year, though there are often special deals available outside the tourist season.

FROM THE MAINLAND

If you want to **fly** to Ibiza, it's best to travel **from Barcelona**, which has more services than any other

Spanish city. Iberia fly four times a day between October and April, rising to nine times a day in July and August; expect to pay around 20,000ptas/€120 for a return ticket throughout the year, though you'll often come across promotional fares that cut the price as low as 15,000ptas/€90 return; these are particularly common in the low season. Air Europa fly three times a day throughout the year, and are usually a little cheaper, with economy fares typically costing around 18,500ptas/€111 return, though again promotions often slash prices to as low as 14,350ptas/€86.23 return.

Though it's a little further from the Balearics, there are also plenty of services to Ibiza **from Madrid**. Air Europa fly twice daily between May and September, and once a day throughout the rest of the year, with economy fares typically around 23,000ptas/€138 return. Iberia have six daily flights between July and mid-September, and three flights a day during the rest of the year, with economy prices set at around 26,500ptas/€159 return. Both companies offer promotions that can periodically cut fares to as low as 15,500ptas/€93.14 return. Iberia also have three daily flights to Ibiza **from Valencia** and a daily flight **from Alicante** all year round; economy tickets from both cities cost around 17,000ptas/€102 return, but promotions can slash this to 13,500ptas/€81 return.

There are regular connections **by sea** between Ibiza and Barcelona, Dénia and Valencia. **From Dénia**, the nearest mainland port to Ibiza, Baleària operate twice-daily ferries to Sant Antoni (6295ptas/€38; 4hr 30min) plus a daily service to Ibiza Town (same prices; 4hr 45min). **From Barcelona**, Trasmediterránea operate four services per week, and Baleària operate three; journey time is nine hours, and both cost 7350ptas/€44.17. **From Valencia**, Trasmediterránea operate a daily hydrofoil between June and late September (6920ptas/€41.58; 3hr 15min), and a weekly Sunday service for the rest of the year (6150ptas/€37; 6hr).

AIRLINES IN SPAIN

The airlines listed below all have bilingual Web sites, which often have details of special offers and last-minute deals, as well as a few English-speaking staff manning the phone lines.

Air Europa ☏ 902 401 501; ⓦ *www.aireuropa.com*.
Iberia ☏ 902 400 500; ⓦ *www.iberia.com*.
Spanair ☏ 902 131 415; ⓦ *www.spanair.es*.

FROM MALLORCA

Getting to Ibiza from Mallorca is simple, with frequent air and ferry services, plus a fast hydrofoil connection in the summer months. **By air**, from Palma, Iberia fly nine times daily between May and late September, and six times daily during the rest of the year; an economy ticket costs around 14,500ptas/€87 return, but fares are sometimes slashed as low as 12,000ptas/€72 return. Air Europa fly twice daily between May and September, and daily in winter from Palma, with economy tickets costing around 11,700ptas/ €70.31 return, while Spanair fly three times daily between June and September, with economy tickets costing around 12,500ptas/€75.10 return.

There are also excellent connections from Mallorca **by sea**. Baleària operate a Palma–Sant Antoni ferry daily in winter, and twice daily between May and October (4350ptas/ €26; 5hr 15min), and another year-round daily service to Ibiza Town (4350ptas/€26; 5hr). Trasmediterránea operate a Palma–Ibiza Town ferry three times a week in winter (3900ptas/€23.50; 5hr) and a daily high-speed hydrofoil between mid-May and mid-September (5750ptas/€36.75; 2hr 15min).

FERRY COMPANIES

Timetables and full details of seat, cabin and vehicle transportation rates are listed on companies' Web sites, though only Trasmediterránea have an English option. Alternatively, call the company offices direct; there are usually some English-speaking staff on hand. It's advisable to book ahead, especially if you plan to travel in the high season, when demand is at its peak.

Baleària ⊤ 902 191 068; Ⓦ www.balearia.com.

Trasmediterránea ⊤ 902 454 645; Ⓦ www.trasmediterranea.es.

Visas and red tape

EU citizens (and those from Norway and Iceland) need only a valid national identity card to enter Spain for up to 90 days. However as the UK has no identity card system, British citizens must travel with a passport. Citizens of the US, Canada, Australia and New Zealand do not need a visa for stays of up to 90 days. Bear in mind, though, that visa requirements do change, and it's always advisable to check the current situation before you travel.

SPANISH EMBASSIES AND CONSULATES ABROAD

Australia,15 Arkana St, Yarralumla, ACT 2600 ☏02/6273 3555.

Britain, 20 Draycott Place, London SW3 2RZ ☏020/7589 8989.

Canada, 74 Stanley Ave, Ottawa, ON K1M 1P4 ☏613/747-2252.

Ireland, 17a Merlyn Park, Ballsbridge, Dublin 4 ☏01/269 1640.

New Zealand, contact the consulate in Australia.

USA, 2375 Pennsylvania Ave NW, Washington, DC 20009 ☏202/728-2330.

VICE CONSULATES IN IBIZA

Italy, c/Joan d'Austria 5, Ibiza Town ☏971 315 428 (Mon–Fri 9.30am–1.30pm).

Netherlands, Via Púnica 2B, Ibiza Town ☏971 300 450

(Mon–Fri 9am–1.30pm).

United Kingdom, Avgda Isidor Macabich 45, Ibiza Town ☏971 301 816 (Mon–Fri 9am–3pm).

For **longer stays**, EU nationals can apply for a *permiso de residencia* (EU residence permit) once in Spain. A temporary residency permit is valid for up to a year, and you'll need an extension after that (valid for up to five years). Applications need to be made first with the Policia Nacional on Avgda de la Pau (the inner Ibiza Town ring road; ☏971 305 313). You'll either need to produce proof that you have sufficient funds (officially around 5000ptas/€30.12 per day) or show a contract of employment.

To **work** in Ibiza legally, whether as a holiday rep, English-language teacher and bar worker, you need to obtain the *permiso de residencia*. During the summer months, hundreds of young Europeans (mainly Brits) illegally work the season without a residency permit, thus avoiding tax and legal employment status; accordingly, most are paid very little – typically 5000ptas/€30 for a night-shift in a bar or as part of a club's promotional team. Though you may have the time of your life, bear in mind that you could face prosecution if you are caught working illegally. If you're a citizen of the US or Canada, you cannot legally work in Spain without a special application from an employer. However, you can apply at the Policía Nacional office for one ninety-day visa extension; you may be asked to prove you have sufficient funds (5000ptas/€30.12 per day), but after 180 days all overseas citizens must leave Spain.

VISAS AND RED TAPE

Information, maps, Web sites and the media

The best general information about Ibiza and Formentera is available from tourist information offices on the islands, or from the Internet. There's little point contacting the Spanish Tourist Board in advance, or visiting their Web site (ⓦ *www.tourspain.es*), as only very general background information about the Pitiuses is available.

In Ibiza, you'll find offices at the airport, Ibiza Town, Sant Antoni and Santa Eulària, as well as La Savina in Formentera, all of which are detailed within the Guide. Staff usually speak English, are generally very helpful, and will dole out leaflets on everything from Carthaginian archeological sites to horse riding as well as accommodation lists, detailing self-catering apartments and campsites; however, they won't make bookings for you. There's also a vast amount of written and Internet-based information about Ibiza and Formentera, covering everything from contemporary politics to the local football leagues, but focusing mostly on the club scene. Six free English language listings magazines are published in the summer months.

SPANISH TOURIST BOARD OFFICES ABROAD

Australia, 1st Floor, 178 Collins St, Melbourne, VIC ☎03/9650 7377 or ☎ /800 817 855.

Britain 22–23 Manchester Square, London W1M 5AP ☎020/7486 8077; ⊛*www.uk.tourspain.es.*

Ireland contact the British office.

Canada, 2 Bloor St W, 34th Floor, Toronto, ON M4W 3E2 ☎416/961-3131; ⊛*www .tourspain.toronto.on.ca.*

New Zealand contact the Australia office.

USA, 666 Fifth Ave, 35th Floor, New York, NY 10103 ☎212/265-8822; San Vincente Plaza Bldg, 8383 Wilshire Blvd, Suite 956, Beverly Hills, CA 90211 ☎323/658-7188; 845 North Michigan Ave, Suite 915-E, Chicago, IL 60611 ☎312/642-1992; 1221 Brickell Ave, Suite 1850, Miami, FL 33131 ☎305/358-1992; ⊛*www.okspain.org.*

MAPS

Free city and island **maps** are available in all the tourist information offices and are generally more accurate than anything available at home. If you do want to buy a map before you leave, Geocenter publish the best (1:75,000) map, while in Ibiza and Formentera, the best option is the widely available 1:76,500 map published by Distri Mapas Telstar. If you rent a car or bike, you'll usually be given a reasonable map from your rental company. In Formentera, the maps issued by the tourist board are generally accurate and should be sufficient for all but the most serious hiker.

To really explore Ibiza by foot or bike, though, you'll need to purchase some Instituto Geográfica Nacional maps. The ten 1:25,000 IGN maps that cover Ibiza include plenty of obscure trails and dirt tracks cost 350ptas/€2.10 each, and are available from outdoor specialists Transit, c/d'Arago 45, Ibiza Town (☎971 303 692), as well as most newsagents and bookstores.

CLUBBERS' MAGAZINES

Ibiza is saturated with **clubbing magazines**, most off-shoots of established UK-based titles, published between June and September, and available free from hip bars and boutiques across the island. The monthly *DJ Magazine* is the best of these publications, and is the only title to focus upon the wider picture of what's going on in the island rather than the narrow British–Ibizan club scene, as well as including comprehensive bar, restaurant and club listings. The other UK-based publications – *Ministry*, *Mixmag* and *Loaded/Muzik* collaboration *The Islander* – are also all worth picking up, though at times they are barely indistinguishable in content, with pages stuffed with messy clubbing misadventures, gurning geezers and lashings of bare flesh. The monthly trilingual *Partisan* also has listings that cover more than the British scene; you'll find it in Ibiza Town at the *Sunset Café*. Finally, *Balearica* is geared more to Mallorcan clubbing, though there's always an article or two about Ibiza, plus record reviews and interviews with DJs.

To sign up for free text message services focused on the Ibizan club scene, register online at Ⓦ *www.worldpop.com* or by calling ☎0906 215 0105 from your mobile phone.

WEB SITES

The island's Web presence is expanding quickly, with a number of local and UK-based sites offering everything from villas to environmental news. The vast bulk are Ibiza sites, though you will find a couple that focus on Formentera.

Architectural Guide to Ibiza and Formentera ⓦ *www .arquired.es/users/Catany /pitiusas/0_home.html.* Informative articles about Pitiusan churches, rural houses and modern architecture.

Club Life ⓦ *www.club-life.net.* Ex acid-house promoter's non-corporate clubbing site, with some Ibiza content and useful links.

Diario de Ibiza ⓦ *www.diariodeibiza.es.* Online edition of Ibiza's leading daily newspaper, with comprehensive news coverage, but in Spanish only.

Formentera Guide ⓦ *www .guiaformentera.com.* Best Formentera-related site, with news bulletins and background on the island's culture, history, beaches, flora and fauna.

Formentera Net ⓦ *www .formentera.net.* Formenteran history, ecology and information; currently in Spanish only – but English translations are promised.

Ibiza Friends of the Earth ⓦ *www.amics-terra.org.* Info on environmental campaigns, past battles, local green issues and lists of events.

Ibiza Holidays ⓦ *www .ibizaholidays.com.* General island information – beaches, bars and accommodation – plus club pictures.

Ibiza Night ⓦ *www .ibizanight.com.* Excellent Ibiza site with extensive historical, cultural and environmental information, plus plenty of useful contact numbers and email addresses for local artistic organizations.

Ibiza Spotlight ⓦ *www.ibiza -spotlight.com.* Leading regularly updated Ibiza site, with good all-round island information, weather and weekly news bulletins courtesy of the *Ibiza Sun*, as well as accommodation and property listings.

Ibizalive ⓦ *www.ibizalive.com.* Rapture TV's Ibiza site has

INFORMATION, MAPS, WEB SITES AND THE MEDIA

video archives, sunset Web cams, club news and gossip.

Ministry of Sound ⓦ *www .ministryofsound.com/life/ibiza*. Keen, professionally organized Ibiza clubbing content, plus info on last-minute holiday and flight deals.

Pitiuses ⓦ *www.pitiuses.com*. Web directory with comprehensive transport schedules and general Pitiusan information, though in Spanish only.

Sant Josep ⓦ *www.sanjose-ibiza.net*. Useful site of the southern Ibiza municipality, with good general background about the region, beach photos and an informative architectural section.

World Pop ⓦ *www.worldpop.com*. Very slick site with impressive content from island-based reporters. Daily club news, reviews, Ibiza documentary clips and Web cams.

Internet cafés are listed on p.278

MAINSTREAM PUBLICATIONS

Though Ibiza and Formentera lack an English-language **newspaper**, you'll find all the British broadsheets, tabloids and many periodicals for sale at shops and newsagents in all the major towns and resorts throughout the islands, usually by 9am the same morning, sometimes a little later in winter. The most popular Ibizan newspaper is the *Diario de Ibiza*, a Spanish-language daily which covers Ibiza and Formenteran news, plus national and international events. It's an essential purchase if you're planning to stay for a while, with dozens of short- and long-term house and apartment rentals. You'll also find the latest bus, ferry and plane timetables, plus *El Rastrillo*, a kind of Pitiusan notice board where everything from bar jobs to scooters are advertised.

Mainly geared toward the expat market, the monthly *Ibiza Now* magazine concentrates on island news, with concise political summaries, comprehensive cultural listings and excellent historical content; it's sold in most newsagents. A breezy weekly freesheet available in most hotels, the rival *Ibiza Sun* is less reliable, but is also geared towards British expats, with island news and events; it's also available online at the Ibiza Spotlight site. *La Carta Totamà* magazine is another useful, if rather dry, source of island news and cultural information; published in Spanish and English, it's also free, but is less widely available. There are no equivalent publications in Formentera.

RADIO AND TV

Cadena Cien (89.1FM) is the liveliest local **radio** station, with mainstream pop and dance in the day and some excellent night-time shows. David Morales, one of Ibiza's leading house DJs, commands the daily evening slot between 9pm and 11pm, and is followed on Saturdays and Sundays by the excellent **Andy Wilson** session, with brilliant Balearic music and island news in English. In the high season, Cadena Cien also has regular link-ups with the UK's BBC Radio One, with Danny Rampling, Pete Tong and others broadcasting live to the UK from Ibiza. The Ministry of Sound also collaborate with Cadena Cien, with live nightly shows from June to mid-September that include DJ interviews and live mixes. There's also an Ibizan Internet radio station (Ⓦ *www.ibizamusica.fm*) that broadcasts live from *Café Mambo* in the summer. Short-wave listeners will find the BBC World Service and Voice of America both come across crisp and clear at most times of the day in the Balearics.

Television is not a Spanish cultural strong point, with lots of inane game shows and Mexican soap operas. However, dozens of bars in the resorts have all the Sky and BBC channels, with live Premier League and European games broadcast on big screens.

Health and insurance

biza and Formentera are generally very safe places to visit in terms of health. No jabs are required, and hygiene standards are high, but you should avoid drinking the tap water, which tastes revolting but isn't dangerous. Alcohol and drug abuse aside the worst thing that's likely to happen to you is an upset stomach.

For minor complaints, go to a **pharmacy** (*farmacia*); signified by a green cross, you'll find these in all the main resorts and towns. Pharmacists are highly trained, willing to give advice (often in English), and able to dispense many drugs which would be available only on prescription in other countries. A night-rota system ensures that there's always a pharmacy open 24 hours a day in Ibiza and Formentera, ready to dole out urgent prescriptions and medical advice; all the local papers print current rotas. In more serious cases, contact one of the English-speaking doctors in the islands (see opposite) or the UK Consulate (☎971 301 816).

For an ambulance (*ambulancia*), dial ☎ 112.

Ibiza's main **hospital** is Can Misses, located in the western suburbs of Ibiza Town at c/de Corona (☎ 971 397 000). Though it's reasonably well-equipped for emergencies, few of the medical staff speak fluent English and communication difficulties are almost inevitable. There's no hospital in Formentera, but the **health centre** (*centre de salut*) at the km3.1 marker on the La Savina–Sant Francesc road (☎ 971 322 357) can deal with most medical problems; in really serious cases, patients are taken to Can Misses in Ibiza. You'll also find health centres in Sant Antoni at c/d'Alacant (☎ 971 345 102), and in Santa Eulària at c/Marià Riquer Wallis 4 (☎ 971 332 453); both deal with minor injuries, and have some English-speaking staff.

Despite Ibiza's status as one of Europe most sexually charged holiday destinations, **condoms** (*condones* or *preservativos*) are not that widely available. All pharmacies stock reliable brands of condoms, and many (but not most) bars have a machine in the male toilets. There's a 24-hour condom machine on c/Antoni Palau in Ibiza Town, just west of the ramp that ascends up the Portal de ses Taules to Dalt Vila.

TRAVEL INSURANCE

Travel insurance is strongly advised if you're not a citizen of an EU state; without it, you'll probably have to pay private hospital rates for any treatment. Spain does have free reciprocal health arrangements with other EU member states; make sure you bring an E111 form (available from post offices) to ensure free treatment. However, EU citizens would do well to take out travel insurance in any case, to cover baggage and tickets in case of theft. However, all travellers should check any existing home or medical insurance policies in case these provide cover whilst abroad. Bank and credit cards often have certain levels of medical or other insurance included, and you may automatically get travel insurance if you use a major credit card to pay for your trip. Lastly, travellers from the UK should bear in mind that though travel agents and tour operators are likely to require some kind of insurance when you book a package holiday, UK law prevents them from making you buy their own policy (other than a £1 premium for "schedule airline failure").

ROUGH GUIDES TRAVEL INSURANCE

Rough Guides now offer their own travel insurance, customized for our readers by a leading UK broker and backed by a Lloyds underwriter. It's available for anyone, of any nationality, travelling anywhere in the world.

There are two main Rough Guide insurance plans: **Essential**, for effective, no-frills cover, starting at £11.75 for two weeks; and **Premier** – more expensive but with more generous and extensive benefits. Each offer European or Worldwide cover, and can be supplemented with a "Hazardous Activities Premium" if you plan to indulge in sports considered dangerous, such as skiing or trekking. Unlike many policies, the Rough Guides schemes are calculated by the day, so if you're travelling for 27 days rather than a month that's all you pay for. Alternatively, you can take out **annual multi-trip** insurance, which covers you for all your travel throughout the year (with a maximum of sixty days for any one trip).

For a policy quote, call the Rough Guides Insurance Line on UK Freefone ☎0800/015 0906 or, if you're calling from outside Britain, on ☎(+44) 1243/621 046. Alternatively, you can get a quote or buy your insurance online at ⓦ*www.roughguides.com/insurance*.

Drugs, safety and the police

Ibiza and Formentera are generally very safe destinations with low crime rates. Most incidents involve bag-snatchers or pickpockets, so it's best to be vigilant with your valuables, and avoid leaving anything on display that will attract thieves to your rental car. Plenty of people do get into self-inflicted trouble of a different nature, though, usually involving alcohol and drugs; bear in mind that drink-driving and drug-dealing are dealt with very severely by the local police and courts.

DRUGS

At times, it's easy to forget that **drugs** are illegal at all in Ibiza. Pills and powders are everywhere, and the main lure for many visitors is the notion that the island is the Mediterranean's best-stocked recreational pharmacy. The reality is that that **Spanish drug laws** are comparable to the UK, most of mainland Europe and North America: cannabis, amphetamines, ecstasy, cocaine, LSD, ketamine, GBH and heroin are all illegal. The maximum penalty for

trafficking drugs is up to twelve years in prison, and possession of drugs is also illegal – every year, dozens of visitors are
arrested for possessing a few pills or gramme or two of coke.
Most are cautioned and released fairly swiftly, but those
caught with larger amounts, not considered to be for personal use, face the bleak prospect of a significant jail term.

If you do decide to indulge, take a few basic **precautions**,
and take great care with who you buy from; while the
chances of being set up by a police informer are slim, the
chances of being sold dodgy powder or moody pills from a
dealer in a club are much higher. It's also important to bear
in mind the dangers of overheating and dehydration after
taking Ecstasy (MDMA), which affects the body's tempera-
ture controls. It's essential to keep drinking sufficient, but not
excessive, fluid – around a pint (568ml) of water or fruit juice
an hour, or a little more if you're dancing all night in the
high-season heat. As a small bottle of water can cost up to
1000ptas/€6 in the big clubs, it's also important to make sure
you have sufficient fluid funds.

The white powder said to have replaced salt as the island's
primary source of wealth, cocaine is omnipresent. Alongside
amphetamines (speed), use is also endemic within the bar
scene of Ibiza Town and Sant Antoni, where some staff survive the season on a nocturnal diet of white lines. Again, if
you do decide to take cocaine or amphetamines, ensure that
you drink enough non-alcoholic fluids. Though of minimal
popularity with clubbers, you may be offered GBH or ketamine; both drugs can be very dangerous if mixed with alcohol – if you suspect you've taken either, stick to water. The
police normally tolerate the possession of small amounts of
cannabis, though don't go waving a spliff around in the
streets. Again, anyone considered to be a dealer faces serious
trouble, and possibly a prison sentence.

There's a massive booze culture in Ibiza's resorts, aided
and abetted by bar-crawls organized by tour operators, and

alcohol abuse is the main reason why most people end up in hospital, either through overindulgence or as a result of an accident. Be especially careful when making your way home at the end of a night out, particularly when crossing the main Ibiza Town–Sant Antoni highway near *Privilege* and *Amnesia* – there have been many deaths on this stretch. It's worth remembering that if you have an accident while drunk (or under the influence of illegal drugs) and end up in hospital, many insurance policies won't pay out, and you could be faced with a large bill.

The emergency telephone number in Ibiza and Formentera is ☎ 112; on getting through, you'll be asked if you want either the police (*policía*), fire brigade (*bomberos*) or ambulance service (*ambulancia*); telephone operators usually speak some English.

Lastly, never drink and drive; quite apart from the safety considerations, the police regularly breath-test drivers in Ibiza and Formentera. The legal alcohol limit is around two alcoholic units for women and three for men. Drivers failing breath tests can expect to pay a fine of 50,000–100,000ptas/ €300.48–€600.96 and face the possibility of a ban.

SAFETY AND THE POLICE

Though **street crime**, such as pickpocketing and mugging, is extremely rare in Ibiza and Formentera, it's certainly wise to take some basic precautions. Be careful in the Sa Penya district of Ibiza Town, which has the highest number of bag-snatching incidents, and avoid walking the dark alleys above (south of) c/de la Verge, close to the city walls, at night. Similarly, inside Dalt Vila, don't amble around the poorly lit streets above Plaça de la Vila late at night, as muggings are not unknown. Pickpockets love crowds, so take extra care at Es Canar market and the La Marina night market in Ibiza Town. Thieves also target pavement cafés, snatching banknotes up from tables, so keep an eye on your money when paying your bill.

You may not find the **police** to be particularly helpful if you do suffer any trouble. The main problem is likely to be that few speak much English, so you'll probably have to wait around until an English speaker is found. Should you be arrested on any charge, you have the right to contact your nearest consulate (see p.22); though British consulate staff are rarely sympathetic, they do keep a list English-speaking lawyers. Remember that if you do have something, you'll have to get a police report in order to claim for the loss on your insurance policy.

Getting around

biza has a good public transport system, with buses and boats linking all the main resorts and towns, and there's a very decent bus service in Formentera considering its tiny population. If you're really planning on exploring the islands, however, you're going to have to rent a car, motorbike or a bicycle, as many of the best stretches of coastline are well off the beaten path.

Hitching is another very popular way to get around the main roads, especially in northern Ibiza. Hitchhikers are not expected to contribute towards drivers' transport costs. Obviously, though, there are risks involved; avoid hitching alone, and never accept a lift if you feel in any way uncomfortable about the driver.

BUSES

Buses in Ibiza and Formentera are inexpensive, punctual and will get you around fairly quickly. Services between the main towns run roughly from 7.30am to midnight between June and late September, and 7.30am until 9.30pm in winter. Smaller villages and coastal resorts are less well-served, with fewer buses running from around 9am to 7pm all year round. While it is possible to get to every village in Ibiza or Formentera by bus (bar Cala Saona in Formentera), services to isolated hamlets like Santa Agnès are pretty infrequent, so it pays to plan ahead and check the current timetables in advance before you set off, especially on Sundays, when there are fewer buses on all routes, and in winter. Copies of timetables are held at tourist offices and bus terminals, and are printed in local newspapers; you can also visit Ⓦ *www.ibizabus.com*. Services to the more popular beaches and resorts are increased between June and late September.

From **Ibiza Town**, there are services to all the main towns, most villages and resorts, and to Salines beach all year round. **Sant Antoni** and **Santa Eulària** are the other two transport hubs, with frequent services to local beach resorts and good intra-island connections. In **Formentera**, there's one main route across the island, from La Savina to La Mola, supplemented by extra services that shuttle between Es Pujols, Sant Ferran, Sant Francesc and La Savina. **Fares** are very reasonable on all routes: Ibiza Town–Sant Antoni costs 200ptas/€1.20, while the longest

GETTING AROUND

●

37

route, Ibiza Town–Portinatx, is 325ptas/€1.95.

Between mid-June and late September the all-night **discobus** service provides hourly shuttles between Ibiza Town and Sant Antoni (passing *Amnesia* and *Privilege*). Additional hourly routes run between Platja d'en Bossa (for *Space*) and Ibiza Town; Sant Antoni and Port des Torrent; Es Canar and Santa Eulària; and Santa Eulària and Ibiza Town. During the rest of the year, the same routes are in operation, but the buses run on Saturday nights only. Tickets cost 250ptas/€1.50 one way; for more information, call ☎971 192 456.

BOATS

Dozens of **boats** buzz up and down the Ibizan coastline between May and late September, providing a delightful – if more expensive – alternative to bus travel. Most services are timed to get tourists to beaches from the main resorts and towns. Boats go from Ibiza Town to Talamanca (375ptas/€2.25 return), and Platja d'en Bossa (700ptas/€4.20) from Sant Antoni to points around the Sant Antoni bay (500ptas/€3 return), Cala Bassa (700ptas/€4.20) and Cala Conta (800ptas/€4.8); and from Santa Eulària to northeast beaches, including Cala Pada (750ptas/€4.50) and Es Canar (900ptas/€5.40). In Formentera there are boats between La Savina and Espalmador via Platja Illetes (750ptas/€4.50 return).

Ferry and hydrofoil services between Formentera and Ibiza Town are detailed on p.60.

TAXIS

Taxi rates are quite reasonable; all tariffs are fixed, and the minimum charge is 500ptas/€3, with an additional

100ptas/€0.60 charge after midnight. To get to Sant Rafel (for *Amnesia* or *Privilege*) from either Ibiza Town or Sant Antoni, for example, the fare is 1700ptas/€9.60, while Ibiza Town to Sant Antoni (15km) will cost 2200ptas/€13.25. You'll have no problems getting a taxi at most times of the year (we've listed reliable companies on the phone below), but demand far exceeds supply on many August nights, when it's not uncommon to wait up to an hour for a ride. Lastly, it's well worth bearing in mind that all Ibizan clubs will pay your taxi fare from anywhere in the island if four of the passengers purchase an entrance ticket to the venue.

TAXI COMPANIES

Ibiza Town ⊤ 971 301 794
⊤ 971 306 602
Sant Antoni ⊤ 971 340 074
⊤ 971 343 764
Santa Eulària ⊤ 971 330 063
Sant Joan ⊤ 971 800 243

Sant Francesc, Formentera
⊤ 971 322 016
La Savina, Formentera ⊤ 971 322 002
Es Pujols, Formentera ⊤ 971 328 016

CAR AND MOTORBIKE RENTAL

Driving along Ibiza and Formentera's smooth network of roads is a pretty straightforward affair, though to really see the islands you'll have to tackle some terrible dirt tracks from time to time. All the major towns and resorts are well signposted, but many small coves, especially in northern Ibiza, are not. Take extra care when **driving at night**, as virtually none of the main roads are adequately lit, including the notorious Sant Antoni–Ibiza Town highway, where accidents are fairly common. In general, local people are not overtly aggressive drivers, and it's the young British boy-racers you'll have to watch out for.

There's no avoiding the fact that **renting a car** is the best way to explore the islands. Daily rental costs are very reasonable, and most companies will give a discount of ten percent or more if you book a full week. Local companies are usually a little cheaper than the international names: for the cheapest hatchback model, expect to pay around 6000ptas/€36 a day in July and August, and around 4500ptas/€27 per day the rest of the year. As rental car numbers are restricted in the Balearics for environmental reasons, it pays to book ahead, particularly in August. All the resorts have a rental company or two, or you can arrange to pick up a car at the airport.

Motorbikes and **scooters** are also a very popular means of getting around the islands independently, with rates starting at around 3500ptas/€21 for the cheapest motorbike, or 2800ptas/€17 a day for a scooter model. In low-lying Formentera, even the least powerful model will be adequate to get two people around, but consider hiring a machine above 100cc to explore hilly Ibiza properly.

LOCAL CAR AND MOTORBIKE RENTAL COMPANIES

All the local companies listed below rent out both cars and motorbikes.

Autos Mari, c/de la Mar 25, Santa Eulària ☎971 330 236; fax ℗971 332 659.

BK, Plaça del Mar 5, Cala Tarida ☎971 806 289.

Comfort Car, c/Alacant 6, Sant Antoni ☎971 340 959; fax ℗971 343 616.

Isla Blanca, c/Felipe II, Ibiza Town ☎971 415 407; harbourside, La Savina, Formentera ☎971 322 559.

Moto Luis, Avgda Portmany 5, Sant Antoni ☎971 340 521; fax ℗971 340 257; ℮ motoluis@arrakis.es.

National Ibiza airport ☎971 395 393.

1GETTING AROUND

INTERNATIONAL CAR RENTAL COMPANIES

Avis (UK ☎0870/606 0100; US and Canada ☎1-800/331-1084; ⓦ*www.avis.com*).

Budget (UK ☎0800/181181; US and Canada ☎1-800/527-0700; ⓦ*www.budget.com*).

Hertz (UK ☎0870/844 8844; US and Canada ☎1-800/654-3001; ⓦ*www.hertz.com*).

National (UK ☎01895/233 300; US and Canada ☎1-800/CAR-RENT; ⓦ*www.nationalcar.com*).

BICYCLES

With few hills, **Formentera** is perfect bicycle territory, and, as illustrated by the rows of bikes for rent in La Savina, Es Pujols and at the big hotels, **cycling** is an easy and popular way to get around the island. Pick up a *Green Routes* leaflet from the tourist office for details of some good cycle excursions along the island's quieter lanes, though bear in mind that most are not signposted. **Ibiza** is much more hilly and its roads more congested, though there are some spectacular routes across the island. Tourist information offices can supply you with leaflets detailing cycling routes, but these tend to be impractical, consisting of vague lines drawn across poor maps, and you're very liable to get lost – to really explore by bike you'll need large-scale IGN maps (see p.26). In both islands, a cheap bike costs around 1700ptas/€10.25 a day, while state-of-the-art mountain bikes start at about 2500ptas/€15.

BICYCLE RENTAL COMPANIES

Autos Ca Mari, harbourside, La Savina, Formentera ☎971 322 921.

Tony Rent, c/Navarra 11, Ibiza Town ☎971 300 879.

Vespas Torres, Sant Jaume 66, Santa Eulària ☎971 330 059.

Costs, money and banks

The Balearics are the most affluent region of Spain with a standard of living above the EU average. Tourist accommodation is around twenty percent more expensive than elsewhere in Spain, while food prices in the supermarkets are also dearer, as most produce has to be imported from the mainland.

However, unless you're planning to go clubbing a lot (a seriously expensive business), it's still fairly easy to have an economical holiday in Ibiza and Formentera. Eating and drinking are generally inexpensive, especially in the village bars and big resorts, but as there are plenty of flash bars and pricey restaurants where your funds can take a real hammering, it pays to be choosy if you're on a budget.

CURRENCY

Spain is one of eleven European Union countries who have opted to join a single currency, the **euro** (€). The transition period, which began on January 1, 1999, is lengthy, however: euro notes and coins are not scheduled to be issued until January 1, 2002, with pesetas remaining in place for cash transactions, at a fixed rate of 166.386 pesetas to 1 euro, until they are scrapped entirely on July 1, 2002.

Even before euro cash appears in 2002, you can opt to pay in euros by credit card, and you can get travellers' cheques in euros – you should not be charged commission for changing them in any of the eleven countries in the euro zone (also known as "Euroland"), nor for changing from any of the old Euroland currencies to any other (French francs to pesetas, for example).

All prices in this book are given in both pesetas and the euro equivalent. Once its in circulation, the euro will come in coins of 1 to 50 cents, €1 and €2, and notes of €5 to €500. The peseta is divided into notes of 1000, 2000, 5000 and 10,000; coins come in denominations of 1, 5, 25, 50, 100, 200 and 500. At the time of writing, £1 is worth 275 pesetas/1.66 euros; US$1 is worth 191 pesetas/1.16 euros.

COSTS

The overall cost of a trip to Ibiza or Formentera depends on what time of year you choose to visit. While it's possible to find a self-catering package deal from the UK to Sant Antoni for under £150 in May or October, the same holiday will double in price by July or August. Similarly, if you're travelling independently, room rates can triple in high season. The hip bars of Ibiza Town and Sant Antoni also crank up drink prices in summer (though elsewhere, bar prices are stable) and car rental costs also increase. Food, restaurant, bus and taxi prices at least remain constant.

If you camp or stay in a simple *hostal* and live frugally, perhaps eating out cheaply once a day, you're looking at a minimum budget of around 6000ptas/€36 a day between June and September, including accommodation. In the winter months, budget accommodation prices drop a little, so you might get by on around 4500ptas/€27 a day. If you plan to stay in a mid-range hotel, rent a car and eat dinner in a good restaurant, you'll spend upwards of 12,000ptas/€72 a day. Bear in mind, though, that with entrance fees to the main venues costing 5000ptas/€30 and over, combined with silly drink prices and taxi fares, it's frighteningly easy to spend substantially more than this if you've come to go clubbing.

BANKS AND EXCHANGE

Banks offer the best rates for changing travellers' cheques and foreign currency – you'll find plenty of branches in all the main towns and resorts and in many villages. The main difficulty is that they have very limited **banking hours** (generally Mon–Sat 9am–2pm), which are not very convenient times if you're planning to dance all night and sleep in the day, so it pays to plan ahead a little if you've only brought travellers' cheques. Bureaux de change, found in all the main resorts, often stay open until midnight, but their commission rates are usually higher. Many large hotels will also cash your travellers' cheques, but you'll rarely get quoted a competitive exchange rate.

Travellers' cheques are probably the safest way to carry money abroad, with cheques in sterling, euros, US dollars and most other major currencies accepted in banks and bureaux de change throughout Ibiza and Formentera; you'll need your passport to validate them.

All international **credit and debit cards** should function fine and allow you to withdraw money from cashpoint (ATM) machines, which are common throughout the islands – you'll even find them in many small villages. Virtually all restaurants and large stores accept credit cards, but don't expect to pay by plastic in a *tapas* bar or at the corner store.

Communications

Telephone connections between Ibiza and Formentera and the rest of the world are generally efficient, but mail can be very slow, especially in the summer months.

You'll find **telephone** booths in towns and villages all over Ibiza and Formentera; these mainly take cash, but some are exclusively geared up for phonecards, which you can buy at tobacconists. Local calls in the ☎971 Balearic area are very cheap, while national calls are quite expensive, at around 125ptas/€0.75 for three minutes. Make sure you have gather a pocketful of change before you dial a mobile number, as calls cost around 110ptas/€0.66 a minute.

International calls can also be made from these booths, at fairly reasonable rates, but the most cost-effective way to dial home is by using an international phonecard – there are plenty of options, but the España Mundo card is one of the cheapest. You can purchase phonecards in any *estanco* (tobacconist) shop; look out for the brown and yellow *Tabac* sign.

Most UK **mobile phones** will work in the Balearics, though users of US-bought handsets may have difficulties. Bear in mind that as you have to pay to receive calls from home, you can run up a hefty bill by chatting on the beach. Text messaging services are detailed on p.26. If you are planning a long stay, consider buying a Spanish mobile phone. Movi Star is the most popular service provider, and you can purchase "pay-as-you-go" handsets from around 7000ptas/€42 – the price usually includes some free calls.

Postal services for international mail are reasonably efficient most of the year, but the system gets clogged in the summer months. Allow a week to ten days for delivery of letters and postcards within the EU, or two weeks for the

DIALLING CODES

To **call Ibiza or Formentera from abroad**, dial 00 plus the relevant country code (00 34 in the UK, Ireland and New Zealand; 011 34 in North America; 0011 64 in Australia) followed by the nine digit number.

To **call abroad from Ibiza or Formentera**, dial 00 followed by the country code (44 for the UK; 353 for Ireland; 1 for the US and Canada; 61 for Australia; 64 then the area code minus its zero for New Zealand), and then the number.

rest of the world, and up to double that time for parcels. Post offices (*correus*) generally open between 9am and 1.30pm Monday to Saturday, and you can also buy stamps from tobacconists and some souvenir shops.

INTERNET CAFÉS

Internet cafés (listed on p.278) are springing up all over Ibiza, but though there are terminals where you can surf and send email in Formentera, like *P.O. Box* in Sant Ferran, no dedicated cafés had opened when this book went to press. Most of Ibiza's cafés are concentrated in Ibiza Town (with three on Avdga d'Ignasi Wallis alone) and Sant Antoni, and you'll even find special photo-pods in clubs like *Pacha* and *Space*, where you can also take a digital photo and email the image home. Rates for Internet access average at 900ptas/€5.42 an hour. Bear in mind, though, that most Internet cafés shut down between October and May.

Sports and outdoor pursuits

I f you can tear yourself away from the clubs and bars, you'll find plenty of opportunities for sporting and outdoor pursuits, from golf to horseback riding, but with a sparkling coastline never more than a short drive away, watersports are especially good. Coastal Ibiza also offers superb scenery for hikers, while Formentera is perfect cycling terrain.

DIVING AND SNORKELLING

Over 70km away from the large cities of the mainland, and virtually free from local heavy industry, the Pitiusan islands can boast some of the cleanest seas in the Mediterranean, the coastlines dotted with blue-flag beaches. With little rainfall runoff, the water is also exceptionally clear for most of the year; visibility of up to 40m is quite common.

Scuba diving is generally excellent, with warm seas and (generally) gentle currents. Boats tend to head for the tiny offshore islands such as Tagomago and Redona that ring the coasts, where sea life is at its most diverse; however, if you've ever been diving on a coral reef, the Mediterranean may seem disappointingly barren. Schools of barracuda and large groupers are reasonably common, though, and you can expect to see conger and moray eels, plenty of colourful wrasse, plus crabs and octopuses. In addition to the marine life, there's some startling underwater scenery, with three shipwrecks around Illot Llado near Ibiza Town and another in Cala Mastella, plus caves and crevices all around the coastline to investigate.

Sea temperatures are at their lowest in February (around 15°C), and highest in late September (around 25°C).

All scuba-diving schools open between May and October only and tend to charge similar prices; a single boat-dive works out around 6800ptas/€41 including all equipment and insurance – you'll save around twenty percent if you bring your own gear. Night dives incur an extra tariff of between 2500ptas/€15 and 5500ptas/€33, depending on the site. If you want to **learn to dive**, expect to pay around 70,000ptas/€422 for a five-day PADI Open Water course; most dive schools offer advanced open-water, rescue-diver and divemaster training, too, plus other specialist courses. You'll find a BSAC school in Port des Torrent, and there's a decompression chamber in Ibiza Town.

SNORKELLING

Armed with a mask, snorkel and fins, you'll find something interesting close to most Pitiusan beaches. Small coves and rocky shorelines offer the most productive **snorkelling** territory: try Cala Mastella Cala Molí and Cala Codolar in Ibiza or Caló de Sant Agustí in Formentera. Perhaps the best area for experienced snorkellers and freedivers is the rugged northwest Ibizan coastline, at bays like Es Portitxol and Cala d'Aubarca where there are very steep drop-offs and deep, clear water. You'll often encounter both coastal fish such as ballan, goby, grouper, brown and painted wrasse, and passing pelagic sea life such as mackerel or even barracuda. Most resorts have a store where you can buy snorkelling equipment, but as much of it is poor quality it's well worth renting or buying from a dive school or a specialist fishing store.

OTHER WATERSPORTS

Windsurfing is a popular sport in the Pitiuses – July and August are often the calmest months, so less challenging for the experienced windsurfer, but conditions are ideal for most of the year. Several of the schools listed opposite rent out boards (around 2500ptas/€15 per hour) or run courses (around 3500ptas/€21 per hour). There are also several **sailing** schools and clubs in Ibiza and Formentera, and the islands host various competitive events. The most famous of these is the Ruta de Sal regatta, held in Easter week, a long-established event that retraces the historic salt route between Ibiza, Dénia and Barcelona.

Operators in most of the main resorts offer **jet-skiing** (around 1750ptas/€10.50 for 15min), **waterskiing** (around 2500ptas/€12 for 15min), a speedy thrill on a blow-up **banana** (1000ptas/€6 per person for 15min) as well as the ubiquitous and very Balearic **pedalos** (around 600ptas/€3.60 an hour). Sea **kayaking** is also quite popular – expect to pay around 5000ptas/€30 for a day's rental plus a hefty deposit. Finally, H2O Sports in Sant Antoni charge 6000ptas/€36 per person for **parasailing**, which includes an hour's power boat trip – book a day in advance.

WATERSPORTS OPERATORS AND STORES

Club de Surf Ibiza, Platja d'en Bossa ⓣ971 192 418. Long-established windsurfing school offering board rental and tuition.

Club Delfin Vela y Windsurf, *Hotel Delfin*, Cala Codolar ⓣ971 806 210. Sailing school, plus windsurf tuition and board rental.

Formentera Diving and Watersports, La Savina, Formentera ⓣ971 323 232. Formentera's best dive school; also rents out kayaks, jet-skis and boats.

H2O Sports, opposite *Hotel San Remo*, Sant Antoni harbourfront ⓣ 616 538 250. Parasailing, plus waterskiing tuition.

Ibiza Diving, Port Esportiu, Santa Eulària ⓣ971 332 949; ⓦ*www.ibiza-diving.com*. Ibiza's only five-star PADI school, with courses that include Nitrox training.

Pesca y Deportes Bonet, c/Pere Francés 20, Ibiza Town ⓣ971 312 624. Fishing tackle and snorkelling gear.

Pesca y Deportes Santa Eulalia, Molins de Rey 12, Santa Eulària ⓣ971 330 838. Snorkelling, spear-fishing and fishing gear.

Sea Horse Sub, Port des Torrent ⓣ 971 346 438. The only BSAC-accredited dive school in Ibiza.

Sirena, c/Balanzat 21, Sant Antoni ⓣ971 342 966; ⓦ*www.ibiza-online.com /DivingSirena*. Dive school offering courses and trips to west coast sites.

Subfari, Es Portitxol beach, Cala Portinatx ⓣ 971 333 183. Scuba school that ventures to many of Ibiza's remote north coast dive sites.

Vela Náutica, Avgda Dr Fleming, Sant Antoni ⓣ971 346 535. Sailing school, with windsurfing equipment, boats and kayaks for rent.

BOAT TRIPS

In all of the main resorts, you'll find companies offering **pleasure-boat trips** around the coastline, most operating from booths along the promenades. The most popular excursion by far is the day-trip to Formentera, and it's well worth doing for the stunning views of the Pitiusan coastline alone. Trips typically leave around 9.30am and return by 6pm, and prices vary depending on the resort you leave from; expect to pay around 1900ptas/€11.50 per person from Figueretes, and 2800ptas/€16.85 per person from Sant Antoni; most visit the island of Espalmador on the way.

The pick of other excursions leave from the Sant Antoni harbour; all are bookable with several companies on the waterfront. The three-hour return trip to Es Vedrà (daily; 2000ptas/€12) is recommended, passing a series of fine beaches and including a snorkelling stop in Cala d'Hort, as is the dramatic day-trip up the northwest coastline to Portinatx, passing lots of isolated coves; boats sail twice weekly, and tickets cost 2800ptas/€16.90 return per person.

HIKING

Ibiza and Formentera's spectacular coastal paths and inland valleys offer exceptional **hiking**. We've detailed several of the best walks within the Guide, all of which have opportunities for a swim along the way; trainers and shorts are adequate equipment. If you plan on doing a lot of walking, you'll need a detailed map – IGN publish the most useful (see p.26). Though the tourist offices do have some hiking leaflets, the information is pretty hopeless, with appalling maps and very vague text. Sunflower Books publish the best specialist walkers' guide to Ibiza and Formentera (see "Contexts", p.321).

The only specialist company offering **organized treks** is Ecoibiza, Avgda d'Isidor Macabich 39, Ibiza Town (℡971 302 347; ⓦ www.ecoibiza.com), which arranges some excellent "Secret Walks" to remote parts of the island. Half-day trips cost around 2600ptas/€15.50 per person; full-day excursions are priced from 3950ptas/€23.80.

HORSE RIDING, GO-KARTING AND GOLF

In Formentera, Sahona Horses (☎971 323 001), based 500m outside Sant Francesc on the road to the Cap de Barbària, offer some excellent **horse rides** on well-looked-after mounts through woodland, along beaches and across the salt flats. In Ibiza, Easy Riders (☎971 196 511), located 200m along the Sòl d'en Serra from Cala Llonga, is another good option, with fine-looking horses and some thrilling beach and hill rides. Both charge around 7500ptas/€45 for a half-day excursion.

Of the two **go-kart tracks** in Ibiza, the hilly 300m Santa Eulària circuit, adjacent to the km6 marker on the main Ibiza Town–Sant Eulària road (daily May–Oct 10am–10pm; no phone), is the better option, with high-power adult karts, junior karts and baby karts. Much flatter and less scenic, the other track is just outside Sant Antoni along the highway to Ibiza Town (daily May–Oct noon–midnight). Kart prices at both tracks start at 1500ptas/€9 for ten minutes.

The only **golf** course in the Pitiuses is Club de Golf Ibiza (☎971 196 152), halfway along the Ibiza Town–Sant Eulària highway at Roca Llisa. It boasts a nine- and an eighteen-hole course, both positioned between patches of pine woodlands under the island's central hills. You don't have be a member to play, but it's an expensive course – green fees are 12,000ptas/€72, and you'll pay extra for a caddy and for renting a golf buggy, though the price does includes club rental.

THE GUIDE

Ibiza Town and around

Elegant and sophisticated, **IBIZA TOWN (EIVISSA)** is the cultural and administrative heart of the island. Superbly set around a dazzling natural harbour, and enclosed by a backdrop of low hills, it's one of the Mediterranean's most cosmopolitan pocket capitals, thick with historic sights, chic bars and restaurants and hip boutiques. In the summer months, the narrow lanes of **La Marina** and **Sa Penya** quarters become an alfresco catwalk, as a good dose of the planet's most accomplished party people, fashion victims and freaks strut the streets in a frenzy of combative hedonism. By the end of September, the pace abates and life becomes a little more languid: most of the restaurants and bars shut up shop, and Ibiza Town's beleaguered residents wind down and look forward to a well-earned winter siesta, counting their euros and recharging for the next seasonal onslaught.

All this sybaritic fury takes place in a setting of breathtaking beauty. Looming magnificently above the portside action is historic **Dalt Vila**, a rocky escarpment topped by a walled enclave, which all the island's invaders have squabbled over since the days of the Phoenicians. The fortress-like Catalan cathedral and craggy Moorish castle that bestride the summit are Ibiza's most famous landmarks, clearly visible from all over the south of the island. Below Dalt Vila, Ibiza Town's stunning **harbour** is the island's busiest port, its azure waters constantly ruffled by a succession of gleaming yachts, fishing boats, container ships and ferries. All this maritime traffic is actually very new, for, as recently as the 1940s, the island's only regular links with the outside world were a sporadic mailboat from Palma and a ferry to the mainland described by British traveller Douglas Goldring as a "deplorable, flea-infested old tub". The scene today could hardly be more of a contrast, with sheik-owned yachts gliding in from the Gulf and vast ferries disgorging hundreds of weekending Spaniards eager to sample the revelry. Occupying the north side of the bay, the **new harbour zone** is an upmarket strip devoted to pleasure and leisure. Here the luxury apartments, yacht marinas, casinos and restaurants attract a suitably moneyed clientele, and the ambience is far less raucous than in the old quarters over the water.

West of La Marina, and extending a kilometre or so inland, the **New Town** is far less appealing. Though the area around boulevard-like Vara de Rey is urbane and attractive, beyond the western suburbs things quickly descend into a featureless commercial sprawl of concrete apartment blocks and traffic-choked streets. Unless you arrive by sea, these banal suburbs will be your first impression of Ibiza Town, and it's easy to wonder what on earth all the fuss is about.

There are a few points of interest **around Ibiza Town**, including a couple of small beach resorts: the appealing, crescent-shaped sandy bay of **Talamanca** is 2km to the north, while the less picturesque **Figueretes**, popular with gay men and holidaying families, is just a fifteen-minute walk to the southwest. Of the villages that border Ibiza Town, **Jesús**, to the northeast, is little more than a suburban overspill of the capital, but Sant Rafel is more absorbing, home to the legendary *Amnesia* and *Privilege* nightclubs and boasting a crop of good restaurants as well as stunning views of the capital from its lofty perch in the central hills to the northwest.

For reviews of accommodation, restaurants, bars and clubs in Ibiza Town, see pp.208, 224, 238 and 253.

Arrival and information

Ibiza's **international airport** (Map 1, F7; ☎971 809 000) is situated 7km southwest of Ibiza Town, close to the Salines salt pans. There's an efficient **tourist office** (May–Sept only Mon–Sat 9am–2pm & 4–9pm, Sun 9am–2pm; ☎971 809 118), with helpful staff and a good stock of leaflets, brochures and maps. There are several car rental companies in the arrival lounge, and **taxis** meet incoming flights; though there are usually plenty available, you may have to wait a while for a ride in August. There's also an efficient **bus** service between the airport and Ibiza Town (hourly 7.30am–10.30pm; 150ptas/€0.90) that operates throughout the year.

Ibiza Town's **bus terminal** (Map 3, A2) is on Avgda d'Isidor Macabich in the New Town, a ten-minute walk from the port area; bear in mind that, as there are no buses into the town centre from here, and no taxi rank, you'll need to call one of the taxi firms listed on p.39 if you don't want to walk to the port area or Old Town. Services from all over the island arrive and depart from bus stops outside the scruffy waiting room. Arriving by **ferry** from the mainland or Palma, you'll dock just east of the Estació Marítima building (Map 3, L3) on the main harbourfont, Passeig Marítim. All Formentera ferries arrive and depart from a separate terminal building (Map 3, I1) on the west side of the harbour.

The efficient **main tourist office** (Map 3, K3) is located opposite the Estació Marítima on Passeig Marítim (June–Sept Mon–Fri 8.30am–2.30pm & 5–7pm, Sat 9.30am–1.30pm; Oct–May Mon–Fri 8.30am–2.30pm; ☎971 301 900).

La Marina and Sa Penya

Ibiza Town's pretty, atmospheric harbourside districts, **La Marina** and **Sa Penya** are rammed with hip boutiques, restaurants and bars, all almost exclusively geared up to tourism. These twin quarters, often lumped together as "the port", are sandwiched between the harbour waters to the north and the walls of Dalt Vila in the south. Smarter La Marina rubs up against the New Town at Vara de Rey in the west; smaller, sleazier Sa Penya almost topples into the Mediterranean waves to the east.

First settled by the Phoenicians in the seventh century BC, and occupied by the Carthaginians and Romans, La Marina and Sa Penya were left virtually uninhabited for a thousand years after Vandals sacked the town in 425 AD. Rudimentary buildings were constructed in the quarters during this period, but again and again they were burned down by bands of plundering Vandals, Visigoths, Moors and Turkish buccaneers. But, by the fifteenth century, despite the continuing threat from pirates, overcrowding inside Dalt Vila forced residents outside the walls, and La Marina and Sa Penya grew steadily as working-class districts, populated by fishermen, tradesmen and privateers. Life in the harbourside districts continued to revolve around the sea and the docks until package tourism revolutionized the Ibizan economy in the 1960s. Today's bombastic bar culture has squeezed out most of the local families, who've relocated to the relative tranquillity of the suburbs, renting out their apartments here to the legions of foreigners in town to work the summer season.

The port area's wonderfully crooked warren of streets, alleys and tiny plazas were built organically, with new buildings being added when population pressure necessitated construction. All the districts' houses are whitewashed, and many streets barely a couple of metres wide, to keep out the glare of the fearsome summer sun. In high season, these almost souk-like streets are some of the most crowded in all Spain, as a tsunami of visitors-on-a-mission come in to shop, feast or hit the bars.

ALONG THE WATERFRONT

The best place to start exploring La Marina is at the southwestern corner of the harbourfront, along Passeig Marítim, where a slightly comical-looking **statue** (Map 3, I2), dedicated to the fishermen of Ibiza, resembles none other than Dopey of seven-dwarf fame. Heading east along Passeig Marítim, a cluster of upmarket café-bars (particularly *Mar y Sol*, long a favoured location amongst Ibizan high society) afford fine views of the yachts and the docks. Midway along the bay, the modern harbour building, the Estació Marítima, juts into the water adjacent to the tourist office and a large stone obelisk (Map 3, K3) dedicated to the corsairs (see p.293), freelance privateers officially licenced to defend territory against pirate attacks. Opposite is a small square, **Plaça d'Antoni Riquer**, named after a legendary corsair who stormed and captured a British pirate ship just offshore in 1806. This plaza is one of *the* places to view the club parades that are such a feature of La Marina's summer-season nightlife; by midnight, the bar terraces are heaving with drinkers gathered to gawp at the outrageous procession of drag queens and costumed PR-people promoting events at the big club venues.

Continuing east from the obelisk, Passeig Marítim is lined with another glut of restaurants and bars, plus market stalls in high season. Almost at the end of the Passeig, the tiny square of **Plaça de sa Riba**, backed by tottering old fishermen's houses, is a popular place for outdoor dining, though more for the views than the food. Though it's firmly a restaurant quarter these days, many Ibizans still refer to this stretch of the harbour as *Sa Riba* (The Shore) – the site of the old docks and shipyards, this was where boats returning from fishing trips would moor up. At the very end of the Passeig Marítim, a twentieth-century breakwater, Es Muro, extends well into the harbour; you can walk right to the end for an excellent view back over the old town. Steps at the beginning of Es Muro lead up into Sa Penya (see p.64).

ESGLÉSIA DE SANT ELM

Map 3, K3.

Just south of Plaça d'Antoni Riquer, c/Sant Elm leads into a tiny triangular cobbled plaza that holds the **Església de Sant Elm**. First built in the fifteenth century, the church acted as a sanctuary for over four centuries, when besieged harbourside residents sought protection from pirate attacks; their efforts were often in vain, though, as Sant Elm has been burned down at least a dozen times. A sturdy, three-storey, functional design with a tiered belltower, the present building was constructed after the last church was destroyed during the Spanish Civil War. The church is only open for Mass, but the cool interior harbours a striking golden statue of a beaming open-armed Christ, and another image, of the haloed **Verge del Carmen** carrying a child, which has long been associated with the Ibizan seamen's guild. On July 16, the statue is removed by the fishermen of La Marina and placed in a boat, which then leads a flotilla around the harbour in an annual ceremony to request her protection at sea for the year ahead.

PLAÇA DE SA CONSTITUCIÓ

Map 3, J4.

South of Sant Elm, La Marina's main shopping street c/del Mar, thick with boutiques and souvenir stalls, leads south to tiny Plaça de sa Font, tight by the city walls and sporting a modest, but now dry, eighteenth-century fountain. From here, head east along c/d'Antoni Palau, nicknamed "pharmacy street" because of its profusion of chemists, to the **Plaça de sa Constitució**, a peaceful square of elegant whitewashed and ochre-painted old merchants' houses that's home to **Es Mercat Vell** (The Old Market), a curiously squat Neoclassical edifice where fruit and vegetables have been traded since 1873. There's little hustle and bustle in evidence today, and the underemployed traders spend most of their time swatting flies from the rows of fruit or selling the odd apple to tourists. Few locals shop here, which is understandable when you see the prices charged; the haggling has shifted to the New Town, where the main market now resides.

The **New Market** (Mercat Nou) occupies a large concrete building on c/d'Extremadura in the New Town (Map 3, A3).

Market aside, leisurely Plaça de sa Constitució is still a great place for a refuelling stop before an excursion into Sa

Penya or an assault on Dalt Vila through the looming presence of the Portal de ses Taules just above. Several **cafés** are
grouped close to the square, including the ever-popular
Croissant Show (see p.239), a legendary but chaotic French-
owned patisserie.

SA PENYA

> *The glamour goes on above the seediness, like a red carpet*
> *over a sewer.*
> Paul Richardson, *Not Part of the Package – A year in Ibiza*

East of Plaça de sa Constitució, the twisted triangle of
crumbling streets, bordered by c/d'Enmig to the north and
hemmed in by the city walls to the south, is **Sa Penya**, the
wildest, sleaziest neighbourhood in the Balearics. Until the
fifteenth century, though, there were few permanent buildings here, and it was only settled in any concerted way
when Ibiza Town began to expand out of the walls.

A run-down and occasionally even threatening place, Sa
Penya is never bland, with an extreme combination of cul-
tures coexisting within its boundaries. Cutting through the
heart of Sa Penya is *the* gay street in Ibiza, **Carrer de la
Verge**, lined with dozens of bars and fetish boutiques,
while the area to the south constitutes Ibiza's main gypsy
district, home to the most marginalized of Spain's population. Most gypsies settled in Ibiza in the 1960s to work in
the construction industry, and have since been subject to
the booms and slumps affecting the building trade more
than any other section of the community. Sa Penya is beset
by social problems – poor housing, high unemployment,
very high levels of drug addiction (particularly heroin) –
and few residents have any stake at all in the tourism sector. Nonetheless, the area does have an unmistakably edgy,
underground appeal, an identity derived from the crum-

bling facades of the dark, warren-like alleys and lanes, and the outrageous streetlife, bars and boutiques, all of which combine into a vibrant and absorbing scene. If you want wander around, though, it's probably best to stick to the area around c/d'Alfonso XII and c/de la Verge, as the area's quieter streets are very poorly lit and can be unsafe at night.

Carrer de la Verge

Map 3, L4.

Despite its inappropriate moniker, **Carrer de la Verge**, or "street of the virgin" (also signposted as c/de la Mare de Déu), is easily the wildest on the island. Barely 400m long, it metamorphoses by night from a sleepy-looking, white-washed Mediterranean lane into a dark, urban ravine of S&M clubs and leather bars, where the night reverberates to pounding trance-techno, trashy drag shows and all-round cacophony.

At its western end, the street begins somewhat tamely with a strip of straight basement bars and an enticing hole-in-the-wall pizza joint, *Pieda Peks*. On the right, c/des Passadís leads past another loose group of bars including *Noctámbula* (see p.241) and ultimately to c/d'Alfonso XII, where many of the club parades finish. Back on c/de la Verge, the ambience steadily changes from here onwards: the road becomes darker, the music and laughter louder and the cave-like boutiques wilder and wilder; check out dildos galore at QG, and the wig specialist Atrevete. Most of the bars are gay, and in high season it's barely possible to squeeze between the mass of perfectly honed muscle that fills the street outside. *GC* is one of the wildest, an exclusively leather and rubber joint that has naked and underwear theme nights. Up in the balconies above the action, drag queens and club dancers preen themselves for the long night ahead.

SA PENYA

The gay bars along c/de la Verge are reviewed on p.275.

The excesses climax at the eastern extreme of c/de la Verge, where the street is barely a couple of paces wide, and rows of bars and their drinkers line up face to face across the divide during summer-season nights. There's a frenzy of flirtation, bravado and mischief in the air as passers-by are assessed, pectorals tensed, and drinks downed like there's no tomorrow. Just before the rocky cliff that signifies the end of the street is *Bar Zuka*, one of the island's most fashionable drinking dens. A few paces beyond here, past the flight of steps down to the Passeig Marítim, is **Sa Torre**, a small stone defensive tower with a pointed roof, rebuilt in 1994, from where there are wonderful views of Formentera and the Botafoc peninsula.

Carrer d'Alfonso XII and around

Map 3, K5.

From the western end of the c/de la Verge, it's a short stroll up c/des Passadís to **Carrer d'Alfonso XII**, actually more of a plaza than a street. Visit in daylight and it's a pleasant but unremarkable corner of Sa Penya – framed by tottering five- and six-storey whitewashed houses on the east side and the city walls just to the south, and dotted with palm-shaded benches. But at night c/Alfonso XII is transformed into one of Ibiza's most flamboyant arenas – the final destination for the summer **club parades**. At around 1am, after an hour or so of triumphant posturing through the streets of La Marina and Sa Penya, the podium dancers, promoters and drag queens move to the almost amphitheatre-like surrounds of c/d'Alfonso XII for a final encore. A surging, sociable throng spills out of some of the most fashionable bars in the island to appraise the parades, comment on the costumes, blag a guest pass and discuss plans for the night's clubbing.

Just below c/d'Alfonso XII, the small octagonal building, dating from 1873, is the city's fish market, **Sa Peixateria**. Disappointingly, it's rarely open these days – most Ibizans head for the glistening displays at the hypermarket to buy their tuna and monkfish. When the traders are there (early mornings are the best bet), the selection of fish laid out on the stainless-steel counters is, in any case, pretty moderate.

Dalt Vila

Occupying a craggy peak to the south of the harbour, the ancient hill of **DALT VILA**, meaning "high town", is the oldest part of Ibiza Town. Colossal Renaissance walls surround this historic enclave, which contains the finest monuments in Ibiza: the **cathedral**, the **castle**, the **town hall** and the island's best **museum**. Alongside these major attractions are numerous other buildings – hidden chapels and tunnels, Moorish fortifications and noblemen's mansions – and a warren of steep streets to explore.

Dalt Vila is one of the quietest parts of the city these days, with nightlife limited to the tasteful bars and restaurants of Sa Carrossa and Plaça de Vila. In winter, the streets are almost deserted, and even in the daylight hours you'll all but have the place to yourself, as many of the families who lived here for centuries have moved out in recent years, preferring the space of the suburbs. The population is a curious mix of disparate classes today: the clergy (who have lived in the area since the Catalan takeover), pockets of Ibizan high society in their imposing ancestral homes and

THE WALLS

Encircling the entire historic quarter of Dalt Vila, Ibiza Town's monumental Renaissance **walls** are the city's most distinctive structure. Completed in 1585 and in near-perfect condition today, the walls – at almost 2km long, 25m high and up to 5m thick – are some of Europe's best-preserved fortifications, and were awarded UNESCO World Heritage status in 1999.

The high ground occupied by Dalt Vila has been fortified for at least 2300 years: the **Carthaginians** first built walls around the very highest point, close to today's castle, and in the fourth century BC traveller-historian Timaeus admired the settlement's imposing defences; later, in 217 BC, a Roman attack led by Cornelius Scipio failed to penetrate the Carthaginian defences. During **Moorish** occupation of the island from the eighth century AD onwards, the city (then Yebisah) was extended to the south, and divided into three fortified quarters (the lower, upper and middle towns), each with its own defences. Protected by all three sets of fortifications, the upper quarter, around the cathedral and castle, remained the safest place to live, and was home to the elite. Remnants of these Moorish walls survive below the Baluard de Sant Jordi on the Ronda de Calvi, and on c/Sant Josep where

wealthy foreigners seduced by the superb views and tranquil atmosphere live alongside poor gypsy families who have moved into the houses in the lower half of town.

Dalt Vila's spectacular summit has been a place of worship for two and a half millennia, crowned by a roll call of edifices, from Carthaginian and Roman temples and a Moorish mosque to the Catalan cathedral that stands there today. The hill's strategic importance is all too clear when you reach the top, which affords magnificent views over the harbour to the open ocean and Formentera, and inland over the central hills.

there's a section that divided middle and lower quarters.

Battered by centuries of pirate attack, the city walls were crumbling by the sixteenth century. Vast new fortifications, strong enough to stand up to the pirates' cannon fire, were planned; the Italian architect Giovanni Battista Calvi produced the designs, and funding came from the Church, the Crown and the sale of salt. Work started in 1554 with the construction of six colossal ramparts (*baluards*) for artillery use, and a ring road, today's **Ronda de Calvi**, atop the broad walls that enabled cannons to be manoeuvred swiftly around the city. By 1575, as the new fortifications were nearing completion, Felipe II's chief architect, Jacobo Fratín, made a crucial modification: the construction of a seventh rampart (**Baluard de Santa Llúcia**), which enabled the precariously situated neighbourhood of Vila Nova to be included within the walls. An impressive new gateway (**Portal de ses Taules**) was designed to accommodate this alteration, and construction was completed by 1585. Perhaps the greatest testament to the success of the architects' design was the security that followed: Barbary pirates deemed the fortifications too formidable to breach, and the residents of Dalt Vila's were never again troubled by marauding buccaneers.

PORTAL DE SES TAULES

Map 4, F2.

The main entrance into Dalt Vila is the appropriately imposing **Portal de ses Taules** (Gate of the Inscriptions), a monumental gateway in the city walls up above the Plaça de sa Constitució. Even the approach is impressive – up a mighty stone ramp, across a drawbridge and over a dried-up moat – all part of the defences necessary to keep out sixteenth-century pirates. A stone *taule* (tablet) mounted above the gate bears the coat of arms of Felipe II and a Latin inscription attesting that the "King of Spain and the East and West Indies" built the fortifications for the benefit of the island. Two white marble statues (a Roman soldier and the goddess Juno) also flank the *portal*, copies of second-century figures found nearby by architect Jacobo Fratín when he was constructing the gateway in 1585 – the originals are now in the archeological museum (see p.75).

Immediately after passing through the Portal de ses Taules, you enter the old **armoury court**, a surprisingly graceful, shady arena – the island's very first hippy market was held here in the 1960s beneath its ten sturdy columns, and there's often a busker and a hairy trader or two here today. At the far end of the armoury court, you pass through a second, less imposing, stone gateway, constructed as an additional defensive measure. Above its arch is a stone cross and two small coats of arms; the upper belongs to Catalunya and Aragón, who controlled the island in the sixteenth century, while the lower is Ibiza Town's own emblem.

PLAÇA DE VILA

Map 4, E2.

The second gateway in the walls leads into **Plaça de Vila**, actually more of a broad, pedestrianized avenue than a town square, its sides graced by elegant old whitewashed mansions, pavement cafés and an assortment of art galleries and boutiques. A fruit and vegetable market was held here until the early twentieth century, but now life in the plaza revolves around enticing the ever-faithful flow of tourists to take a breather on their way to the historic treats above. The restaurants and cafés here reflect this, and though the setting is wonderful, the menus offer somewhat bland pan-European food, printed in a babble of languages that would keep an EU translator busy for weeks.

Heading west along the Plaça de Vila, the first path on the right leads up to the **Baluard de Sant Joan**, one of the seven turrets depicted on Ibiza Town's flag. From the manicured gardens on top of the rampart, there are excellent views over the Mercat Vell and La Marina quarter to the harbour, and beyond to Ibiza's rounded central hills.

MUSEU D'ART CONTEMPORANI

Map 4, E2. Tues–Fri 10am–2pm & 4–6pm, Sat & Sun 10am–1.30pm; 400ptas/E2.40.

From the Baluard de Sant Joan, it's a short stroll along the edge of the walls, past a tiny pyramid-topped watchtower, to the **Museu d'Art Contemporani**, housed in a two-storey rectangular building originally constructed in 1727 as an arsenal, and later used as a barracks and as the stables of the Infantry Guard. Its conversion, in 1969, made it one of Spain's very first contemporary art museums, and the collection, though small, is well worth taking in.

You enter into the upper floor of the building, the old arms hall, an expansive space with a lofty beamed roof where temporary exhibitions are staged. The lower floor (the old ammunition store and former stables) comprises two rooms separated by a metre-thick dividing wall. This is where the pick of the museum's collection is displayed; mostly the work of artists with an Ibizan connection of some kind. The exhibits are frequently shuffled around, but the work of island-born Tur Costa and the challenging abstract art of Ibiza visitors Will Faber, Hans Hinterreiter and Erwin Broner stand out.

WEST TO PLAÇA DEL SOL

Continuing west from Plaça de Vila, c/Santa Creu passes another row of restaurants, including the fine *Sa Torretta*

(see p.226), and narrows as it passes through what was originally part of the lower town of Moorish Yebisah, before
leading into **Plaça del Sol** (Map 4, B2). A small, shady
square directly above city walls overlooking the harbour and
Ibiza Town, it's an ideal place to take a drink or a snack.
The *Plaza del Sol* restaurant commands the best views, but
you'll pay a bit over the odds because of this.

West of Plaça del Sol, a flight of steps just before the
adjoining rampart of Baluard des Portal Nou leads down
into the New Town, passing through the Portal Nou itself
and into the Parc Reina Sofia, a small paved arena below
the walls that's popular with skateboarders.

TOWARDS PLAÇA DE LA CATEDRAL

From Plaça del Sol, most people head to the top of Dalt
Vila to see the castle and the cathedral. The most direct
route is along the Ronda de Calvi, the ancient ring road on
the top of the walls that girdle Dalt Vila, which passes
Baluard de Sant Jaume and Baluard de Sant Jordi. However,
you'll suffer in the summer sun, and a shadier (and more
interesting) alternative is to work your way through the
heart of the Old Town. From the southwest corner of the
square, climb the broad stone staircase of c/Portal Nou. At
the top, turn left into c/Sant Josep, its upper side lined by
10-metrehigh remnants of the original Arab-built fortifications, including a defence tower. At the corner of c/Sant
Josep and c/Santa Faç is the unadorned whitewashed facade
of the fifteenth-century **Església de l'Hospitalet** (Map 4,
C3), originally a hospital for the poor, but now a low-key
cultural centre that serves as a venue for amateur dramatics
and occasional art exhibitions.

Adjacent to the steps at the end of c/Sant Josep is the
imposing, angular old **Seminari** (Map 4, C3). The Jesuits
first used the building as lodgings for their monks between

1669 and 1767, but after they were thrown out of Spain by Carlos III it served as a seminary until the late 1990s, when it was converted into the luxury apartments of today. From the top of the staircase, pretty c/Conquista on the right derives its name from the Catalan takeover of the island in 1235 – some of the heaviest fighting took place on this street. The road also houses the most eccentric hotel in Ibiza, *El Palacio*, a temple to kitsch and chintz that sniggeringly acclaims itself to be "the hotel of the movie stars"; each of the rooms has a celluloid theme (from Charlie Chaplin to Marilyn Monroe), and assorted Teutonic wannabe guests have left their handprints on clay plaques hung on the wall outside, but this is about as close to Hollywood as things get.

At the end of c/Conquista, more steps lead up to the left into c/Sant Ciriac, the first street inside what was once the old Moorish upper town. A few metres along and on the right is a curious little chapel, the **Capella de Sant Ciriac** (Map 4, C5), which is little more than a shrine, set into the wall, protected by a metal grille and embellished with pot plants, candles and incense burners. The chapel is said to be the entrance to a secret tunnel through which the Catalan and Aragonese stormed the upper quarter of the Moorish citadel on August 8, 1235. The arch of a sealed-up passage is clearly visible below the painting of Sant Ciriac on the back wall of the chapel, but local opinion is divided as to the accuracy of the story – the invaders may have used a number of entrances. Whatever the truth, the legend is remembered on August 8 every year with a special mass held here.

Today the upper town is probably quieter than it's ever been, the garrison and market having relocated (along with many of the aristocratic original inhabitants) to the suburbs. Some reminders of the glory days remain, though: **Carrer Major** (Map 4, D5), the continuation of c/Sant Ciriac and

TOWARDS PLAÇA DE LA CATEDRAL

the main thoroughfare to the cathedral, boasts numerous grand houses adorned with family coats of arms.

The luxurious *La Torre de Canónigo* apartments on c/Major are reviewed on p.211.

PLAÇA DE LA CATEDRAL

Map 4, E5.

At the eastern end of c/Major, **Plaça de la Catedral** is the epicentre of Ibizan civilization. Phoenicians were the first to settle this spot in around 600 BC, attracted by the pivotal position above the island's best harbour, and by 400 BC Ibiza Town (then Ibosim) was a crucial city in the Carthaginian empire, with a temple dedicated to the god Eshmun gracing today's plaza. In 283 AD, the Romans also built a temple to Mercury here, followed by an Arab mosque that was torn down after the Catalans took over in 1235 to make way for the Gothic cathedral that dominates the small plaza today. A cluster of historic buildings also line the north side of the plaza, including the archeological museum and the courthouse, but it's the sublime **view** of Ibiza Town from the lookout between these buildings, with the sparkling waters of the harbour and forested hills beyond, that's the plaza's most arresting aspect.

Until 1838, when the town hall offices were moved to today's Ajuntament building, Plaça de la Catedral was also the focus of Ibizan political power, home to the Universitat (island government) building, to the right of the lookout, which is now occupied by the **archeological museum**. The late Gothic-style courthouse, and the former seat of the judiciary, the **Reial Curia** building is just to the left of the lookout; it's a modest whitewashed building, but the honey-stone coat of arms (belonging to Felipe V) above the double doorway gives the semi-derelict building a certain presence.

Museu Arqueològic d'Eivissa i Formentera

Map 4, E5. April–Sept Tues–Sat 10am–2pm & 5–8pm, Sun 10am–2pm; Oct–March Tues–Sat 10am–1pm & 4–6pm, Sun 10am–2pm; 300ptas/€1.80.

To the right of the Plaça de la Catedral lookout is one of the two buildings that make up the **Museu Arqueològic d'Eivissa i Formentera**. The other (currently closed) site in the New Town concentrates on the Carthaginian necropolis, the Puig des Molins and other Punic treasures, while the collection here provides an overview of Pitiusan history from prehistoric to Islamic times. It's not wildly exciting, but the logically arranged, well-presented exhibits are worth a browse; you'll need around an hour to have a good look around.

Consisting of four different constructions, the simple-looking **museum building** is itself of some interest, it's low, simple stone facade belying a much bigger interior. The middle portion of the structure is mid-fifteenth-century, built in a very functional, unadorned Mudéjar (Spanish Islamic) style, though the old entrance is now bricked up. It housed the **Universitat**, the seat of government for over 300 years until 1717, when Madrid downgraded its power to town hall (Ajuntament) status. On the left, and now serving as the museum's entrance hall, the fourteenth-century **Capella del Salvador** boasts a fine ribbed vault roof and was the seat of the seamen's guild until 1702, when it was moved to the Església de Sant Elm in La Marina (see p.62). On the right, the sixteenth-century **Capella des Joans** is more modest in scale, and now houses the Phoenician exhibits. The final section of the museum, con-

PLAÇA DE LA CATEDRAL

taining the Punic, Roman and Medieval rooms, extends down into the **Baluard de Santa Tecla**, the southeastern rampart which overlooks the harbour.

The museum's first room deals with prehistoric remains and the initial Phoenician colonization. The earliest exhibits, from around 1500 BC, consist mainly of pottery cooking vessels, stone and bone tools and copper axeheads, used by farmers, fishermen and hunters who lived in caves and in high locations, such as the Puig de ses Torrents near Santa Eulària and the Cap de Barbària (see p.190) in Formentera. Dating from the seventh century BC onwards, the **Phoenician** exhibits are more cosmopolitan, reflecting the sophisticated trade routes established by these powerful seafarers: red-glazed ceramic plates and amphorae from mainland Spain, Italian perfume bottles, and alabaster vessels and scarabs from Egypt stand out. Most of the Phoenician pieces were collected from Sa Caleta (see p.171) and the Plaça de la Catedral, the two main Phoenician settlements in the Pitiuses.

However, it was under the Phoenician's distant relatives, the **Carthaginians**, that Ibiza really flourished. Ibosim, as Ibiza Town was then called, was a key settlement in the Carthaginian (or **Punic**) empire until the mid-second century BC, with several thousand inhabitants, extensive docks from which figs, dates and wool were exported, and potteries that supplied the western Mediterranean with amphorae on an industrial scale. From the first room, steps lead down to the small Punic collection, housed in the tunnel that extends under the Baluard de Santa Tecla from under the old Universitat. Almost all of Ibiza's finest Punic artefacts, however, are in the (currently closed) Puig des Molins museum; here, there's an ordinary-looking stela, carved from local limestone, with an image of an unknown robed male figure and a religious inscription dedicated to the fearsome god

Baal, around whom a cult developed that included offerings of wine, olive oil and the sacrifice of children. Earthenware images of the fertility goddess (and wife of Baal) **Tanit**, who had her own sanctuary at the cave of Es Cuieram near Sant Vicent (see p.112) are also on display alongside plenty of local pottery and coins, and imported curiosities including painted ostrich eggs – a symbol of resurrection for the Carthaginians.

Ibiza was little more than an island backwater within the mighty **Roman** empire and would have had very limited geopolitical significance; hence there are few items in the Roman room of the museum, at the end of the Punic corridor. If the Roman statues look familiar, that's because you'll have passed the replicas mounted on the walls of the Portal de ses Taules. There's also an interesting Roman coin or two – Ibiza had had its own mint from the third century BC and the Romans maintained production within the island during the reigns of Tiberius, Caligula and Claudius. They continued using an image of the Carthaginian god Bes on the reverse side, reflecting the dual cultural nature of the island (there were also separate cemeteries) and the fairly harmonious crossover between Punic and Roman times.

The meagre **Islamic** collection, housed in a small room under the Baluard de Santa Tecla, is also fairly unassuming, again reflecting the Pitiuses' relatively unimportant status during the Moorish era. Silver and gold coins minted in Córdoba and Morocco, glazed pottery and assorted epigraphic oddities make up the bulk of the artefacts.

The cathedral

Map 4, F5. Daily 10am–1pm; Sunday service 10.30am; free.
Visible from all over the south of the island, the **cathedral** and adjacent castle that crown Dalt Vila are Ibiza's most

PLAÇA DE LA CATEDRAL

prominent landmarks. The former parish church of Santa Maria was granted cathedral status in 1782, after centuries of petitioning by the Ibizan clergy. Somewhat oddly, in that Ibiza only ever gets a light dusting every ten years or so, it's dedicated to Santa Maria de les Neus (Mary of the Snows).

Built mostly in the mid-fourteenth century in Catalan Gothic style, the cathedral is a simple, rectangular structure topped by a mighty belltower. Its sombre, uncluttered lines are at their most aesthetically pleasing from a distance, especially at night from across the harbour when the structure is floodlit. Whitewashed throughout, the interior is much less attractive, with somewhat trite Baroque embellishments added between 1712 and 1728 that detract somewhat from the hushed, austere atmosphere typical of Catalan Gothic churches. The cathedral's small **museum**, housing assorted ecclesiastical relics, including some impressive silver- and gold-plated altar pieces and Catalan art, is currently closed for renovation; no one seems sure when it'll reopen.

THE CASTLE AND AROUND

A rambling strip of buildings constructed in a fractious contest of architectural styles, the **castle** (Map 4, E6) squats atop the very highest ground in Dalt Vila, just south of the cathedral. Built between the eighth and eighteenth centuries, the heavily fortified castle complex housed the governor's residence and contained its own garrison. During the Spanish Civil War, the castle was the setting for one of the darkest chapters in Ibizan history, when mainland Anarchists, briefly in control of the island, massacred over a hundred Ibizan Nationalist prisoners here before fleeing the island. The incident is seen as the basis for decades of local opposition to leftist politics, which was broken only by the election of the leader of the Left-leaning Pacte Progressita coalition as president of the Consell Insular (island government) in June 1999.

Despite its historical significance, the castle complex has been left to decay for years while the Consell Insular, which owns the site, squabble over what to do with the place – various ideas have been mooted, including conversion into a museum or a luxury hotel. The latest plan is to turn the entire complex into a museum of Ibiza, putting all the island's historical treasures and documents under one roof, a task that will involve several years of building work.

Barriers, locked gates and all-round structural instability mean it's not possible to enter the complex at the moment, but for the best perspective of its crumbling facade head south to the **Baluard de Sant Bernat** rampart (Map 4, E7). To get there from the Plaça de la Catedral, follow c/de l'Universitat, a short passageway squeezed between the castle and cathedral buildings. On its right side, the modern staircase cut into the sandstone walls of Sa Torreta tower (one of the original Moorish fortifications) will serve as an entrance to the castle if the renovation work is ever completed; a little further on, another staircase cuts down through the walls to the scrubland of Es Soto below. The broad stone-flagged apex of the Sant Bernat rampart, jutting over the edge of the walls, is just to the right, from where the decaying profile of the castle complex is laid bare. Just left of the Sa Torreta tower is the sixteenth-century former governor's residence – slab-fronted, dusty pink and with three iron balconies, and rising above this to the left are the towers of the **Almudaina**, the Moorish keep. Smack in the middle of the castle complex is the tower of homage, another original rectangular Moorish fortification. Finally, dropping down in elevation to the left, are the wonky-windowed eighteenth-century infantry barracks.

The southerly views from Sant Bernat are also spectacular, with Formentera clearly visible on the horizon and the

THE CASTLE AND AROUND

Ibizan resorts of Figueretes and Platja d'en Bossa just a couple of kilometres away.

VILA NOVA

Retreating back to the Plaça de la Catedral, then onto c/Major, you'll quickly come to a small passageway on the right, some 50m down the street. Known as **Sa Portella** or "Little Gate" (Map 4, D5), this modest little archway is the only remaining Arab entrance to the old city, and today divides the historic upper town from the newer quarter of **VILA NOVA** to the south. Belatedly included in the city walls by Fratín, Vila Nova encompasses the Plaça d'Espanya, the Plaça de Vila and the Baluard de Santa Llúcia.

Through the gateway, the cobbled street ahead, c/Santa Maria (so named because it's the traditional route from La Marina and Vila Nova to the cathedral) passes the legendary **El Corsario** hotel on the left (see p.209), where Picasso is said to have stayed in the 1950s. On the same side of the road is a surviving section of Calvi's walls, rendered ineffectual after Fratín extended the defences south to include the Vila Nova area.

C/Santa Maria ends at **Plaça d'Espanya** (Map 4, G5), a small, open-ended cobbled square shaded by palm trees. The imposing arcaded building with the tiled, domed roof which dominates the plaza was originally built as a Dominican monastery in 1587, and also housed a school, providing free education for the poor until the Dominicans were expelled by the Spanish Crown in 1835, and the building was converted to today's **Ajuntament**, or town hall.

The tunnel opposite the Ajuntament cuts through the walls
to the scrubland of Es Soto beneath the castle.

At the eastern end of the plaza is a recumbent statue of Guillem de Montgrí, a crusading Catalan ecclesiastic who helped drive the Moors from Ibiza in 1235. It's a short walk from here along the edge of the walls and around to the left into c/General Balanzat, home to the **Església de Sant Pere** (Map 4, H4), open only for services (Sat 7pm, Sun noon & 7pm). This whitewashed sixteenth-century church, constructed by master Genoese craftsmen, is one of Ibiza's most handsome, topped by a bulbous crop of red-tiled domes. It was built as the Dominican monastery's church, and is still referred to the Església Sant Domingo by many Ibizans. Opposite the church, vast, five-sided **Baluard de Santa Llúcia** (Map 4, H3) is the biggest of all the seven ramparts that define the perimeters of Ibiza Town's walls. It was constructed by Fratín thirty years after the other six were built, then connected to Baluard des Portal Nou via an extension of the city walls from Baluard de Sant Joan.

West of the Baluard de Santa Llúcia, pretty **Sa Carrossa** (Map 4, F3–G3) heads back down toward the Portal de ses Taules. A triangular grassy bank, planted with palm trees and flowering scrubs, graces the centre of the street. Amongst the foliage is a miserable-looking statue of local historian and author of a formidable four-volume history of the island, **Isidor Macabich**, who, despite being known for his sense of humour, is depicted as a rather serious figure, with a book at his side. When asked if he was descended from one of Ibiza's most noble families, he replied "In Ibiza there are no nobles, we are sons of seamen, of peasants, or of a bitch." Though Sa Carrossa has a slumberous feel during the day, it transforms during high-season nights into one of the liveliest gay spots on the island, when the adjoining city walls serve as prime cruising territory.

VILA NOVA

The New Town

The suburban **NEW TOWN** (also known as the *Eixample* or "extension") west of Dalt Vila and La Marina has sprung up over the last thirty years, and holds little of interest. The one appealing area surrounds boulevard-like **Vara de Rey**, bordered with attractive streets brimming with cafés and quirky boutiques; just east of here is the Carthaginian necropolis of **Puig des Molins**, though its museum and tombs are currently closed. The further you get from this central zone, the worse things get – the outer suburbs are a depressing world of bland, faceless apartment blocks and broad, traffic-choked avenues. Somewhat surprisingly, though, these dormitory zones are the most lively part of town in the low season, when the no-nonsense bars and cafés buzz with business while the hip joints in the port enjoy a long winter slumber.

Taking up the entire northern and western sides of the port, the **new harbour** area is also short on sights, but it does at least provide marvellous views of the old town across the water. The docks and marinas can also be fun to explore and, in any case, you'll have to pass this way to get to the **Botafoc peninsula** and Talamanca beach.

VARA DE REY AND AROUND

An imposing and graceful tree-lined boulevard, **Vara de Rey** (Map 3, H3–D4) is the hub of modern Ibiza, and the logical place to start exploring the area. It's here that you'll find the island's oldest cinema, the Lux, the island's most famous café-bar, the *Montesol*, numerous banks and a compendium of fashionable boutiques. Vara de Rey can't compete with Barcelona's Ramblas, but the beautiful five-storey, early twentieth-century buildings, many in Spanish colonial style, give the street a certain status and character. Like the Ramblas, the central portion of Vara de Rey is pedestrianized; shaded by palms and poplar trees, it's thick with tourists in high season. Smack in the middle of the avenue is a large stone-and-iron monument dedicated to Ibizaborn **General Joachim Vara de Rey**, who died in the Battle of Caney fought between Spain and the USA over Cuba in 1889.

Just a block to the south, the **Plaça des Parc** (Map 3, H4) is an even more inviting place for a coffee or a snack, night or day, with six café-bars and a restaurant grouped around a square shaded by acacias and palms. There's no traffic at all to contend with here, and the small plaza attracts an intriguing collection of characters: ageing New Agers, clubbers and hippies. The bars all have a lot of character and atmosphere, each catering for different punters – pre-club favourite *Sunset Café* (see p.241) and classy, comfortable *Madagascar* (see p.240) are the most popular.

PUIG DES MOLINS

Map 3, D6.

East of Plaça des Parc on Via Romana, **Puig des Molins** (Hill of the Windmills) was one of the premier Punic burial sites in the Mediterranean, favoured by Carthaginians, whose burial requirements specified a site free from poisonous creatures; there are no snakes and scorpions in Ibiza. Noblemen were buried in this A-list necropolis in their thousands, their bodies transported here from all over the empire.

Today, Puig des Molins looks like little more than a barren rocky park, scattered with olive trees and rosemary bushes, and there seem to be few clues as to why it should be UNESCO-listed. If you can get inside the fences (the site is currently closed), you'll find the hillside riddled with

PUIG DES MOLINS

over three thousand tombs; excavations over the years have unearthed some splendid terracotta figurines, amphorae and amulets. Most of the finds have been gathered inside the grand halls of the site's imposing Neoclassical museum, the **Museu Arqueològic d'Eivissa i Formentera**, but it's currently closed for renovation and no one seems to know when it'll reopen.

NEW HARBOUR

Map 2, F2–G2.

Occupying the western and northern sides of Ibiza Town's bay, the **new harbour** (or Port d'Eivissa) is another modern extension to the city. This area was one half of the capital's vegetable patch, **Ses Feixes** (see box on p.86), until the late 1950s, when the town began to expand to the north. Today, it's a wealthy enclave that holds the yacht club, several marinas, the casino and the clubs *El Divino* and *Pacha*.

From the western end of Passeig Marítim (opposite the *Café Mar y Sol*), the harbour promenade of Avgda Santa Eulària heads north past the Formentera ferry terminal building and the yacht club. Continuing around the north side of the harbour, you'll pass rows of gleaming yachts in the bay and a line of luxury apartment blocks inland. The Art Deco-style *Ocean Drive* hotel (see p.209), jogging tracks, exercise stations, palm trees, Rayban-toting yachties and seemingly year-round sunshine hereabouts are reminiscent of Miami and, to a degree, even the vice is here too, in the form of the casino, the *El Divino* nightclub (see p.256) and an upmarket brothel or two.

BOTAFOC PENINSULA

From the *Ocean Drive* hotel, the thin, kilometre-long **Botafoc peninsula** stretches southeast into the harbour, with a road running along its length and a lighthouse defining the final rocky extremity. The three main bodies of land are now connected by strips of beach, the result of infilling in 1885; before this, all three were offshore islands. Over a century later, the environment is set to change again – despite protests from the green lobby, a vast new dock capable of accommodating cruise ships is under construction, slated to stretch from the lighthouse into the harbour.

There's certainly no reason to linger long at the first hill, the residential **Illa Plana** (Map 2, H3–H4), which was used as a plague colony in the fifteenth century. Even further back, in Carthaginian days, it was the base of a fertility cult centred around the goddess Tanit; dozens of figures dug up here can now be seen in Dalt Vila's archeological museum (see p.75). The tiny, pebbly slither of a beach, **Platja des Duros**, just below the road, is nothing special, though it does benefit from spectacular views of Dalt Vila. There are more great views of the old town and the ocean from the **Illa Grossa** (Map 2, I6) and **Botafoc** (Map 2, H6) promontories, the latter, a much smaller adjunct of Illa Grossa, defined by the sentinel-like **Far de Botafoc** lighthouse at its end. The new Botafoc dock and widened road will spoil the scene considerably, however, and it remains to be seen if revellers will continue the custom of congregating here to witness the first sunrise of the New Year.

Around Ibiza Town

The suburbs, resorts and beaches that ring the flat land around the capital are not Ibiza's best aspect, but if you desperately need to cool down, there are plenty of places to swim and chill. **Hikers** will find fine coastal walking, too,

SES FEIXES

It hardly looks historically important, but the large, seemingly barren patch of land west of Talamanca beach is actually a UNESCO World Heritage site. Now choked with giant reeds, scrub bush and dumped, rusting fridges, **Ses Feixes** (The Plots) were developed by the **Moors** over a thousand years ago using innovative agricultural methods. The farmlands were irrigated via an incredibly complex network of *acequias* (dykes), *fiblas* (subterranean water channels) and crop rotation systems thought to be unique to Ibiza, which enabled the land to produce two harvests per year.

The *feixes* remained Ibiza Town's most important farmland until the late 1950s, when the fringes of the fields began to be developed and tourism replaced agriculture as the island's main industry. Onions, cabbages, beetroot and melons were the main crops, plus, after the fifteenth century, maize and peppers. From the edge of the plots, it's still possible to make out the *feixes*, *fiblas* and water gates (*compuertas*) amongst the reeds, and the area is also rich in birdlife: grebes, the black-winged stilt, redshanks, egrets, herons and other waders. In August 2000, the island government announced plans to clean up the two *feixes* (there's another smaller area behind the yacht club on the western side of the harbour) alongside the environmental group GEN, but as industrial contaminants have been discovered, the work is likely to take some time to complete.

with the shoreline north of **Talamanca** beach almost untouched. Historical interest is thin on the ground, but the village church of **Jesús** in particular is worth investigating.

Physically, the suburbs extend to Talamanca and Jesús in the north and **Figueretes** to the south. In the west Ibiza

Town is at its most ugly, with a bewildering tangle of roundabouts, industrial estates and hypermarkets scarring the indeterminate fringes of the town. Eight kilometres to the west, the village of **Sant Rafel** is worth a quick visit for its ceramic workshops and church, though it's most famous for the **clubs** on its doorstep: the legendary venues of *Amnesia* and *Privilege*.

TALAMANCA

Map 2, H2.

A sweeping sandy bay 2km north of Ibiza Town, **Talamanca** beach rarely gets overcrowded, despite its close proximity to the capital. Development has been fairly restrained here, with hotels mainly confined to the northern and southern fringes, and it's not impossible to imagine the paradiscal pre-tourism environment. A smattering of bars and some good fish restaurants occupy the central part of the shoreline, which is popular with European families – the gently shelving beach is ideal for children.

Talamanca's *Bar Flotante* is reviewed on p.225.

To **get there**, you can walk from Ibiza Town (it'll take around 30min) via the new harbour along Passeig de Juan Carlos I or, in the summer, catch one of the hourly boats that depart from the docks close to the statue of the fisherman in La Marina (April–Oct only 9am–9.30pm; 370ptas/€2.22 return; 10min).

JESÚS

Map 1, F5.

Just northeast of Ibiza Town along the road to Cala Llonga, **JESÚS** is a messy overspill of the capital suspended in

A WALK FROM TALAMANCA TO CALA D'ESTANYOL

This easy hour-long, four-kilometre hike from Talamanca around the coastal cliffs north of Ibiza Town passes pine forests and a tiny secluded cove, and ends at the little bay of Cala d'Estanyol, where there's good swimming and a beach café selling snacks. If you want to shorten the hike, take one of the buses that run hourly to Cap Martinet from Agvda Santa Eulària in Ibiza Town.

Just beyond the crumbling *Paraíso del Mar*, the last hotel on the north side of Talamanca bay, a path follows the shore, passing a string of huts housing fishing boats, a scruffy, name-less, summer-only café-shack and a rocky outcrop, **Punta de s'Andreus**, that's popular with naturists – sharp rocks and strong currents don't make the swimming here especially pleasant, though. Past here, the path stays close to the sea, hugging the shoreline as it climbs the cliffs around the *Paradise Club* villa complex. Walk around the cliff side of the complex, and then head inland to avoid the firing range ahead; the path then heads east (right) back to the sea by the main entrance to the *Paradise Club*, where municipal buses termi-nate. Jutting into the waves ahead is **Cap Martinet**, a thin, saw-toothed rocky promontory.

From Cap Martinet, head north toward the slightly ridiculous white villa with the mock turret, then down through the woods ahead for a couple of minutes to a tiny stony bay that's ideal for a swim, a snorkel around the rocks or a picnic lunch. From the bay, walk up the right-hand side of the valley directly behind, following a pretty trail lined with rosemary bushes, and turning right after five minutes down a short dirt track bordered by stone walls. At the end of this trail, you reach the driveway of a cluster of villas; turn left into the drive, and walk for 200m until you reach the villa gateway; turn sharp right here along a dirt lane. Follow the lane for a couple of minutes, then skirt round the second of two sets of black gates and pick your way through a stretch of scrubland towards a gap in the stone wall some 100m ahead. Pass through the hole, and head uphill, taking the middle path that swings to the left; this steep trail climbs quickly though some woods and follows a crevice in the cliffs. After three minutes' walking, the trail levels out and affords views over the sea, with two jagged rocks visible just offshore; from here, the path descends to an old lime kiln, and after another five minutes or so you reach a sandy-coloured farmhouse. A track swings to the right below the farmhouse, and it's a further five minutes' walk to **Cala d'Estanyol**, a tiny, quiet cove with a patch of fine pale sand and sheltered swimming. It's undeveloped apart from a hand-ful of fishermen's huts and the funky *Juanela* café-restaurant (May–Oct only).

To return to Talamanca via a different route, retrace your steps to the farmhouse, then walk straight ahead through the farm's gate and take the left-hand dirt road uphill through a pine forest. Ignore two left turns and continue uphill along the winding track, which soon levels out to reveal superb views of Formentera on the horizon. The route is all downhill from here, passing the sandstone walls of a stupendous *casament*-style house below, until you reach a crossroads adjacent to a cluster of houses. Take the right turn, and a narrow paved road soon starts to descend toward the castle and cathedral of Dalt Vila ahead. It's a further five minutes' walk to the coast below past the concrete villas of *Puig Manya*, protected by razor wire and guard dogs. Once you reach the seashore, Talamanca is just 200m to the west along the coast path.

suburban no-man's land; just urban enough to boast a happening late-night bar, *La Alternativa* (see p.242), but rural enough to ensure that roosters disrupt all chance of a lie-in.

Right on the highway, but almost hidden amongst an anonymously ugly sprawl of boxy apartment blocks, is the whitewashed village church, **Nostra Mare de Jesús** (Thurs 10am–noon, plus Sunday Mass), a wonderfully simple Ibizan design that's brilliantly illuminated at night. The church building dates back to 1466 and was originally a convent, but construction work continued under Franciscan friars, who established themselves here in 1498, and wasn't completed until 1549. The church boasts Ibiza's finest altar painting, by Valencians Pere de Cabanes and Rodrigo de Osona. An impressive and expansive work spread over seven panels, with images of Christ, the Virgin Mary and the Apostles, it was deemed of sufficient artistic merit to be spared during the Civil War, when most of the island's ecclesiastical art was destroyed. Right opposite the church is a good, no-nonsense café-bar, *Bon Lloc* (see p.242) where there are some interesting old photographs of the church and village on the walls and a very swish terrace café, *Croissanteria Jesús*, which is one of the best breakfast spots in Ibiza.

FIGUERETES

Map 2, A5.

The suburb-cum-resort of **FIGUERETES** may be just a fifteen-minute walk southwest of the capital, but any urbane cultural influence is absent. Strangely, Figueretes was *the* most happening place in Ibiza during the early 1960s, when the area was the focus of the early beatnik scene and the haunt of jazzmen including the bassist Titi and trumpeter Pony Poindexter, who settled here to jam throughout the summer seasons. However, there's no evidence of this funky former life in Figueretes today; nightlife is limited to

A SCENIC WALK TO FIGUERETES

Though the simplest way to **walk** to Figueretes from Ibiza Town is via the fume-filled Agvda d'Espanya, a much more attractive alternative is to take the route around the coast, a fifteen-minute walk from the centre of town. From the western end of Vara de Rey (Map 3, F4), turn left up c/Joan Xico, keeping the city walls on your left. After 200m the road splits; take the left-hand turn through the short tunnel ahead, then the first right up a potholed dirt track. You emerge in a near-rural corner of the city, scattered with pine trees and rosemary bushes, and with the Mediterranean directly ahead.

Follow the dirt track for 150m or so, and you'll reach the coastal cliffs, where you'll see a phone box. Uncluttered by the sprawl of the modern city, the walls of Dalt Vila to the north look especially impressive from here, while to the south are sublime vistas of Figueretes and Platja d'en Bossa, and over the sea to Es Cavallet and Formentera. Just below the phone box, a spiky tangle of prickly pear cacti and spear-leaved agave plants disguise a precipitous path that snakes down to a tiny sandy **beach**, popular with gay men. Figueretes is just 500m away from the phone box, down the wide dirt track that clings to the cliffs. This track joins up with c/Ramón Muntaner after a couple of minutes, from where steps lead down to Figueretes' promenade and beach below.

a tired bunch of expat-run bars and some very mediocre Chinese and Italian restaurants. The sandy beach isn't one of the island's finest, either, and is certainly not flattered by the dense concentration of unruly apartment blocks that frame the double bay, but it does have some basic seaside appeal, with an attractive palm-lined promenade that gives the waterfront a welcome slice of charm. Unlike many Ibizan resorts,

FIGUERETES

there is a small resident population here, and in winter elderly Ibizans reclaim the streets, stroll, chat and take some sea air.

The other main draw here is the location: as it's so close to the capital, it's easy to use Figueretes as a convenient and economic base for some serious forays into the dynamic night scene just around the bay. **Gay** visitors have known this for years, and many return every year to the same apartments.

SANT RAFEL

Map 1, E5.

Perched atop the central hills 8km from the capital, **SANT RAFEL** is a largely featureless village just north of the Ibiza Town–Sant Antoni highway that's all but overshadowed by the mighty clubbing temples of *Amnesia* and *Privilege* just to the south. You'll find a moderate collection of stores, cafés and restaurants strung out along its modest high street, Avgda Macabich, which was originally a section of the main road across the island until the current highway between Ibiza Town and Sant Antoni was built. Though Sant Rafel's appeal may seem a little thin, the town does boast several **ceramic workshops** – a couple of which originally set up by Argentinian leftists fleeing from the military junta in the 1970s – leading the Consell Insular to (somewhat ambitiously) declare the village a *zona de interés artesanal*, or artisan zone. Hype notwithstanding, there are a few good potteries in town; head for Cerámica Es Moli or Kinoto on Avgda Macabich, or Icardi Martinez on the main highway, adjacent to the km4.2 marker. Local ceramics are usually on show at the annual October 24 fiesta.

Sant Rafel's restaurant is reviewed on p.226; *Amnesia* and *Privilege* are reviewed on pp.253 & 259.

SANT RAFEL

Just 300m east of the high street is the nicest part of the village, centred around the **church**. Built between 1786 and 1797, it's typically Ibizan, with metre-thick white-washed walls that are visible for miles around, and impressive buttresses. From the churchyard there are stunning views down to Dalt Vila and the sea, as well as glimpses of *Privilege* and *Amnesia*.

The East

From the slender, pebbly beach of Sòl d'en Serra, some 5km north of Ibiza Town, to the rugged cliffs around the hamlet of Sant Vicent in the extreme northeast, Ibiza's **east coast** represents the sane side of the island's tourism industry, with a shoreline dotted with family-orientated resorts and sheltered coves. Many of the most spectacular sandy beaches, including lovely **Cala Llonga** and **Cala de Sant Vicent**, both handsomely backed by towering coastal hills, were developed decades ago into bucket-and-spade holiday resorts, where the nights reverberate to karaoke and 1980s hits rather than pounding techno-trance, but plenty of wild, pristine places remain. North of the busy, built-up environs of the lively resort of **Es Canar**, it's just a few kilometres' drive to the tiny, sheltered cove beach of **Cala Mastella**, and the invigorating surf- and cliff-backed sands at **Cala Boix**. A little further north, the kilometre-long sands of **Aigües Blanques** are *the* place to bare all in the north of the island.

The region's main hub, and its municipal capital, **Santa Eulària des Riu** is a pleasant but slightly mundane town that acts as a focus for the east coast's resorts, with a good restaurant strip and a clutch of appealing bars, cafés and shops. The town has a friendly, family-orientated appeal, with an atmosphere that's markedly different to the teenage histrionics that can plague Sant Antoni or the wild street theatrics of Ibiza Town. Aside from the historic hilltop **church**, there's little in the way of sightseeing, but the **harbourfront**, with its extensive promenade, is an agreeable place for a wander, and the bars and restaurants in the port zone have a fair degree of bustle in the summer months. To the north, the pretty village of **Sant Carles** is worth a visit, with a historic church, a half-decent Saturday hippy market and a good bar or two. Heading towards the extreme northeast tip of the island, around the hamlet of **Sant Vicent**, you'll find some of Ibiza's most spectacular scenery: steep, forested hillsides and sweeping valleys as well as rugged coves like **Port de ses Caletes**.

Getting around the east is fairly easy. One of Ibiza's main transport hubs, Santa Eulària is connected to the area's main resorts and villages by regular bus and boat services. To get to the more remote beaches, though, you'll have to procure your own wheels – there are car, scooter and bicycle rental outlets in all the resorts – or take taxis. After midnight, the discobus (see p.38) runs between Es Canar, Santa Eulària and Ibiza Town.

Reviews of accommodation and restaurants in the east start on pp.212 and 227 respectively.

CALA LLONGA AND AROUND

Heading northeast from Ibiza Town, you're best off avoiding the heavy traffic on the main C733 highway to Santa Eulària in favour of the far more scenic minor road to Santa Eulària that runs via the village of Jesús (see p.87) – the right-hand turnoff is 1km along the C733, beside the pink *Manumission Motel*. Beyond Jesús, this road climbs up the eastern hills, twisting and turning through dense forests of aleppo pine, skirting the lush greens of the **Roca Llisa** golf course (see p.53) and providing sweeping views of the island's interior. Some 8km past Jesús, there's a turnoff on the right for the small family resort of **CALA LLONGA** (Map 5, B9). Superbly set in a spectacular, fjord-like inlet below soaring forested cliffs, Cala Llonga is purely a holiday enclave, and though the 300-metre-wide bay is blessed with fine creamy-coloured sand and translucent water, the place closes down completely for six months after the last visitors have left in late October. Unfortunately, the bay's natural beauty is tainted somewhat by a nasty rash of off-white hotels and apartment blocks insensitively dumped on the northern cliffs, a concrete legacy of rampant development in the 1960s.

Infrastructure aside, the gently-shelving sands are superb, and the shallow water is usually unruffled by waves. There are full beachside facilities including sunbeds, umbrellas and pedalos, and a **tourist information** kiosk just behind the sands (May–Oct Mon–Sat 10am–2pm). As in many Ibizan resorts, the cuisine scene here isn't especially inspiring, with little variety amongst the fairly bland menus. The best bet is the *Wild Asparagus*, well-signposted down a track at the rear of the bay.

Sòl d'en Serra

Map 5, A9.

Just 800m south of Cala Llonga, down a bumpy dirt track (you can drive as far as the path that leads down from the cliffs to the beach), **Sòl d'en Serra** is a slender, undeveloped 500-metre-long pebble beach backed by high golden cliffs. The shore is quite exposed here, and the sea can get choppy when there's a strong wind – perfect for an invigorating dip if you're a confident swimmer, but not ideal if you're travelling with with small children. The beach never gets busy, even in high season; visit between October and May and you're almost guaranteed to have it to yourself. Good **meals** and **snacks** are served in the Dutch-owned *Sòl d'en Serra* restaurant above the waves, where there's also a chillout terrace complete with hammocks and sunbeds.

SANTA EULÀRIA DES RIU

Map 5, B7.

In an island of excess, **SANTA EULÀRIA DES RIU**, Ibiza's third largest town, is remarkable for its very ordinariness. Pleasant and provincial, the town clings tight to the eastern shoreline beside the banks of the only **river** in the Balearics, the Riu de Santa Eulària, from which the town takes its suffix, *des riu* (of the river). Apart from an attractive fortified church and modest museum perched on the **Puig de Missa** hilltop just northwest of the town centre, there's little of specific interest. Santa Eulària's sparkling shoreline is its best aspect – the two town **beaches** are kept clean and tidy, with gently-sloping sands that are ideal for children, while the recently redeveloped **Port Esportiu** in the harbour bristles with yachts, bars and restaurants.

The grid-like network of streets abound with functional rather than fashionable stores and bars, most open throughout the year, giving the town a modest degree of urban hustle and bustle. Architectural treats are all but absent in the town centre, but the wide **Passeig de s'Alamera**, running from the town hall south to the shore, helps compensate, providing Santa Eulària with an agreeably leafy focal point.

There's a good selection of atmospheric, moderately priced places to **eat** along the main restaurant strip, c/Sant Josep, but the **nightlife** is pretty tame, with most locals and visitors content with an amble along the palm-lined promenade or a quiet drink in one of the many seafront café-bars.

Some history

Isolated pottery fragments found close to the Santa Eulària River indicate that there was a minor Punic presence here during the first millennium BC, but there's no evidence of a sizeable settlement. The **Romans** constructed a bridge over the river (now the rebuilt Pont Vell), but they left the Santa Eulària bay alone. The region remained a rural backwater for six hundred years, until the **Moors** took control of the island in the tenth century and intensively farmed the Riu Eulària valley, but again, they didn't establish an urban centre. Following the **Catalan** conquest in 1235, a simple chapel was constructed atop the Puig de Missa, but Santa Eulària's population remained hamlet-sized for another five hundred years as **pirates** terrorized the eastern coast, burning down the first chapel in 1550.

Santa Eulària's first streets, c/de Sant Jaume and Passeig s'Alamera, and the **Ajuntament** (town hall) building, were constructed in 1795, but the population remained tiny, growing to only around a couple of hundred inhabitants by 1920. The first foreign **travellers** – mainly writers and artists – also began arriving in the early years of the twentieth century, but tourism didn't really become an important factor in the local economy until well after the Spanish Civil War, which fractured the town politically.

Elliot Paul's *Life and Death of a Spanish Town* (see Contexts, p.324) documents Santa Eulària's extreme poverty and social divisions at the time of the Spanish Civil War.

New hotels began to be constructed after 1950, and Santa Eulària's economy slowly began to rely on **tourism** rather than its fishing boats and market. In the 1960s and early 1970s, the relatively unspoiled nature of the place, combined with the presence of the legendary bar, *Sandy's*, enticed a fair slice of European jetsetters. Laurence Olivier and John Mills were regulars, while Diana Rigg, Terry Thomas and Denholm Elliott even settled and bought houses in the area. As the town has expanded and dedicated itself to mass tourism, though, the glamour has faded: *Sandy's* has closed, and today Santa Eulària is an appealing family resort rather than a chic, glamorous destination.

Plaça d'Espanya and Passeig de s'Alamera

Smack in the centre of town, pretty little **Plaça d'Espanya** (Map 3, F3), planted with palms trees and lined with benches, is the quiet hub of the Santa Eulària municipality and a good place from which to start exploring the town. The graceful **Ajuntament** (Town Hall) dominates the north side of the plaza. Built in 1795, this sober building exudes provincial restraint, with a stout-arched colonnade flanked by two simple municipal coats-of-arms. In front of the Ajuntament is a small stone monument, put up by the city of Palma in neighbouring Mallorca to thank the local seamen who came to the rescue of the steamboat *Mallorca*, which caught an underwater reef near the island of Redona, just offshore, in 1913.

Just below Plaça d'Espanya, over the busy, traffic-choked high street of c/Sant Jaume, **Passeig de s'Alamera** (Map 6, F3–F4) is easily Santa Eulària's most attractive thoroughfare. Laid out at the same time as the Ajuntament, boulevard-like s'Alamera has a shady pedestrianized centre, planted with a healthy collection of well-tended trees and flowering shrubs. In the summer season, the dozens of market stalls set up here add a splash of colour, selling jewellery, sarongs and tie-dye Thai garb.

SANTA EULÀRIA DES RIU

Along the harbourfront

At the end of Passeig s'Alamera, Santa Eulària's **harbourfront** commands wonderful views of the glistening, turquoise Mediterranean and the steep wooded hill, Puig d'en Fita, that frames the bay to the south. Below the promenade are the town's two slim, crescent-shaped **beaches**, packed in high season with families enjoying the fine golden sands and safe swimming. The seaside scene is somewhat tainted, though, by the obtrusive, slab-like apartment blocks that form a concrete curtain above the sand, and the unremarkable bunch of café-bars that line the promenade.

Heading northeast along the harbourfront, you'll soon arrive at the **Port Esportiu** (Map 6, H4; signposted in Castilian as the "Puerto Deportivo"), an upmarket, yachtie-orientated enclave set around a modern marina. Thick with restaurants and bars, it's a popular place for a drink or something to eat, though many of the menus are on the bland side, and the location ensures high prices.

Continuing east, the harbourfront takes you past rows and rows of shimmering yachts before reaching a rocky point some 500m from the beaches, in front of the bulky *Hotel Ses Estaques*, from where there are spectacular **views** back along the Santa Eulària bay. Local legend attests that the small hill beside the huge, modern *Hotel Los Loros*, a couple of minutes further on, was the site of an ancient chapel that collapsed seconds after the congregation had left the building after Mass. There's no evidence to back this up, but the unremarkable site still appears on most maps as **Punta de s'Església Vella** (Point of the Old Church). It's been earmarked as the spot of a new municipal edifice, with an auditorium and cultural centre – work should begin in 2001.

Puig de Missa

Map 6, C2.
Behind Plaça d'Espanya, at the back of the Ajuntament, c/Sant Josep is the first leg of the walk up to **Puig de Missa**, the little hill to the west that holds the town's sixteenth-century church and ethnological museum; it's an easy ten-minute walk to the top. Pink signs proclaim the route a *paisatge pintoresc* (picturesque path), but it's far from scenic initially, passing shops and long, ordinary suburban streets. The route continues to the right into c/Sol, and then left along c/Pintor Barrau, passing close to the town's main **market** (Map 6, E2; Mon–Sat 8am–6pm) underground on the corner of c/del Sol and Camí del Missa – it's not a wildly exciting commercial hub, but fine for a quick browse amongst the glistening fish displays and piles of fruit and veg.

Museu Etnològic d'Eivissa i Formentera
Map 6, C3. May–Oct 10am–1pm & 5–8pm; Nov–April 10am–1pm & 4–6pm; 300ptas/€1.80.
Half way up Puig de Missa, the **Museu Etnològic d'Eivissa i Formentera** is focused around Pitiusan rural traditions, but unless you have a passion for the rustic tools of yesteryear the exhibits are not especially interesting. The **museum building** itself is something of a draw, though: a classic example of the traditional flat-roofed Ibizan *casament*. You enter via the outdoor terrace (*porxet*) that would have been the centre of family life in the hot summer months. Moving inside, the

ticket office is located in the cool, beamed **porxo** (long room), the engine room of the household for most of the year, where corn would have been husked, tools sharpened and *festeig* (courting rituals) held. Most of the exhibits here are either carpentry tools or musical instruments, such as oleander wood flutes (*flautas*) and *tambor* drums made from pine and rabbit skin.

All the other rooms lead off from the *porxo*. Up a short staircase, **room 4** houses sombre black nineteenth-century *gonella* skirts and several flamboyant, billowing dresses from the early twentieth century, made to wear at weddings and fiestas; some are adorned with spectacular *emprendadas* – ceremonial necklaces made from silver, gold and coral. Downstairs, **room 5** is the most unusual feature of the house – a damp natural cave, perfect for wine storage, with a grape press, vat, cask and decanter on display. The **kitchen** (room 6), dominated by a massive hearth and chimney hood, has a modest collection of meat cleavers, mincers, coffee roasters and gourds. All things agricultural have been amassed in **room 7** – ploughs, shovels, yokes, pitchforks and hoes – while the attraction in **room 8** is a huge old-olive oil press. Up another flight of stairs from the *porxo*, **room 9** has a nautical flavour, with fishing spears and a framed privateer's licence, the legal certificate granted to Ibizan corsairs (see p.102) by the Crown which authorized them to attack pirate vessels. Adjoining room 9, **room 10** was originally a tiny bedroom, and a small cot and a bridal chest are displayed today.

Església de Puig de Missa

Map 6, C2. May–Sept daily 9am–9pm.

Puig de Missa's 52-metre summit is dominated by the sculpted lines of Santa Eulària's magnificent fortress-cum-church, **Església de Puig de Missa**, a white-painted, rectangular building constructed, after pirates destroyed the original chapel, to a suitably impenetrable design by the Italian architect Calvi, who was also responsible for the Dalt Vila walls. Dating from 1568, the church has a semicircular tower built into its eastern flank that formed part of Ibiza's coastal defences. In around 1700, two side chapels and magnificent porch were added, and the latter is the church's best feature, a wonderfully cool arena with eight arches and mighty pillars supporting a precarious-looking beamed roof. Inside, everything is very simple: whitewashed throughout, with little decoration apart from a series of images of a suffering Christ and a huge, typically gaudy, *churrigueresque*-style seventeenth-century altar brought here from Segovia by the Marqués de Lozoya in 1967 – the original interior was torched in the Spanish Civil War. Below the church, just to the north, the **cemetery** is worth a quick look, thick with verdant foliage and spilling down the hill over several different levels. In amongst the predominantly Catholic monuments, one tombstone displays a Star of David, presumably in honour of a member of the tiny Jewish community that has been established in Ibiza since Carthaginian times.

Along the river

Descending from the Puig de Missa via a footpath just before the Ethnological Museum, you soon reach busy c/de Sant Jaume, the old Roman road that connected the capital with the lead mines near Sant Carles (see p.106); today, it's Santa Eulària's main thoroughfare. Cross to the other side of c/de Sant Jaume and turn right along it towards the **river**; after 100m, take the path that leads down to **Pont Vell** (Map 6, B2), with its three simple seventeenth-century stone arches. It's a footbridge these days - traffic continues along c/de Sant Jaume and crosses the river via the modern roadbridge just upstream. The river itself is usually little more than a minor stream these days, though there's enough water to keep the resident population of ducks happy.

Heading downstream from Pont Vell towards the sea, an attractive, manicured **path** lined with giant reeds and the odd bench follows the course of the wide riverbed to the town's promenade and southern beach. Just before you reach the river's mouth, a startlingly modern blue suspension bridge (Map 6, A5) connects Santa Eulària with the suburb of **Siesta**, once a rural retreat where the English actress Diana Rigg owned a house, and now a faceless modern housing estate.

NORTHEAST TO PUNTA ARABÍ

From the seafront promenade in Santa Eulària, an attractive, easy-to-follow **coastal path** follows the serrated shoreline northeast to the modern resort of Es Canar. It's a six-kilometre, two-hour walk, with plenty of opportunities for a swim along the way. Walking east along the promenade, you'll reach the rocky promontory of **Punta de s'Església Vella** (Map 5, C7) in about fifteen minutes. The path then loops around the bulky, landmark *Hotel Los Soros*, and passes above quiet **Cala Niu Blau**, or "Blue Nest Cove" (Map 5, C7), where there's a 100-metre arc of fine, sunbed-strewn sand and a simple fish restaurant.

Continuing along the coast path, past a cluster of pricey-looking villas, you'll arrive at **Cala Pada** (Map 5, D7) in about twenty minutes; the 200m of fine, pale sand and shallow water here are popular with families, and there are three café-restaurants. It's also a surprisingly well-connected beach, with hourly **boats** to Santa Eulària and Ibiza Town during the summer, when boat operators also offer excursions to Formentera.

Some 500m beyond Cala Pada, the path skirts **s'Argamassa** (Map 5, D7), a compact, fairly upmarket family resort where a scattering of large modern three- and four-star hotels loom over the shoreline, and then heads inland, bypassing the wooded promontory of **Punta Arabí**, which juts into the Mediterranean opposite two tiny rocky islets, Redona and Santa Eulària. From here, it's a ten-minute stroll into Es Canar, passing the *Club Arabí* resort, where Ibiza's biggest hippy market (see below) is held.

ES CANAR

Map 5, D7.

A quick 5km dash across the well-watered plain northeast of Santa Eulària, **ES CANAR** is a medium-sized resort of four- and five-storey hotel blocks with a sandy, blue-flagged beach. A recently built promenade stretches north to the beach of Cala Nova (see p.106), lined with a strip of British and Irish pubs, souvenir shops and fast-food joints toward the centre of the resort.

There are good hourly boat and bus connections between Es Canar and Santa Eulària, as well as discobuses in the evenings (see Basics, p.38).

Es Canar is generally a family-orientated place, where children are well catered for and nights revolve around "Miss and Mr Es Canar" competitions and quiz shows. However, it's the weekly **hippy market** (May–Oct Wed 9am–6pm), held just south of the centre in the grounds of the *Club Arabí* resort, that draws most people to this part of the coast. First held in the early 1970s, it's unquestionably the biggest in the island these days; each July and August, Ibiza's worst traffic jams form amongst the convoys of coaches and rent cars in town to peruse some four hundred stalls. If you join them, bear in mind that you'll be extremely lucky to find anything that you haven't seen at

ES CANAR

105

home. The whole affair has become very sanitized, and most of the stalls sell the same kind of overpriced tack, from gaudy nylon Bob Marley and Che Guevara banners and junk jewellery to "I love Ibiza" T-shirts. Since the cookshacks were cleared out a few years ago following a health scare, there's nothing very interesting to snack on either.

Cala Nova

Map 5, D6.

A kilometre north of Es Canar around the rocky coastline, the wide sandy bay of **Cala Nova** is one of Ibiza's most exposed beaches, with invigorating, churning waves at most times of year; when there's a northerly wind blowing, it's one of a handful of places in Ibiza where it's possible to **surf** – there are no boards available for rent, though. As offshore rocks and the pounding wave action can make swimming tricky, Cala Nova isn't a favourite with families and the sands never get too crowded. There are sunbeds and umbrellas for rent, a small snack bar (May–Oct) and a large, very well-equipped **campsite** (see p.218) at the entrance to the beach.

SANT CARLES

Map 5, D5.

Of all Ibiza's villages, the pretty, whitewashed hamlet of **SANT CARLES**, 7km northeast of Santa Eulària and set a couple of kilometres back from the coast, is probably the most steeped in hippy history. It first became associated with early bohemian travellers in the 1960s, when a glut of vacant farmhouses in the unspoiled surrounding countryside attracted hippy settlers, who quickly made Sant Carles, and specifically the legendary *Anita's* bar, the focus of a lively scene. *Anita's* remains open (see p.243), though these days the scene is less in evidence here than in the *Las Dalias* bar (see p.243), just south of the village on the Santa Eulària road, which stages an interesting Saturday **market** (see p.268) that's strong on ethnic trappings; there's also a chai tea stall and a merry bunch of crystal-ball merchants, navel-gazers and rebirthers in attendance.

The only other point of interest is the village **church**, Església de Sant Carles, a very fine eighteenth-century construction with a broad, arcaded entrance porch supported by six squat pillars, and a simple white interior with a single nave and a side chapel on the left dedicated to Santa Mare del Roser. The church is most notable as having witnessed a bloody chapter in the **Spanish Civil War**, which led to the death of the village curate and his father in 1936. Until recently, the best-known version of events came from Elliot Paul, an American writer based in Santa Eulària, who reported in his book *Life and Death of a Spanish Town* (see Contexts, p.324) that the Nationalist curate was so at odds with his staunchly Republican parishioners that he was forced to barricade himself inside the church, and even opened fire on the villagers from the belfry before being captured and executed. An alternative view, with more widespread local support, has been put forward by Ibizan historian Rafael Sainz. He asserts that when Republican forces arrived in the village demanding water from the church cistern, the curate refused them entry unless they disarmed. This provoked an argument between the curate and his father (who appeared on the scene with a rifle), and the Nationalist troops. Sainz charges that neither father or son fired a shot, but were both quickly overpowered before being executed. Whatever the truth, they were both hung from the carob tree which still stands outside the church.

SANT CARLES

S'ARGENTERA MINES

Travelling around Ibiza, especially the north of the island, you can't help but notice the astonishing rust-red hue of the earth, or *terra rossa*, so called because of its high metallic content. The s'Argentera hills south of Sant Carles were quarried from Roman times until 1909 and, alongside salt, mining represented the island's only other export industry for two millennia. The crumbling brick chimneys of the **s'Argentera mines** still stand 3km south of Sant Carles on the road to Santa Eulària; here, two hundred Ibizans were employed on nine different seams, removing over a hundred tons of lead a year as well as small amounts of silver. The mines are not currently open to the public, but there are plans to develop the site into a tourist attraction, with guided tours and a museum.

THE NORTHEAST CORNER

East of Sant Carles, Ibiza's rugged **northeastern corner**, between Cala Llenya and Aigües Blanques, is strewn with beautiful sandy beaches, low amber cliffs and patches of thick woodland. With only two small, upmarket hotel complexes along the entire shoreline, limited public transport links and no towns in the vicinity, many of the beaches on this exposed coastline are empty for most of the year, and even in the high season things never get too crowded. Waves often pound the sands at the beaches of **Cala Llenya** and **Cala Boix**, while the surf can get really strong at **Figueral** and **Aigües Blanques**, especially in winter. The coves of **Cala Mastella** and **Pou des Lleó**, however, are more sheltered, and for most of the year there's barely a ripple in the pellucid water.

Cala Llenya to Cala Boix

Southeast of Sant Carles, a signposted road weaves 4km downhill through small terraced fields of olive and carob trees, and skirts the *La Joya* holiday village – one of the island's less brutal developments – before depositing you at **Cala Llenya** (Map 5, E6), a two-hundred-metre-wide, bite-shaped sandy bay positioned between low sandstone cliffs that are scattered with white-painted villas. Like many of the beaches on this stretch of the island, the sea can get choppy here and, perhaps because of this, the fine sands never get too crowded – you should have no problem finding a sunbed or umbrella for the day. There's a beachside café (May–Oct) for snacks and more formal evening dining, when tables are placed on the sand. Two daily **buses** run between Cala Llenya and Santa Eulària, via Sant Carles.

Working north along the coast, the next accessible beach is **Cala Mastella** (Map 5, E5), some 3km from Cala Llenya and reachable via the same road from Santa Carles, from where you take a signposted right turn and follow the road down through an idyllic terraced valley. Barely 40m wide, the sandy beach is sublime, set at the back of a deep coastal inlet with pine trees almost touching the sheltered, emerald waters. There's a tiny snack-kiosk by the shore, from which you can rent out sunbeds, but for fine seafood and grilled fish lunches walk 50m around the north side of the bay to the *Cala Mastella* restaurant (see p.227); you can't see it from the main section of the beach.

North of Cala Mastella, a coastal road meanders for 1km or so through pine forest, affording panoramic views over the Mediterranean below, to **Cala Boix** (Map 5, F5). Set below high, crumbling cliffs, Cala Boix is a beautiful sliver of a beach, with coarse sand and pebbles, and the obligatory umbrellas and sunbeds for rent. Three simple restaurants

THE NORTHEAST CORNER

line the headland high above the shore – the *Restaurant Cala Boix* commands the best views – and there's also the excellent inexpensive *Hostal Cala Boix* if you need a place to stay.

For reviews of hotels and restaurants in Cala Boix, see p.212 and 227 respectively.

Pou des Lleó and around

Inland of Cala Boix, a lone country road scythes northwest for 1km or so, past large terraced fields separated by honey-coloured dry-stone walls, until you come to a signposted junction for the diminutive bay of **Pou des Lleó** (Map 5, F5), named "Lion's Well" after a sweet spring close to the shore which is now all but dry. A tiny, pebble-and-sand-strewn horseshoe-shaped inlet, surrounded by low-lying, rust-red cliffs and lined with fishing huts, Pou des Lleó is popular amongst Ibizan families, who come here for barbecues on summer evenings, but is usually deserted in winter save for a fisherman or two. A tiny snack bar (May–Oct) that serves delicious grilled fish and cold beers, and the decent *Restaurant Salvadó* (see p.227), comprise the entirety of the facilities here. Walk around to the left of the bay (north), above the fishing huts, and you'll come upon two completely deserted coves, both covered with banks of compressed seaweed that form a natural, comfortable mattress for sunbathing.

From the restaurant, it's a further kilometre down a winding road that strikes east towards the coast to a seventeenth-century defence tower, **Torre d'en Valls** (Map 5, F5). Set atop of one of the few patches of lava rock in Ibiza, the tower is in fine condition, but even though metal rungs ascend its wall the door is kept locked. There are panoramic views over the ocean from here, towards the humpback

island of **Tagomago** (Map 5, G5), 153 acres of privately
owned beach and scrubland. Trips around the island leave
from Cala de Sant Vicent (see p.112).

Figueral and Aigües Blanques

After a two-kilometre detour inland from Pou des Lleó, the
road loops back to the exposed northeast coast at **FIGUER-
AL** (Map 5, E4), a small, fairly prosperous, but somewhat
bland family resort characterized by its clump of hotels,
nondescript restaurants and postcard and lilo-proffering souvenir shops. The narrow, 200-metre stretch of exposed sands
is swept clean by churning waves, but conditions can get a
little rough and there are some jagged rocks offshore.

  If you're after a day by the sea, though, you're far better
off heading for the naturist beach of **Aigües Blanques**
(Map 5, E4), or "White Waters", separated from Figueral's
slender sands by eroded, storm-battered cliffs. To get there,
retreat inland for 1km, and then turn right (north) and follow the coastal road north towards Cala de Sant Vicent; 1km
further north and you're at Aigües Blanques, signposted in
Castilian as "Agua Blancas". The kilometre-long slice of
dark sand here, interspersed with rocky outcrops and crumbling cliffs and buffeted by the ocean, is usually pretty
empty, and the beach offers Ibiza's most consistent **surf**,
with three-kilometre swells some winters; conditions are
only ever ideal for a few days a year, though. Aigües
Blanques is also the only official **nudist** beach in the north
of the island, and very popular with the hippy crew, who
gather at the *chiringuito* at the southern end of the shore – a
favoured place to watch the sun rise over the Mediterranean.

**Both Figueral and Aigües Blanques are on the Santa
Eulària–Cala de Sant Vicent bus route.**

THE NORTHEAST CORNER

111

CHAPTER ONE

Cala de Sant Vicent and around

Map 5, E3.

Ibiza's isolated northeastern tip harbours some of the island's most dramatic highland country, dominated by the plunging valley of Sant Vicent, west of the resort of **Cala de Sant Vicent**, the only tourist development in this near-pristine area. Getting there is an attraction in itself: the coastal road north of Aigües Blanques offers one of Ibiza's most magnificent drives, clinging to the contours of the corrugated coastline and weaving through thick pine forests, with sparkling waters offshore. After 3km you catch a glimpse of Cala de Sant Vicent, its sweeping arc of golden sand enclosed by the 303-metre-high peak of **Sa Talaia** to the north, and steep cliffs to the south. Unfortunately, property developers have filled Cala de Sant Vicent's shoreline with a row of lumpish concrete hotels, but the waters here still offer some of the most exhilarating swimming in the area. Minimarts, cafés and restaurants sit below the hotels on the otherwise featureless promenade. Cast a glance behind the prom, however, and you'll see the derelict remains of a concrete house, which served as the hideout of French assassin Raoul Villian after he killed the socialist leader **Jean Jaurès** in 1914 and fled to Ibiza. Villian lived here in near-total seclusion for almost two decades before he was finally tracked down and murdered in 1936.

There are regular buses between Cala de Sant Vicent and Santa Eulària.

Cova des Cuieram
Map 5, D2.

From the shoreline at Cala de Sant Vicent, a good paved

road heads inland, slowly climbing westward up the broad, U-shaped valley of Sant Vicent. A kilometre from the bay, there's a small lay-by on the right side of the road, where a sign points the way up a vertiginous path up to a cave, **Cova des Cuieram**. A site of worship in Carthaginian times, hundreds of terracotta images of the fertility goddess Tanit were unearthed here when the cave was rediscovered in 1907; some are displayed in the archeological museum in Ibiza Town (see p.75). Consisting of several small chambers, the modest cavern is thought to be in danger of collapse, partly due to the damage inflicted by a dynamite-wielding, treasure-seeking lunatic some decades ago. It's currently closed, but the views from its mouth (almost 200m above the road) are exceptional enough to warrant the very stiff fifteen- to twenty-minute trek through dense forest.

Sant Vicent

Map 5, C3.

As Ibiza's smallest village, **SANT VICENT**, 3km up the valley from the coast on the road to Sant Joan (see p.117), is easily missed. Consisting of a handful of houses and a fenced basketball court, there are no sights except for the modest, minimalist village **church**, built between 1827 and 1838, with a double-arched porch and an appealing setting in its own tiny plaza, with a solitary palm tree for company. The facade is unembellished except for a small plaque, which confidently proclaims, in Castilian Spanish, "house of God and gate to heaven". Just downhill from the church is Sant Vicent's only other feature, an orderly, dark little bar, *Es Café*, which also functions as the valley's post office and shop.

Port de ses Caletes

Map 5, C2.

A tiny pebbly cove, barely 50m across, **Port de ses Caletes** is reachable only via a torturous (but signposted) road from Sant Vicent village that ascends via switchbacks to 250m and then plummets to the sea; it's a bumpy fifteen-minute drive from Sant Vicent. With a ramshackle collection of dilapidated fishing huts as its only buildings, the cove is dwarfed by soaring coastal cliffs, and it's a blissfully peaceful spot, where there's nothing much to do except listen to the waves wash over the smooth stones on the shore or snorkel round the rocky edges of the bay.

THE NORTHEAST CORNER

Ibiza Town

IAIN STEWART

Cala de Sant Vicent, Ibiza

ROBERT HARDING

Sant Miquel, Ibiza

Balàfia, Ibiza

Cala d'en Serra, Ibiza

Chupito-downing, Ibiza Town

Manumission at Privilege, Ibiza

The Northwest

From the tiny cove of Cala d'en Serra at the island's northernmost tip to the diminutive inland village of Santa Agnès in the southwest interior, rugged **northwest Ibiza** is the wildest, most isolated part of the island. An awesome, almost unbroken barrier of towering cliffs and forested peaks, the coastline only relents to allow access to the shore in a few places. Just two bays – **Port de Sant Miquel** and the small family resort of **Portinatx** – have been developed for tourism; elsewhere, the coastal environment is all but pristine, with formidable cliffs, some over 300m high, offering more possibilities for **hiking** than for beachlife – and even in the height of summer sea breezes usually intervene to alleviate the heat. Though the area is short on sand, the rocky coastline below the cliffs is ideal for **snorkelling**, with 30-metre-plus visibility and rich marine life: spiny lobsters, dogfish, moray and conger eels, and peacock wrasse are all commonly seen.

Best of all, the relative inaccessibility of much of the northwest coast means that most of the pebble bays and inlets are usually all but deserted, and even in July and August the few sandy beaches never get really crowded. For total isolation, you can hike to the untouched coast around **Cala d'Aubarca** and **Portitxol**; while, for a bit more action, the stunning beaches of **Cala d'en Serra** and **Cala Xarraca** each have snack bars and sunbeds to rent. Beautiful **Benirràs** is the island's premier hippy beach, where the sinking sun is synchronized with the beat of bongo drummers. Inland, the thickly forested inland terrain is interspersed with small patches of farmland where olives, carob, almonds, wheat and citrus fruits are nourished by the rust-red earth.

The northwest is the most sparsely populated part of Ibiza – of the handful of tiny, isolated settlements, only picturesque **Sant Joan** and slumberous **Sant Miquel** could realistically be described as villages, though all the other hamlets boast a whitewashed, fortified church and a bar or two. Many of the villages tend to be associated with a particular crop: **Santa Agnès** is known for its almonds, **Sant Mateu** is famous for its wine, and orchards grace the countryside around **Santa Gertrudis**. Ancient Ibizan rural customs and traditions, some Carthaginian in origin – including dance rituals at remote springs and wells – still survive in the remotest areas. On many hillsides, traditional Cubist Ibizan *casaments* still outnumber modern villas and chalets, while in the village bars the rhythmic Ibizan dialect of Catalan (see p.312), rather than Castilian Spanish, remains the dominant tongue.

Reviews of accommodation and restaurants in the northwest
start on p.213 and p.228 respectively.

There's no **public transport** hub in northwest Ibiza and, while buses do serve virtually every village and resort between May and late September, there are only one or two daily services to the smaller settlements. In winter, schedules are even less frequent, though you can at least get to the main villages (Sant Joan, Sant Miquel and Sant Agnès) by bus. With the exception of one cross-island service that connects Sant Antoni and Port de Sant Miquel via

THE NORTHWEST

Santa Agnès and Sant Mateu, all services originate in either Ibiza Town (see Chapter 1) or Santa Eulària (see Chapter 2).

To really explore the northwest, you'll need your own transport; **car rental** companies are listed in Basics (see p.40). As many of the best bays are well off the beaten track, at the foot of atrocious dirt tracks, you'll also have to be prepared to do some walking.

SANT JOAN

Map 5, 3A.

High in the lofty northern hills of the Serra de la Mala Costa, the pretty village of **SANT JOAN** (San Juan in Castilian) clings to the main highway from Ibiza Town to Portinatx. Though only a couple of hundred people live here, the village is capital of the Sant Joan municipality, which comprises most of northern Ibiza, and boasts its own modest little Ajuntament (Town Hall), just above the highway. You'll also find a good, very cheap pension (see p.213), a small supermarket and a bar, and, with regular buses linking the village to Ibiza Town and Portinatx, Sant Joan makes an excellent, tranquil base to explore the attractions of the remote north of the island.

Along with Sant Carles (see p.106), Sant Joan has served as a focal point for northern Ibiza's **hippies** since the 1960s, when the scene developed around the Can Tiruit commune. Later it became a centre of operations for the Bhagwan Rajneesh cult (later renamed the Osho Commune International), where snippets of Sufism, Buddhism, Zen and yoga were blended with a good dose of hedonistic sexual libertinism. Rave folk history has it that Bhagwan Rajneesh devotees from California were the first people to bring ecstasy to Ibiza in the late 1970s, when there was the first mass ritual use of drugs.

Evidence of Sant Joan's left-field credentials is somewhat muted today, though the counter-cultural spirit survives to a certain extent in the New Age-ish *Eco Centre* café, located in

SANT JOAN

117

a pretty terraced row in the heart of the village. The region remains popular with a bohemian bunch of artists and writers, however, and the hills around the village are a favoured destination for Ibiza's clandestine psychedelic-trance party scene.

Sant Joan's bar is reviewed on p.244.

Dominating the skyline, Sant Joan's eighteenth-century **church**, just off the main highway, boasts typically high, whitewashed walls and an arched side porch. The slim steeple that rises slightly awkwardly from the main body of the building is a twentieth-century addition, which detracts a little from the wonderfully minimalist simplicity of the original design. Inside, there's an unadorned single nave, with a barrel-vaulted roof and a small dome, comprising several segments painted with images of Christ.

NORTH TO XARRACA BAY

Map 5, A2.

North of Sant Joan, the main highway to Portinatx wriggles down to the coast following a beautiful, fertile valley flanked by olive-terraced hills and orderly almond and citrus groves. The route affords sweeping views of **Xarraca Bay** below, one of Ibiza's most expansive at 2km wide. Dotted with tiny rocky islands, the translucent waters are backed by low cliffs, and there are three small beaches. Four kilometres along the road, a short signposted turnoff at the km17 road marker loops past some villas to the quiet beach of **Cala Xarraca**, a thin strip of coarse sand no more than 150m long, with a few sunbeds and umbrellas to rent. The solitary bar/restaurant sells good snacks and *tapas*, and is a fine spot to watch cormorants and spear-fishermen diving for fish at the end of the day.

Though Cala Xarraca is a nice place to chill out, you're far better off pressing on if you want to swim. A kilometre further along the Portinatx road, **s'Illot des Renclí** is a beautiful 30-metre-wide slice of well-raked sand and very shallow, azure water that holds the tiny islet after which the beach is named. There's a decent fish restaurant, also called *s'Illot des Renclí*, just above the shore, with tables positioned to give stunning views over the ocean, but no snacks are available. Another kilometre around Xarraca Bay, look out for the signpost to **Cala Xuclar**, a sandy, horseshoe-shaped inlet sprinkled with fishing huts that lies at the mouth of a seasonal river. It's usually very tranquil here, and there are plenty of rocks to the west ideal for sunbathing, while the waters offer good snorkelling possibilities.

PORTINATX AND AROUND

Map 5, B1.

At the end of the highway, and separated from Xarraca Bay by the sharp contours of Punta de sa Torre, moderately sized, low-rise **PORTINATX** is one of Ibiza's more attractive resorts. Set around a double bay, and blessed with three small sandy beaches, this friendly, family-orientated holiday centre, with its well-spaced hotels and apartment blocks built between mature pine trees, may not be an especially happening place – there's a dearth of stylish bars and boutiques – but it's pleasant enough for a day by the sea; and with several other good beaches nearby it also makes a good base.

Somewhat unconvincingly for such an innocuous holiday destination, Portinatx adopted the self-bestowed suffix "*Des Rei*" (royal) after King Alfonso XIII made a fleeting visit in 1929. More impressively, in terms of celebrity cachet, scenes from *South Pacific* were also filmed in the gin-clear waters of the two bays. The largest of these bays, Port de Portinatx, has two golden patches of sand, **s'Arenal Gross** and **s'Arenal Petite**, where rows of sunbeds are rotated on an hourly basis in high season. The other beach, **Es Portitxol**, at the end of a narrow inlet 500m west of s'Arenal Gross, boasts superbly sheltered water, perfect for swimming and snorkelling; there's also a dive school here (see p.51).

Cala d'en Serra

Map 5, C1.

East of Portinatx, a glorious road climbs up the low, sloping hills that rise above Ibiza's northern tip, threading through woods and past isolated luxury villas. After 3km, there's a magnificent view of diminutive **Cala d'en Serra**, a remote, exquisite cove framed by green hills that's reachable via a poor, but signposted, and just about driveable, dirt road. The only scar in the paradisal scenery is the ugly, half-built shell of an abandoned hotel project just above the beach, the concrete remains beginning to be reclaimed by the forest after a decade of decay – mercifully, it's all but hidden once you're down at the sandy shore. Cala d'en Serra's translucent waters are perfect for swimming, and offer rich snorkelling pickings; there's another tiny pebbly cove to explore over the rocks to the south. Between May and October, a German-run café-shack dispenses superb seafood, *bocadillos* and drinks, all served up just above the water.

You can also reach Cala d'en Serra via a signposted road from Sant Joan, that passes though exhilarating, remote highland scenery.

BALÀFIA TO SANT LLORENÇ

South of Sant Joan, the linear north–south highway to Ibiza Town beats a path to two historic inland hamlets that are well worth a quick peek. Six kilometres along the highway, **BALÀFIA** (Map 1, D3), characterized by a crop of castle-like defence towers, is often cited as Ibiza's only surviving Moorish village, though the only thing that's definitely

Arabic about the place is its name. It's certainly one of the most unusual settlements in the Ibiza, though – a cluster of ancient, interlocking whitewashed homes, and amber-coloured towers where the population once sheltered from pirates. This layout, a common defensive arrangement else-where in Europe, never really caught on in Ibiza, where the diffused population relied instead on coastal watchtowers to warn them of possible danger well before it arrived on their doorstep. Though there are a few "*Privado*" (Private) signs, there's nothing to stop you walking around the hamlet's two alleys to get a closer look at the houses and towers; however, bear in mind that the buildings are private homes.

The Can Sort organic food market is held each Saturday in the hills between Sant Joan and Balàfia. To get there from the the C733 Ibiza Town–Sant Joan highway, take the turnoff signposted for the "Mercado del Campo".

Sant Llorenç

Map 1, G3.

A kilometre west of Balàfia, down a signposted dirt road off the highway, remote **SANT LLORENÇ** (San Lorenzo in Castilian) is one of Ibiza's least-visited settlements. There's nothing here but a couple of village bars, a handful of hous-es and a large **church** that seems out of proportion with the rest of the place. A fine eighteenth-century construc-tion, it boasts a broad single-arched entrance porch lined with stone seating, and blindingly white exterior walls. Inside, the nave is divided into five bays and topped with a barrel-vaulted roof, with a single nineteenth-century chapel dedicated to the Virgin Mary.

The wooded hillside above the church has been set aside as the **Can Pere Mosson country park**, a spacious recreation spot with good, waymarked walking trails, barbecue areas and three lookout points offering fine views of the hilly heart of the island. The park is popular with Ibizan families at weekends, but deserted the rest of the week.

BENIRRÀS

Map 7, H1.

Three kilometres west of Sant Joan, along the road to Sant Miquel, a signposted right-hand turnoff leads to one of Ibiza's most idyllic beaches, **Benirràs**, a 300-metre-wide sandy cove set against a backdrop of high, densely forested cliffs. Development has been restricted here for decades, and buildings are currently limited to three unobtrusive beach cafés (open summer only) and a handful of villas in the hills above. More houses are proposed, but the plans are currently being vigorously contested by the green lobby.

Legendary in Ibizan **hippy** folklore, and said to have been the site of wild drug-taking-and-free-sex orgies in the 1960s, Benirràs's distinctly bohemian tendency persists today, and it remains the New Age community's favourite beach. Summer afternoons (particularly Sundays) see the bongo brigade gathering here to bang a drum at **sunset** or at full-moon time, a tradition that reaches its zenith at the annual August drumfest (see box). Just offshore, the small rock at the mouth of the bay is somewhat revered by the mystically minded, and is said to resemble, variously, a woman at prayer, a giant baby, or the Sphinx; however, in the cold light of day, it's difficult to see what all the fuss is about.

SANT MIQUEL

Map 7, G6.

Perched high in the glorious Els Amunts hills, which isolate the northwest coast from the interior, **SANT MIQUEL** is

THE DAY OF THE DRUMS

Since the hazy days of the hippy trail to Marrakesh, Benirràs has been the scene of sporadic **full-moon parties** staged by Ibiza's bohemian population. The assembly declined somewhat in the 1980s, but in 1990, as tension in the Persian Gulf reached fever pitch following Iraq's invasion of Kuwait, the congas and bongos were dusted down, brought to the beach and bashed in a huge rhythm-driven protest for world peace. Since then, the **Day of the Drums**, held on August 28, has become an annual fixture, performed with inimitable crusty gusto. In the last few years, though, the festival has been threatened by the party-pooping local government, which has spoiled the fun somewhat by laying down strict guidelines: bonfires have been banned, vehicles restricted (to ensure access for the emergency services) and the whole future of the event is dependent upon delicate negotiations between the organizers and the authorities.

Future uncertainty notwithstanding, the Day of the Drums is a spectacular occasion, and one of the premier social celebrations for Ibiza's hippy denizens. Dozens of sarong-clad drummers descend to the bay, and a furious rhythm is maintained from before sunset until after sunrise, often developing into a reggae-style sound-clash situation, with two competing teams amassed below the cliffs at the opposite ends of the bay. Benirràs takes on a somewhat magical air, bathed in blue light from the moon and illuminated by hundreds of candles, while the sweet smell of cardamom-scented *chai* and vegetarian feasts from the cook-shacks fills the night air. The celebration has developed into one of Ibiza's unique events, a non-commercial festival that's as much a part of Ibizan culture as the clubs' closing parties and the village fiestas. For a flavour of the occasion, check out the *Waves in the Air* CD on the island-based Ibizarre label, which features many Benirràs percussionists.

THE DAY OF THE DRUMS

the largest of the villages in this sparsely populated, thickly forested region. The village is not especially picturesque, its main street lined with tiny old cottages that sit somewhat uneasily amongst five-storey apartment blocks, but Sant Miquel does retain plenty of unhurried, rural character, and you'll find a good mix of locals and visitors in the bars.

The settlement dates back to the thirteenth century, when the first walls of the fortified church, **Església de Sant Miquel**, were constructed high on the Puig de Missa hill, a superb defensive position some 4km from the sea, which gave the original inhabitants a little extra protection from marauding pirates. Parish status was granted in the early eighteenth century, when a few families were encouraged by (then) Bishop Abad y Lasierra to build houses around the hilltop. It's a short stroll to Puig de Missa from the main street, past a neat little row of terraced cottages and a small plaza, which commands magnificent views over the pine forests and terraced groves of the interior. Opposite the plaza is a tiny post office, which conveniently doubles as a **bar**, where you can gaze over the hills with a glass of Rioja. From the plaza, you enter the church via the arches of a walled patio, then pass through a broad porch, which leads into the southern side of the barrel-vaulted nave. The simple altar is to the right, flanked by two large side chapels. The recently restored **frescoes** of the Benirràs chapel, to the right of the altar, are the church's most unusual feature – swirling mono-chrome vines and flowers that blanket the walls and ceiling which date back to the late seventeenth century, when construction was finally completed. Below the frescoes is a layer of superb stonework of tessellated crosses and octagons.

Ball pagès (folk dancing) displays are staged in the church patio all year round (May–Oct 6.15pm; Nov–April 5.15pm; 500ptas/€3).

PORT DE SANT MIQUEL AND AROUND

Map 7, H2.

From Sant Miquel, a scenic road meanders 4km north to **Port de Sant Miquel**, a spectacular bay that was a tiny fishing harbour and a tobacco smugglers' stronghold until tourism took over in the 1970s. Enclosed by high cliffs that shelter the inlet's dazzlingly blue, shallow waters, and boasting a fine sandy beach that's well-suited to children, Port de Sant Miquel's beauty is tainted considerably by the portentous presence of two lumpish, incumbent concrete hotels insensitively built into the eastern cliff. Catering almost exclusively to the captive package tourist trade, Sant Miquel's **bars** and **restaurants** are also disappointing, ranging from the *Happy Friar* English pub to a Wild West-themed saloon bar. The only recognizably Spanish bar/restaurant, the *Marin Dos*, is the best of a bad bunch, with decent *menú del día* – unlike all the others, it's also open all year.

In the summer season, things are pretty lively, with sarong and jewellery vendors wandering along the shore, dodging the pedalos racked up for rent; you can also arrange boat trips to neighbouring beaches from a desk on the sand.

Cala des Moltons and Torre des Molar

Map 7, G1.

From the western edge of Port de Sant Miquel's beach, a path loops around the shoreline for 200m to a tiny cove, **Cala des Moltons**, where there's a small patch of sand and fine, sheltered swimming. The same, easily followed trail continues past the beach, climbing through rocks and crossing a dirt road, then passing through patches of woodland. After ten minutes' walk, you'll reach a well-preserved stone defence tower, eighteenth-century **Torre des Molar**, from where there are good views of the rugged northern coast towards Portinatx.

Cova de Can Marça

Map 7, H2. Daily 11am–1.30pm & 3–5.30pm; 800ptas/e4.81.

Nuzzled into the steep eastern cliffs above Port de Sant Miquel, just past the monstrous hotels, **Cova de Can Marça** is a modest-sized cave system that, though unlikely to get speleologists drooling with excitement, is the biggest in Ibiza. Tobacco and liquor smugglers used its one main chamber and several smaller ones until the mid-twentieth century, after which the cavern was developed as a tourist attraction, with lighting installed and a staircase and pathway constructed. Once you've paid your entrance fee, guides conduct an interesting, informative twenty-minute tour through the dripping chambers.

The cave is about 100,000 years old, and was formed by an underground river that once flowed through the hillside. There are some impressive stalactites and stalagmites, many sniggeringly phallic, and one specimen that looks like a fat Buddha. An entertaining sound and light show ends the tour, with an artificial waterfall synchronized to cosmic electronic music from 1970s band Tangerine Dream, who remain big in Ibiza. There's a small café next to the ticket office, where tables afford wonderful views over the sparking, turquoise waters below.

From the Cova de Can Marça, a well-signposted, potholed two-kilometre dirt track leads east to Benirràs (see p.122).

Na Xamena and around

Clinging to the vertiginous cliffs east of Port de Sant Miquel, and commanding spectacular vistas over the north shore, tiny **NA XAMENA** (Map 7, F2) consists of nothing more than a small development of holiday villas, and the palatial *Hotel Hacienda* (see p.213). Nonetheless, if you're in the area it's worth a detour for the views alone, or for a quick drink in the hotel, popular with supermodels and assorted Euro-showbiz types.

To get to Na Xamena from Port de Sant Miquel, head 800m south toward Sant Miquel village along the main road, and take the signposted paved turnoff on the right. This twists and turns through dense pine forest, passing a turnoff for Playa Blanca after 1km – this route leads north toward **Illa des Bosc**, an islet in the Port Sant Miquel bay. The islet, capped by an exclusive private villa, is connected to Ibiza's northern shore via a tiny, sandy **beach**, where there's good swimming. Back on the road to Na Xamena, the tarmac climbs steeply through the pines until you reach the scattered, small whitewashed villas that make up the main body of the settlement, and then the imposing frontage of the *Hacienda*. Adjacent to the hotel, a steep, rough trail descends over rocks, roots and shoots to the foaming, exposed waters below, where you can take an invigorating dip. To reach the trailhead, walk south through the hotel car park, then right down a dirt track after the second holiday cottage, named *Ses Sevines*; it'll take fifteen minutes to walk to the shore. There's no beach, just an assemblage of boulders and rocks, but there's excellent **snorkelling** in the deep, cobalt waters offshore.

Swinging to the right just before the hotel, a bumpy but sealed road heads north to the lofty peninsula of **Punta de sa Creu** (Map 7, F1), where a heliport serves the rich residents of the luxurious houses hereabouts. The views from the heliport are some of the most spectacular in all Ibiza, the jutting promontory enveloped by the Mediterranean on three sides, with a brilliant perspective of the golden sands of Benirràs over in the east, and the mighty ochre cliffs around Portitxol and Cap Rubió just to the west.

PORTITXOL AND AROUND

Map 7, D2.

Some 5km northwest of Sant Miquel, the hidden bay of **Portitxol** is one of the most dramatic sights in Ibiza – a fifty-metre-wide, horseshoe-shaped pebbly cove, strewn with giant boulders and dwarfed by a monumental backdrop of cliffs that seem to isolate the beach from the rest of the world. Entirely free of villas and concrete eyesores, the only structures are a ring of tiny stone-and-brushwood huts, owned by fishermen who use the bay as a sanctuary from the rough but rich waters, which plummet to over 90m in depth just a short distance from the beach. In high season, a few adventurous souls work their way to this remote spot for a spot of secluded snorkelling, but for most of the year Portitxol is completely deserted, a pristine – but also sunbed-and refreshment-free – zone. There's plenty to explore, however: tracks sneak past colossal amber-coloured boulders of earth and rock, and past weird rock formations; the craggy peak that looms 315m above the bay to the west is **Cap Rubió** (the blonde cape), named for its sandy colour.

Getting to Portitxol is a bit tricky. From Sant Miquel, take the Sant Mateu road to the west, then after about a kilometre and a half, turn off onto a paved road to the right, which zigzags up through woods to *Isla Blanca*, a small, unlovely complex of half-built, whitewashed holiday villas high in the coastal hills. Past here, the road starts to descend to the sea; park up at the small bar-kiosk (summer only), as the road is in terrible condition from here onwards. From the kiosk, walk for fifteen minutes along the potholed road until you reach an unmarked path, which heads west by a high stone wall just before the second of two hairpin turns. Twenty minutes' more walking along the path, through some stunning cliffside scenery, and you're at the seashore.

Entrepenyas and s'Àguila

Map 7, E2.

There are two equally secluded places to swim within walking distance of Portitxol, both reachable via the same rough road from the kiosk at Isla Blanca. Five minutes' walk past the point where the Portitxol path turns off, the road divides by an abandoned stone hut. To the left, there's more excellent snorkelling in the deep indigo waters of **Entrepenyas** (Between Cliffs), a small rocky bay strewn with boulders and rocks. The right turn from the hut leads to **s'Àguila** (The Eagle), the more impressive of the two bays, surrounded by grey cliffs etched with rusty orange rocks that plummet into the Mediterranean. There's no beach here, but plenty more giant boulders for sunbathing. Even in August, there's only ever a handful of people in this lonely spot.

SANT MATEU D'AUBARCA AND AROUND

There's little to the tiny village of **SANT MATEU D'AUBARCA** (Map 7, A5), 7km west of Sant Miquel and some 3km inland, other than a confusingly aimless collection of lanes, a solitary but friendly store-cum-bar and a typically well-fortified, whitewashed **church**. Completed in 1796, it boasts a slim, squarish belfry and a fine triple-arched entrance porch, supported by two rows of compact columns, the latter added in 1885. Two tiny chapels, dedicated to the virgins of Montserrat and Rosario, are set at the end of the draughtboard-tiled nave, on the right.

A dreamy, rustic landscape, with small fields of brick-red earth separated by low sandstone walls, tourism has barely touched the countryside around Sant Mateu. Much of the land is used to foster the village's one cottage industry, **wine**, and each December, the village hosts an annual festival in honour of the humble but delicious local *ví pagès* (country wine). It's an unmissable event, with around a thousand people gathering from all over the island to slurp the new vintage from teapot-shaped glass jugs called *porrós*, and gobble down *sobrassada* and *butifarra* sausages barbecued over pine and apricot wood fires lit on the village football pitch. Unsurprisingly, given that all the *ví pagès* is free, there's a tremendously sociable atmosphere, aided by some folk dancing and a live band that usually concentrates on Dire Straits and Spanish rock cover versions.

At other times of the year you'll have to be content with **visiting a vineyard** and sampling the cellars in a slightly less festive fashion. One and a half kilometres west of the village, the **Sa Cova** vineyard (Map 7, A5; ☎971 187 046) run by the Bonet family, produces 22,000 bottles a year – two reds, a rosé and a white. They have plans to build a information centre for tourists and start tours, but will give you an unofficial look around and a taste in the meantime. It's best to call ahead to arrange a visit, particularly in the quiet winter months.

CALA D'AUBARCA

Map 7, B4.

Once the main point of sea access for Sant Mateu, the stunning, untouched bay of **Cala d'Aubarca**, 4km north of the town, is one of Ibiza's most magnificent. In an island of diminutive cove beaches, its sheer scale is remarkable: a massive tier of cliffs envelop the three-kilometre-wide bay, and a thundering ocean batters the brutal, rocky shore. There's no beach, and it's quite tricky to fathom out a path to the sea, and this unforgiving feel helps to ensure that Cala d'Aubarca remains one of Ibiza's best-kept secrets, completely deserted for most of the year.

Whether it's an internal Ibizan conspiracy to keep the place clandestine, or an oversight by the island's tourism department, there's only one official sign to direct you to Cala d'Aubarca. To **get there** by car or on foot from Sant Mateu, follow the road beside the church that's signposted "Camí d'Aubarca"; after 700m, you reach a junction. Bear left (you'll soon pass a tree on the right with "Aubarca" daubed onto the bark), and follow the road through a large vineyard until you pass a white house with yellow windows on the right. Turn right just after this house, up a dirt road that leads to the wooded cliffs above Cala d'Aubarca. Past the cliffs, the road is in terrible condition, so park up in the woods and walk the final fifteen minutes down to the beach.

When you reach the rugged promontory at the bottom of the dirt road, look out for the **natural stone bridge** that's been carved out of the rock by the waves. With the sandy and amber formations of Cap Rubió to the northeast, and brilliant white patches of chalk at the back of the bay, the multicoloured cliffs are also pretty striking. Several tricky paths lead to the sea to the left of the bridge, but for an easier route, backtrack uphill along the dirt trail for three minutes and you'll meet a clear path that cuts through the woods to the shore, directly below the chalky section of cliffs.

SANTA AGNÈS

Map 1, B5.

Southwest of Sant Mateu, a road bumps 7km towards the coast and to the tiny village of **SANTA AGNÈS** ("Santa Inés" in Castilian), made up of a couple of streets, the simple *La Palmera* restaurant, a decent *Can Cosmi* bar (see p.244) and a loose dispersal of houses. There are no specific sights other than the village **church**, which dates from 1806. It's properly known as **Santa Agnès de Corona** (Saint Agnès of the Crown) a reference to the 200-metre-high plain, enclosed by low hills on all sides, that surrounds the village. With a patchwork of small, stone-walled fields of ochre earth densely planted with figs, fruit

SANTA AGNÈS COASTAL HIKE

This circular walk (8km; 2.5hr) explores some of the remotest coastal scenery in the island – along high cliffs and through thick forest, past valleys and gorges – and offers several chances for a dip in the sea. There are no refreshments along the route, so you'll have to carry everything you're likely to need.

From the church in Santa Agnès, follow the paved Cami des Pla de Coruna for 600m until it bends to the left, beside an old stone **well** with a pointed roof. At this fork, continue straight ahead up the dirt track, past farm buildings and through some woods. The track cuts through two clearings; keep the dry-stone wall on your left and, ten minutes' walk from the fork, you'll catch a glimpse of the narrow **Ses Balandres gorge**, nicknamed "heaven's gate" by Ibizan hippies, with the sea glinting below. It's an adrenaline-charged fifteen-minute descent to the water through the gorge – certainly not a route for vertigo sufferers. The rocky path is quite good at first, but you'll soon have to make use of a wooden ladder and the steps that have been cut into the cliff. Though there's no actual beach at the base of the gorge, it's a great place for a swim or snorkel below near-vertical cliffs. If this all seems like too much effort, forgo the climb down to the beach and head instead for the lookout (*mirador*) 100m north of the gorge entrance, which affords outstanding views inland to the pine-topped hill of Puig de Joan Andreu, the fortress-like rocky summit of Es Castellar to the right, and the horseshoe-shaped island of **Ses Margalides** below.

Backtracking from the lookout, another path, directly opposite the gorge entrance, sneaks through a patch of woodland that's popular with mushroom collectors, who come to seek out delicious orange *cepes* each Autumn. After five minutes' walk you'll arrive at a wide dirt road. To the right, it's a steep but easy fifteen-minute hike down to the shore at **Sa Illot**, though there's no beach at the bottom – just a strange, almost apocalyptic world of rusty abandoned cars, smashed stone huts and giant cuboid boulders. Alternatively, ignoring the Sa Illot route, turn left up the same wide dirt road and it's a five-minute stroll back to the Camí des Pla de Coruna.

Turn right along the Camí des Pla de Coruna, and walk for 800m past some villas and farmhouses. The **Corona** plain is beautiful around here, with fields of vines, fruit and almond trees divided by limestone walls all around. Just after, the road dips towards the coast, there's a clearing on the right, marked by a white electricity box – it's a popular picnicking spot, with sea views. From here, head to the left (west) along a good path that continues around the cliffside, dotted with scrub pine and juniper bushes, about 100m above the sea. After another ten minutes' walking, the trail passes through the rocky outcrop of **Cap Negret**, then gets a little vague as you make your way through overgrown farm terraces before descending to a lovely clearing in the pines, where there's a long-abandoned farmhouse with a stone bread oven. Continuing west, you'll reach a series of large, overgrown farm terraces, propped up by substantial stone walls. Walk through the terraces past some old water-storage tanks; after the last terrace, some 30m above the sea, you'll meet a stone wall and glimpse the next rocky bay, **Corrals d'en Guillem**. It's tempting to cross the wall and head down for a dip, but the path is treacherous. Instead, turn to the left before the stone wall and head inland up the wooded hillside. The steep route is ill-defined at first, but soon joins a dried-up stream bed before continuing up the right-hand side of the pine-clad valley. Some fifteen minutes from the stone wall, the trail levels out and descends gently to the Camí des Pla de Coruna; turn left, and it's a fifteen-minute walk back to Santa Agnès.

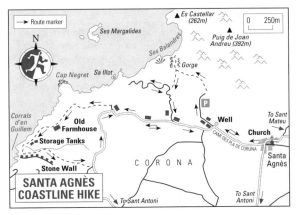

and thousands of *ametlla* (almond) trees, the plain is supremely beautiful. If you visit in mid-January, the sea of pinky-white almond blossoms is an unforgettable sight, a dreamy vision almost as celebrated in Ibiza as the cherry-tree flowers in Japan.

SANTA GERTRUDIS DE LA FRUITERA

Map 1, D4.

Smack in the centre of the island, 11km from Ibiza Town and just off the highway to Sant Miquel, **SANTA GERTRUDIS DE LA FRUITERA** is a diminutive village that holds a glut of bars, restaurants and boutiques out of all proportion to its size. Despite this somewhat bourgeois nature, the village doesn't lack character, or characters. Even in the winter months, tank-like 4WDs and ancient Citröen 2CVs joust for prime parking positions, and an incongruous collection of moneyed expats (particularly Germans), farmers, artists and artists-who-farm fill the streetside café terraces of *Bar Costa* and *Es Canto*.

Santa Gertrudis's bars and restaurants are reviewed on p.244, and p.229 respectively.

Beside the bars and boutiques, with their Indonesian and Indian threads, trinkets and handicrafts, there's also an excellent **auction house**, the English-owned *Casi Todo* (☎971 197 023), a few doors down from *Bar Costa*, where everything from gypsy carts and antiques to plastic garden furniture to rusty 1950s motorbikes goes under the hammer once a month. Auction day is something of a social event, as triple air kisses are exchanged, property prices discussed and exhibits examined.

Just outside the village, on the road to Sant Mateu, there's yet another rather chi-chi group of stores, including Can Daifa, a very exclusive art dealer, and Nino d'Agata, a pricey boutique that specializes in jewellery and sculpture. Appropriately enough there are also two **cashpoints** (ATMs) along Santa Gertrudis's main street – convenient if you want to embark on a serious spending spree.

The landmark eighteenth-century **Església de Santa Gertrudis**, in the centre of the village, is less austere than most Ibizan churches, with an elevated two-storey frontage and small windows picked out with yellow paint. Their interior, though hardly ornate, does have a few sculptural decorations, including some apples and figs on the ceiling (Santa Gertrudis has long been a fruit-growing centre), which add a splash of colour. If you're in Ibiza in November, try to time your visit to coincide with the village's annual **fiesta**. Aside from the usual Ibizan dancing and folk-rock bands, animals are exhibited, which inevitably undertake a global flavour – the prize pigs in 1999 included a Vietnamese pot-bellied porker.

SANTA GERTRUDIS DE LA FRUITERA

Sant Antoni and around

Labelled as the Mediterranean's premier rave resort by the British media, the sex, drugs and techno package unique to **SANT ANTONI** (**SAN ANTONIO**) is as dynamic as you'll find anywhere in Europe. High-rise, concrete-clad and shamelessly brash, San An (as it's usually called) primarily draws crowds of young clubbers bent on relentless pursuit of unbridled hedonism, the scene propelled by a combustible cocktail of cheap booze and copious pills and powders. Things can get seriously out of control in the Brit-only enclave of the **West End**, with its unbroken chain of bars, disco-bars and fast-food fryers, but this is really only one side of the story – there are less frenetic sides to the resort, such as the stylish chillout bars of the **Sunset Strip**, where the ambience is far more measured.

The Sant Antoni municipality has been trying hard to shake off its less-than-wholesome reputation in recent years, introducing restrictions to the notorious holiday-rep-piloted bar-crawls and drinking competitions, and belatedly attempting to attract "grey pound" winter visitors. Though the essential character of the resort remains unchanged, the atmosphere has become a little more refined since the excesses of the 1980s, when alcohol-fuelled street brawls were nightly occurrences in the high season. Environmental improvements have also been enacted: further hotel development is now restricted, several streets have been pedestrianized and the harbour has been given the beautification treatment, with a new palm-lined promenade that's soon to be extended as far as Cala Gració. Cosmetic improvements aside, Sant Antoni's harbour, prized by the Romans, remains the island's finest – a sickle-shaped expanse of sapphire water framed to the south by the crest of 475-metre Sa Talaiassa (see p.160), and to the north by the wooded uplands of Santa Agnès (see p.134).

Around Sant Antoni, away from the crowded sands at the heart of the resort, you'll find some spectacular **cove beaches**; north of town, gorgeous **Cala Gració**, **Cala Gracioneta** and **Cala Salada** are all within a couple of kilometres of the centre. To the southwest, **Sant Antoni bay** is heavily built-up, a continuous, happy-holiday-geared sprawl that stretches as far as the pretty swimming spot of **Port des Torrent**. Travel a little further west, and there's a string of stunning beaches, including **Cala Conta** and **Cala Bassa**, where you can swim in some of the cleanest water in the Mediterranean.

Some history

The cave paintings at the Cova de les Fontanelles, just north of Sant Antoni, thought to be either **prehistoric** or dating from the early **Bronze Age**, are the earliest evidence of human presence in the region, but there's nothing to suggest a significant settlement here at this time. Though local legend attests that **Carthaginian** general Hannibal was born on the island of Conillera, just west of Sant Antoni's bay, it seems that the area was more or less bypassed by his people, as Punic pottery fragments found at the cave chapel of Capella de Santa Agnès are the only proof of their presence here. The **Roman** invaders were certainly impressed by Sant Antoni's natural harbour, naming it *portus magnus* (great port), but they never settled here in numbers either. Their name did stick, however; most rural Ibizans still call the town "Portmany", a corruption of the Latin moniker.

For more on Ibiza's early history, see Contexts, p.283.

For the next two thousand years, Sant Antoni was never anything grander than a small fishing village. The **Catalans** constructed a rudimentary chapel in 1305, as a focal point for the scattered population of no more than fifty families living around the harbour, but the area remained something of a backwater. Successive islandwide waves of bubonic plague took their toll, as did periodic pirate raids, and it wasn't until the seventeenth century that the town got a little protection in the form of a defence tower added to the church which had been built on the site of the Catalan chapel.

In the early twentieth century, curious travellers from overseas arrived, and **tourism** began to impact upon the local economy. The first substantial construction projects began in the late 1950s, and hotels quickly mushroomed around the bay; as in the other mainland Spanish resorts, Franco-directed mass tourism initiatives, characterized by unregulated building and planning controls, unleashed a frenzy of ugly construction. Fishing boats became sightseeing cruisers, and an army of waiters and support staff were recruited from rural Andalucía and Murcia to pamper the needs of northern European visitors who were starting to arrive in droves. By the 1970s, Sant Antoni's high-rise skyline was barely distinguishable from Benidorm or Magaluf, its success built on a "sell 'em cheap" package-holiday menu of bacon and eggs, *The Birdie Song*, the sun and *The Sun* – all washed down with jugs of sangria and barrels of San Miguel.

Sant Antoni became a mecca for the Club 18–30 holiday crowd in the 1980s, and the serious problems began. Drunken rampages by Union Jack-bedecked British louts hit the headlines in Spain and the UK, as policemen and non-British tourists were regularly beaten up. Tourism dipped considerably, and by the early 1990s Sant Antoni had a formidable PR problem, described by one guide-book as a destination characterized by "booze-ups, brawls and hangovers", because "even soccer hooligans need holi-days". Unquestionably, the British **clubbing revolution** kickstarted the resort's recovery. Though Sant Antoni was a pivotal part of the acid-house scene in the late 1980s, the resort was quite polarized: specialist venues such as the *Milk Bar* reverberated with Balearic Beat classics while the West End pubs rang to the strains of drunken football chants. However, by 1994, as clubbing became much more mainstream in the UK, the word was out: Ibiza was *the* place to party, with the best club venues, the cream of the DJs and a seemingly liberal attitude towards drug use. Propelled by a wave of publicity, young British tourists descended en masse.

Today, non-British visitors are rare in Sant Antoni, and the town is totally dependent on the seasonal influx of thousands of UK clubbers. An army of PR teams comb the streets day and night to maintain the hype, and ensure that pre-club parties, clubs and after-hours venues are all packed to the gills. The tourism authorities know all their eggs are in one basket – future prosperity is dependent upon the strength of the pound and the continued magnetism of British club culture – but, for now, Sant Antoni remains *the* Mediterranean party destination.

For reviews of accommodation, restaurants, bars and clubs in Sant Antoni, see p.214, p.229, p.245 and p.253.

The Town

Sant Antoni's **layout** is simple. The **Egg** (Map 8, H6) is the most useful landmark, at the centre of the roundabout at the eastern end of the harbourfront where the roads from Ibiza Town and Sant Josep converge. Northwest of the Egg is the main body of the town, including the church and the busiest shopping district, the latter concentrated around c/Sant Antoni. South of here, the waterfront promenade (**Passeig de ses Fonts** at its western end and **Passeig de la Mar** to the east) skirts the ferry docks, the marina and the bus terminal, while the rocky coast that encloses the west side of town is occupied by the bars of the **Sunset Strip**. Finally, south of the Egg, another promenade loops down past more bars and hotels to the new maritime museum at the **Punta des Molí**.

Arrival and information

Sant Antoni's small open-air **bus terminal** overlooks the harbour at the western end of the Passeig de la Mar. Though it appears to be little more than a glorified bus stop, this is the point where all buses arrive and depart for destinations throughout the island. The **ferry dock** for services to and from mainland Spain is almost opposite the bus terminal, while boat services around the San An bay leave from the eastern end of the Passeig de ses Fonts, near the Egg. If you're arriving by **car**, you're best off leaving your vehicle in the car park just off Avgda Dr Fleming, 100m south of the pyramid-topped *Es Paradis* club.

The efficient **tourist information** kiosk (May–Oct Mon–Fri 9.30am–2.30pm & 3–8.30pm, Sat & Sun 9.30am–1pm; Nov–April Mon–Sat 9.30am–1pm; ☎971 314 005) is at the eastern end of the Passeig de ses Fonts, just west of the Egg, and has a good stock of leaflets about the

THE EGG

Smack in the centre of town, in the middle of a grassy round-about, San An's prominent flat-bottomed, ovoid sculpture, universally known as the **Egg**, was erected by the local government in the early 1990s in honour of the somewhat tenuous claim that **Christopher Columbus** was born on the island. Inside the hollow, creamy-white structure is a miniature wooden galleon, modelled on the fifteenth-century vessels in which the explorer sailed.

The origins of the sculpture's unusual shape lie with Columbus himself. The story goes that, when ridiculed for suggesting there was a westerly route to the Indies, Columbus countered by saying he could also make an egg stand upright. Challenged, he promptly cracked the base of an egg and placed in on a table.

island and municipality. What with the island's four main listings magazines (see p.26) all covering Sant Antoni fairly comprehensively, and teams of "flyerers" patrolling the streets dispensing leaflets, it doesn't take much effort to find out what's going on in the club scene.

PASSEIG DE SES FONTS

Map 8, F6–G6.

The eastern portion of Sant Antoni's harbourside prome-nade, broad **Passeig de ses Fonts** benefited from land-scaping in the early 1990s, when the luxuriant collection of tropical palms, rubber plants and flowering shrubs were planted. To the west, past the tourist information kiosk, the messy string of concrete office and apartment blocks that line the prom are occupied at street level by rows of pavement cafés, where you can munch on American fast food or tuck into a full English breakfast while gazing at the harbour. All but lost in this near-featureless architectural sprawl is the whitewashed **Ajuntament** building, on the corner of c/Bisbe Cardona, identifiable by its fluttering municipal flags and modern clock, where the town's transformation from fishing village to full-blown resort was mapped out.

West of here, Passeig de ses Fonts continues past a series of flashy modern fountains, dramatically illuminated at night, and the docks from which ferries shuttle to various points around the bay. On summer evenings, the street lined with street sellers and caricaturists, and thick with drinkers heading to up c/Santa Agnès to the bars of the West End (see opposite).

ESGLÉSIA DE SANT ANTONI

Map 8, G5.

From Passeig de ses Fonts, c/Ample leads north to the small plaza that houses the town's historic church, **Església de Sant Antoni**, a handsome, whitewashed structure with a twin belfry and a pleasantly shady side porch. What sets the church apart from others in the island is its two-storey, rectangular **defence tower**, integrated into the southeast side of the building; until the early nineteenth century, cannons were mounted at the top of the tower to defend the town from marauding pirates. Today's building mainly dates from the late seventeenth century, and was constructed over the remains of two simple chapels – the first built in 1305 and the latter in 1570 which were badly damaged by pirate attacks.

You approach the church through the twin arches of a cobbled, courtyard-like patio, with the porch and priest's quarters on the left, and an old well to the right. Inside, the calm, sombre interior is dimly lit by three small stained-glass windows. A collection of dark oil paintings of Sant

Francesc and Sant Antoni line the nave; the altar, coated in gold leaf, replaced a previous Baroque piece that was destroyed during the Spanish Civil War.

THE WEST END

The Blackpool of Ibiza, cheerfully vulgar, unashamedly unglamorous.
Paul Richardson, *Not Part of the Package – A Year in Ibiza*

The island's most raucous bar zone, Sant Antoni's infamous **West End** is spread over a network of streets centred around **Carrer Santa Agnès** (Map 8, F5–F6), plus the southern end of c/Bartomeu Vicent Ramón and c/de Cristòfol Colom. There's nothing very subtle or complicated about this almost entirely British enclave of wall-to-wall disco-bars and English- and Irish-style pubs, interspersed with the odd hole-in-the-wall kebab joint or Chinese restaurant doing full fried breakfasts. In the summer months, a "Brits abroad" mentality comes to the fore, with the streets transformed into a seething mass of football-shirt-clad, pink-fleshed humanity; understandably, few Ibizans would dream of drinking around here. Once the morning cleaners have the swept up the broken bottles and cleaned up the puke, there's nothing at all to see in the day, and most of the bars are closed.

Attitudes towards the West End tend to be strictly polarized, and after a quick glance at c/Sant Agnès by night you'll be able to tell if it's the kind of place you'll love or hate straight away. If you do decide to hit the bars here, you'll find that, in general, drinks are priced well below Sunset Strip or Ibiza Town averages, and as disco-bars are usually free to enter it's an economic place to strut your stuff. Though the music is generally party-anthem, happy-holiday house, plenty of decent DJs have cut their teeth and gained a reputation in the better bars, which include the *Simple Art Club* for its

House Nation nights, and *Kremlin,* where you'll hear UK garage – both are located on c/Santa Agnès.

PASSEIG DE LA MAR

Map 8, E7.

Back along the harbourfront, the promenade narrows west of c/Santa Agnès, becoming **Passeig de la Mar** once you've passed a statue of a fisherman, complete with nets and catch, who stands beside a crop of gaudy Chinese restaurants and a glut of banks. Opposite the statue, take a quick look at the **Moll Vell**, the old dock, where you'll often see fishermen mending their nets and fixing reed lobster pots. Further west, you pass the marina and modern Yacht Club building, the main bus terminal and a group of bars before you reach the **Moll Nou** (Map 8, C8), the extensive, 400-metre-long dock that juts into harbour, from where huge ferries steam for mainland Spain. At the end of the Passeig de la Mar, a flight of steps leads northwards up into c/Alemanya, from a where it's a short walk to the left along c/General Balanzat to the bars of the Sunset Strip.

THE SUNSET STRIP

Map 8, B6.

Stretching for 250m along the rocky shoreline between c/General Balanzat and c/Vara de Rey, Sant Antoni's legendary **Sunset Strip** of urbane chillout bars is the town's most cosmopolitan place to drink. In the day, the setting appears far from ideal – the bars cling to a jagged, low-lying rocky shelf some 50m away from the sea, and it's a tricky scramble over the rocks to take a swim. However, the location starts to make sense towards sunset, when all eyes face west to watch the sun sinking into the blood-red sea, to a background of ambient soundscapes.

Until 1993, there was only one **chillout bar**, the infamous *Café del Mar*, along this entire stretch of coast, and it was very much the preserve of in-the-know clubbers and islanders. By the following year, though, the renowned *Café Mambo* had opened, and by the late 1990s a barrage of publicity led by massive success of the seminal *Café del Mar* CDs had spread the word, and other bars were quick to get in on the act. Today, there are half a dozen chillout bars here, and the area is very much on the map, with the sunset spectacle an essential part of the "Ibiza experience" for most visitors.

For reviews of bars in Sant Antoni, see p.245 onwards.

It's undeniable that the original vibe, created by José Padilla at the *Café del Mar* and nurtured by a small clique of like-minded chillout DJs and producers, has been considerably diluted. Though little can detract from the appeal of spectacular sunsets and superb chillout music, the hype is incredible in the height of summer, when thousands of visitors congregate, television crews stalk the strip and Web cams beam the sunset scene around the globe. The commercialism is unavoidable – all the bars now sell their own T-shirts and CD mixes – but in spite of these changes a certain unique atmosphere does survive, especially early and late in the summer season, when things are less high-octane.

Construction of a promenade north from the Passeig de la Mar to Cala Gració, passing through the Sunset Strip, is due to start in 2001.

THE SUNSET STRIP

CALÓ DES MORO

Map 8, B2.

Some 500m north of the Sunset Strip, the rocky shoreline gives way at **Caló des Moro**, a tiny cove with a minuscule patch of sand that's surrounded by a loose scattering of hotel and apartment blocks. It is possible to take a swim here, but few people bother, as you have to negotiate your way over the sharp rocks that surround the bay. Instead, most come for the **bars**. Caló des Moro is fast becoming a worthy alternative to the Sunset Strip, with a clutch of recently established places including the funky *Kanya* and neighbouring *Kasbah* proving popular amongst an older crowd of seasoned clubbers and dance-industry professionals seeking a less frenetic atmosphere.

To get to Caló des Moro from the Sunset Strip, you'll either have to negotiate the 500-metre-long patch of rocky shoreline that lies between the two, or head to the right along Vara de Rey and then left into Avgda Isidor Macabich, turning left again into c/Santa Rosalia, which leads to the bay.

S'ARENAL TO PUNTA DES MOLÍ

From the Egg, a newly landscaped, palm-lined harbour-side promenade runs around the southern fringes of Sant Anton, slicing another few metres off already slimline **s'Arenal beach** (Map 8, H8–H10), which begins just south of the Egg. Barely a couple of metres wide in places, s'Arenal is nevertheless the closest stretch of sand available to Sant Antoni-based tourists, and despite the less-than-pristine harbours waters the entire 500-metre stretch is packed in the summer months. Bordering the sands at the northern end of the beach are three very stylish bar-cafés, *Kiwi*, *Bar M* and *Itaca*, all popular places offering good snacks and tunes.

Just inland from s'Arenal, on the other side of Avgda Dr Fleming, are the town's two vast temples of trance, pyramid-roofed *Es Paradis* and domed *Eden*; nearby is the disfiguring steel shell of a half-built club, *Idea*, which has been left incomplete for years. South of the clubs, the promenade skirts a row of slab-like hotel complexes and a scruffy, seldom-used row of fishing huts before skirting an imposing old **windmill** (Map 8, G11), with a white tower, a conical brushwood-roof and warped wooden sails. The windmill crowns the **Punta des Molí** (Map 8, G12), a quiet, landscaped spot jutting into Sant Antoni's bay, which houses the island's new Museu Marítim, due to open in 2001 – for more details contact the tourist office (see p.140). Beside the fenced-off museum enclave, a restored well and an old water wheel afford panoramic views over the entire Sant Antoni bay.

North of Sant Antoni

There are several diverting attractions **north of Sant Antoni**, all reachable via turnoffs from the main road to Sant Agnès, which leaves the grim suburbs of the town swiftly behind and climbs steeply towards Ibiza's wooded interior. Though they're within a fifteen-minute walk of Sant Antoni, relatively few visitors get to the cave-chapel **Capella de Santa Agnès**, or plump for the twin sandy beaches of **Cala Gració** and **Cala Gracioneta** over s'Arenal, while hardly anyone visits idyllic **Cala Salada**, some 5km away and accessible either by road or the wonderful coastal hike detailed on p.150.

CAPELLA DE SANTA AGNÈS

Map 9, H3. Sat 9am–noon; 200ptas/€1.20.

A chapel set in a cave, the **Capella de Santa Agnès**, down a signposted turnoff 1.5km north of town along the Sant Antoni–Santa Agnès road, has been a place of worship since the third or fourth century AD. Carthaginian pottery fragments found here also suggest that humans visited the site much earlier, but it's not known whether the cave had any religious significance during the Punic era. There's little evidence of the chapel's historical importance today, though: the walls of the tiny, rectangular nave are built into the cave mouth, and there's just about enough room for a dozen worshippers in addition to the low stone altar and statues of Christ and the Virgin Mary.

Capella de Santa Agnès sits beside the car park of a much larger eighteenth-century church, which was never consecrated, and has now been converted into the esteemed *Sa Capella* restaurant (see p.230).

CALA GRACIÓ AND CALA GRACIONETA

Map 9, F3.

From Caló des Moro, just north of the Sunset Strip, a path winds around the rocky edge of Sant Antoni bay, beside the leafy grounds of some of the resort's most upmarket hotels; 1km from town, you emerge above an small but gorgeous beach, **Cala Gració** – a somewhat unexpected sight given that you can't see its deep inlet at all from San An. Gració's elongated patch of fine white sand stretches back 100m from the sea, and the shallow water is wonderfully calm and clear. The beach is popular with British and German families holidaying in the smart hotels and villas close to the bay, but things only get busy at the height of summer. A small snack bar rents out pedalos, sunbeds and umbrellas between May and October.

Set in an old smugglers' cave on the south side of the bay, Cala Gració is also home to the modest **Aquarium Cap Blanc** (daily 10.30am–7pm; 500ptas/€3), where a collection of sluggish-looking Mediterranean sea life, including lobster, moray eels and plenty of fish, has been amassed. The whole thing is fairly well set up and is popular with children, though you have to spot the spiny and scaly creatures from wooden walkways built above pools in the cave floor.

Adjacent to the fishing huts on the north side of Cala Gració, a path clings to the shoreline, leading 100m to a second hidden bay, **Cala Gracioneta**. Astoundingly beautiful and peaceful, Cala Gracioneta, at barely 30m wide, is even smaller than its neighbour, with a minute patch of exquisitely fine, pale sand nestled between a low shoreline dotted with pines, and shallow, sheltered waters that heat up to bathtub temperatures by late summer. Few people know about this little gem of a beach, and it rarely gets crowded, despite the presence of the wonderful *El Chiringuito* restaurant (see p.230), where food is served almost on the sand.

If you don't want to walk, you can also **get to** the beaches by road. From the town centre, follow c/Ramon y Calal (Map 8, G5), which becomes the Sant Antoni–Santa Agnès road. Follow the signpost for both the bays, which takes you off the Santa Agnès road and left along c/Johann Sebastian Bach (Map 8, G1), round a roundabout (Map 8, D1), and then west along Carreterra de Cala Gració for another 1.5km to Cala Gració. To get to Cala Gracioneta by road you have to do a loop around the coast: follow the same route to Cala Gració, but turn right after 1km on Carreterra de Cala Gració, up Carreterra de Cap Negret. The road

CALA GRACIÓ AND CALA GRACIONETA

A HIKE TO CALA SALADA

The 5km of coastline between Cala Gració and Cala Salada makes a lovely forty-minute hike, passing a series of small, rocky coves. Starting at **Cala Gració** (Map 9, F3), the trail quickly reaches **Cala Gracioneta**, then weaves past jagged coastal rocks and through a scrubby landscape of stunted pines and juniper bush, skirting the smart detached villas of **Cap Negret** (Map 9, F2) after ten minutes' walk. Sticking close to the shore, the trail continues north, reaching **Punta de sa Galera** (Map 9, G2), a slender, crooked sandy-coloured finger of rock that jabs into the sea, in another ten minutes. Past here, the path winds above two miniature pebbly coves; the second, and the larger of the two, known as **Cala Yoga** (Map 9, G1), is popular with nudists and hippies. Completely undeveloped, with bizarre eroded cliffs of stratified rock and a series of shelf-like rock terraces (many painted with New Age doodles) that are good for sun-bathing, the sapphire waters make this a good spot to break your walk with a swim. In summer, there's even a resident reiki masseur and reflexologist, available (in theory) daily from 7pm to 8pm.

From Cala Yoga, it's a further fifteen minutes' walk to Cala Salada. Continue uphill along the poorly surfaced road, leaving the shoreline and ignoring the first turnoff by a villa's large electrical box. Take the next left down a leafy road lined with the exclusive houses of luxury development, passing the *Artesia* villa and its 250-metre-long dry-stone walls, and following the road to the left past a tennis court. Here, a green perimeter fence marks the rough path down through a copse to **Cala Salada** (Map 9, G1). You'll emerge just above the beachside *Restaurant Cala Salada*, from where you can phone for a taxi to take you back to Sant Antoni.

heads northeast for 1km, then west for 2km towards Cap Negret; just before you get to Cap Negret, a signpost on the left directs you south to Cala Gracioneta.

To get to Cala Yoga by road, take the Cala Salada turnoff from the Sant Antoni–Santa Agnès highway, and bear left downhill towards the sea, where the road splits by a white arched gateway across the road; you can park above Cala Yoga.

CALA SALADA

Map 9, G1.

Ringed by a protective barrier of steep, pine-clad hills, and reachable via the coastal hike detailed opposite or a serpentine road through the trees, signposted off the Sant Antoni–Santa Agnès road, the small, all-but-undeveloped cove-beach of **Cala Salada** is an idyllic escape valve from the crowds of Sant Antoni, just 5km to the south. A deep turquoise colour, the inviting waters here lap at a fine 100m strip of pale sand, and there's a low rocky shelf good for sunbathing. Apart from a line of stick-and-thatch fishermen's huts, a solitary villa and a simple seafood restaurant that's popular with locals (May–Oct daily; Nov–April Sat & Sun), there's nothing here but the sea and sand. Across the bay to the north is an even more peaceful sandy beach – you can either swim over or follow a path that winds around the fishing huts.

Cala Salada is one of the most spectacular places in the Pitiuses to watch the **sunset**, though you'll have to shuffle around the shore for the optimum view, depending on the season. Winter is possibly the best time of year, when the sun sinks into the ocean between the gateway-like outline of the islands of Conillera and Bosc. Just above the beach, the setting rays paint a villa (appropriately named *Casa Roja*) almost ridiculously intense shades of red, crimson and purple.

COVA DE LES FONTANELLES

Map 1, B5.

Half a kilometre inland from Cala Salada, a signposted dirt track strikes off the main to **Cova de les Fontanelles**, named "Cave of the Springs" for the spring water that used to bubble up from the cliffs along this part of the coast. Protected by a metal fence (the interior is off limits to the public), the cave is a modest affair, at around 10m wide, but it harbours the only ancient **petroglyphs** in the Pitiuses. Unfortunately, the designs can barely be made out due to centuries of weathering, but you can just about make out boats, and the grapes which have given the cave its other name, Cova des Ví (Cave of Wine). Scholars disagree about the age of the rock art, but the images, which have been copied onto display panels, are thought to be either prehistoric or from the early Bronze Age. Dates aside, Les Fontanelles' setting is magical, tight beneath the bulbous 255-metre hill of Puig Nunó, and overlooking the sea towards the island of Conillera. The best time to be visit is at **sunset**, when the place is usually deserted except for the odd hippy and his joint. From the cave, a short path winds 100m down to the waves below, where the rocky shore provides a blissfully isolated spot for a swim.

To **get to** the Cova de les Fontanelles, follow the sign from Cala Salada along a signposted dirt track that snakes up the hills. Ignore the first (private) right turn, and after 2km take the second right, where a signpost guides you down another poor dirt track. You'll have to park and walk the last few hundred metres.

Southwest of Sant Antoni

Southwest of the Punta des Molí, a continuous, seemingly endless sprawl of slab-like hotels and apartment blocks, supermarkets and souvenir shops and bars and restaurants creep around **Sant Antoni bay**. Giant carcasses of half-built hotels loom over the coast road, and the rocky shoreline is broken only by patches of pine woods and a sprinkling of man-made beaches. These small patches of sand are convenient for a dip if you're staying locally, but if you're after a day by the sea you're far better off continuing west to the far superior **beaches** to the southwest of Sant Antoni; all are reachable via a short drive, bus journey or boat trip from the centre of town.

Travelling southwest around the bay, the closest seashore, **Port des Torrent**, can get very busy with families in the high season. Further west across the dry, flat littoral plains, things are a bit less hectic at sandy **Cala Bassa**, but the very best stretches of sand – the stunning stark expanses of **Cala Compte** and neighbouring **Cala Conta** – are in the far west opposite the arid offshore islands of Conillera and Bosc; just to the south, the bite-shaped cove beach of **Cala Codolar** provides a little variety.

PORT DES TORRENT

Map 9, E5.

The facility-filled coastal road around San An bay comes to an abrupt halt beside the *Seaview Country Club* holiday village, some 5km from the centre of town. A short pathway from the roundabout beside the *Seaview* descends to the pretty, sandy cove of **Port des Torrent**, named after a seasonal stream that originates atop Ibiza's highest peak, Sa Talaiassa (see p.160), and empties into the small bay. Nestled at the end of a deep inlet, Port des Torrent's sands are packed with families lounging on sunbeds and splashing about in the calm water during the summer, when snack bars open up to feed and water the crowds; for the rest of the year, it's empty save for the odd fisherman.

CALA BASSA

Map 9, C5.

A striking half-moon bay, ringed by low cliffs and sabina pines, the fine, 250-metre-wide sandy beach of **Cala Bassa** is one of the most popular in the Sant Antoni surrounds, with plenty of sunbeds and umbrellas to rent and three large café-restaurants. The inviting, sparkling waters have been awarded Blue Flag status, and there are plenty of watersports on offer, from waterskiing to banana rides. Cala Bassa does tend to get very busy in high season, when it's well-served by regular boats and buses from San An, but peace returns and the beach clears by 7pm, when the last transport departs. To get to Cala Bassa by road from town, take the southbound Sant Antoni–Sant Josep highway; after 5km, take the signposted right-hand turnoff opposite the small village of Sant Agustí – Cala Bassa is 6km to the northwest.

- -

Cala Bassa's peaceful **campsite** is reviewed on p.217.

- -

CALA CONTA AND AROUND

After a three-kilometre loop around the remote rocky fringes of western Ibiza, the Cala Bassa road ends at exposed, blue flag-bestowed beach of **Cala Conta** (Map 9, B6), which, together with neighbouring Cala Compte, is generally considered to be one of Ibiza's very best. Though there are only two small patches of golden sand, it's easy to see why people rave about the place: gin-clear water, superb ocean vistas and sunsets that are rarely less than spectacular.

Just 100m or so to the north is a second bite-like bay, **Cala Compte** (Map 9, B6), where there's a good fish restaurant, *s'Illa des Bosc*, named in honour of **Illa des Bosc** (Map 9, B5) directly offshore – though the name means "island of woods", it's now completely deforested, the trees having been felled for charcoal burning over a century ago. A popular place for nude sunbathing, Illa des Bosc is reach-able via a 400-metre wade and swim across shallow water dotted with three tiny islets, but, though the crossing is easy when the sea is calm, beware the currents that can sweep along this section of the coast when things get choppy. Just beyond Illa des Bosc, the much larger island of **Conillera** (Map 9, A3–A4) is visible from most points of Sant Antoni bay, from where its elongated profile resembles a giant beached whale. Many local legends are attached to the island – it's said to have been the birthplace of Hannibal, the Carthaginian general and archenemy of Rome, and also the best source of the *beleño blanco* psychoactive herb, col-lected by pagan practitioners each year and burned during the night of Sant Joan (see p.271). Topped by a lighthouse, the island is uninhabited today, though scuba divers often visit the waters just offshore.

Two kilometres north of Cala Conta is beachless, empty **Cala Roja** (Map 9, B5), named after the burned red colour of its low sandstone coastal cliffs. To get there, you'll have to bump through a tangle of dirt tracks that cut through the parched scrubland. A few lonely fishing huts lurk beneath Cala Roja's corrugated shoreline, and it's easy enough to scramble down to the sea for a blissfully peaceful dip; if you have a snorkel, you can swim to some coastal caves, rich with crustaceans, under the bay's protruding coastal rocks.

CALA CONTA AND AROUND

Looming above Cala Roja, the eighteenth-century **Torre d'en Rovira** watchtower crowns the Cap de Torre, a barren, rocky outcrop that affords spectacular views back over Sant Antoni bay and to the islands of Conillera and Illa Bosc.

CALA CODALAR

Map 9, B7.

Two kilometres inland of Cala Compte, the road takes you past a dirt road signposted for the minuscule cove of **Cala Codalar**, 1km away. It's a pretty little bay, just 40m wide, with fine, pale sand and waters sheltered by the rocky Punta de s'Embacador headland to the north. The beach can get crowded in high season, when it's popular with tourists from the *Club Delfin* hotel just above the bay. There's a simple, nameless snack-shack and a **windsurfing** school (see p.51) here, both open between May and October only.

The South

Adramatic patchwork of soaring hills, thick forests and exquisite beaches, **southern Ibiza** is wildly beautiful, and thankfully, much of the landscape remains untouched by developers. It's the island's the most geographically diverse region, with the highest peak, **Sa Talaiassa**, the shimmering flats of the **Salines salt pans** and drowsy one-horse villages as well as a craggy coast staked with defence towers.

Virtually the entire coastline is dazzlingly picturesque, the shore lapped by balmy, pellucid water and endowed with more than a dozen beautiful **beaches**: from secluded, diminutive Cala Llentrisca, Cala Carbó and Cala Molí, to family-friendly bays like Sa Caleta and Es Cubells and the outrageous posing zones of Es Cavallet and Salines. The area holds only three resorts – the quiet bays of Cala Vedella and Cala Tarida in the west, and big, brash Platja d'en Bossa in the extreme east; the rest of the shore is more or less pristine. The most dramatic coastline is around Cala d'Hort in the southwest, an isolated, remote region of soaring mountains and bizarre cliff and rock formations; here, the mysterious island of **Es Vedrà** and an ancient quarry known as **Atlantis**, a place of pilgrimage for Ibiza's mystic crew, form a kind of "cosmic corner", where fishermen, farmers and hippies have been reporting UFO sightings and weird happenings for decades. Beachlife and unexplained phenomena notwith-standing, southern Ibiza is well worth exploring for the sweeping views and unspoiled landscape alone.

Inland, the rolling, forested countryside is dotted with small villages – serene **Sant Agustí**, prosperous **Sant Josep**, and suburban **Sant Jordi**, home to the prettiest church in Ibiza. There are also some very funky **bars** spread across the south (especially at **Cala Jondal**, Salines beach and along the Sant Josep–Ibiza Town highway), plus some great dining options – everything from simple shoreside *chiringuitos* to elaborate country restaurants. **Getting around** the south is easy with your own vehicle, as there's a decent road network and plenty of signposts, while buses run along the main highway and to some beaches.

Reviews of accommodation, restaurants and bars in the south start on p.214, p.231 and p.246 respectively.

Sant Josep and around

The attractive municipal capital of southern Ibiza and the hub of the area, refreshingly **Sant Josep** is surrounded by high, thickly forested hills that include **Sa Talaiassa**, the island's highest peak. To the south of Sant Josep is the slumberous hilltop village of **Sant Agustí**, capped by a fortified church and affording sweeping views over the southwest coast. Regular **buses** run through the region, passing Sant Agustí and Sant Josep as they trundle along the glorious southern highway between Sant Antoni and Ibiza Town;

however, unless you plan to walk to Sa Talaiassa, you'll need your own transport.

SANT JOSEP

Map 10, E2.

Pretty, prosperous **SANT JOSEP** boasts a delightful setting, suspended 200m above sea level in a valley between the island's central hills and, to the south, the green, forested slopes of Sa Talaiassa. Though the village itself is of no great size, with a population of just four hundred, it is the largest settlement in the region, and if you're staying in the south you're likely to visit both for its banks, boutiques and restaurants and for its easy-going, unruffled ambience. There's a tidy, orderly self-confidence here, best illustrated along the attractive, pint-sized **high street**, where you'll find the arched modern Ajuntament, and just to the west around the delightful little central plaza, where the Moorish-style tiled benches are shaded by pines. From this plaza you have an excellent perspective across the main road to the imposing, whitewashed **Església de Sant Josep**, one of the largest churches in the island, which dates from 1726. Its most arresting aspect is its superb three-storey facade, with a triple-arched porch that extends out from the main body of the building. The church is only open for Mass, but if you do get to take a look at the capacious, delightfully cool interior, check out the wooden pulpit painted with biblical scenes, a reproduction of the eighteenth-century piece that was destroyed when the church's interior was gutted in the Spanish Civil War.

SANT AGUSTÍ

Map 10, E1.

A couple of kilometres north of Sant Josep, a signposted turnoff from the main road to Sant Antoni climbs up to the pretty hilltop village of **SANT AGUSTÍ**, an almost absurdly tranquil place where all signs of life seem to have been frazzled by the Mediterranean sun. Grouped around the fortified church at the heart of the settlement are a clump of old farmhouses, one of which has been beautifully converted into the *Can Berri Vell* restaurant (see p.231), as well as the village bar, a solitary store and an ancient stone defence tower where the locals once hid from pirates. The views across the interior of the island and down to the southwest coast are captivating from the little plaza next to the **Església de Sant Agustí**, built in the late eighteenth century to a design by Spanish architect Pedro Criollez.

SA TALAIASSA

Map 10, D2.

Towering above Sant Josep is the 475-metre peak of **Sa Talaiassa**, the highest point in the Pitiuses, reachable either by an hour-long hike or a ten-minute drive from town along a well-signposted dirt track that turns off the road to Cala d'Hort and Cala Vedella 2km west of Sant Josep. Thickly wooded with aleppo and Italian stone pines, the summit offers exceptional views of southern Ibiza from gaps between the trees; you should be able to pick out the humpback cliffs of Jondal and Falcó, the Salines salt pans and plateau-like Formentera pretty easily – on very clear days, the mountains of the Dénia peninsula in mainland Spain are also visible, some 50km distant. There's a wonderfully peaceful feel here, the silence broken only by the buzz of cicadas and hum of a set of television antennae. The summit was the scene of legendary full-moon parties staged by the hippy population in the 1960s; misty-eyed survivors talk about watching the sun set into the ocean beyond the island of Conillera and the moon rising over the Mediterranean in the east; such gatherings are illegal these days, but there's nothing to stop you driving up to take in the sunset or moonrise.

The southwest coast

One kilometre west of Sant Josep, a turnoff from the road to Sant Antoni bristles with brown signs directing you to the string of lovely sandy beaches that lie along the southwest coast. **Cala Vedella** and **Cala Tarida** have been developed into attractive, small-scale family resorts, while cliff-backed **Cala Molí** and **Cala Carbó** are almost pristine, and are more peaceful places to spend a day by the sea. An isolated, remote region of soaring mountains and bizarre cliff and rock formations, the area also holds special significance for New Age types, drawn to the weird rock-island of **Es Vedrà**, which lies opposite the fabled beach of **Cala d'Hort**, and the ancient quarry known as **Atlantis**.

CALA TARIDA

Map 10, B1.

A wide arc of golden sand broken by two low rocky outcrops, **CALA TARIDA** plays host to one of Ibiza's more appealing resorts, a small, family-orientated collection of low-rise hotels surrounding a pretty bay. In high season, the **beach** gets very busy with German and Spanish holidaymakers, and you'll have to pick your way through rows of umbrellas and sunbeds for a swim. There are plenty of fairly unexciting bars and restaurants to choose from; the best seafood is served up at the expensive *Cas Mila*.

Regular **buses** run between Cala Tarida and Ibiza Town via Sant Josep all year round.

CALA TARIDA

CALA MOLÍ

Map 10, B2.

Two kilometres south of Cala Tarida, the coast road barrels past **Cala Molí**, a fine beach at the foot of a seasonal river bed. Steep cliffs envelop the pebbly cove, which is undeveloped except for a solitary eyesore, *Restaurant Cala Molí*, placed insensitively close to the shoreline, which sells snacks and has a big swimming pool for use of its patrons. The sheltered, deep green waters are a much better place for a dip, however – if you swim across to the cove's southern cliff, you can also explore a small cave. Despite its relatively close proximity to the popular resorts of Tarida and Vedella, Cala Molí never seems to get too busy, probably because it's not served by buses – if you've can get there independently, you'll find it's perfect for a chilled-out day by the sea.

CALA VEDELLA

Map 10, B2.

Continuing south from Cala Molí, the precipitous, shady road twists through the coastal pines for 3km, passing pricey-looking holiday homes and the beautifully positioned *Hostal Cala Molí* (see p.214) before emerging above the long, narrow-mouthed inlet that harbours **CALA VEDELLA**. One of Ibiza's smallest and most attractive resorts, Cala Vedella's profusion of good-quality villas and well-spaced, low-rise hotels are separated into two main developments dotted around the low hills that frame the bay. The sheltered, sandy beach is ideal for families, with calm, very shallow water and a collection of snack bars and restaurants backing onto the sands. Between May and late September, Cala Vedella is served by regular **buses** from Sant Antoni and Ibiza Town via Sant Josep.

CALA CARBÓ

Map 10, B4.

A tiny, tranquil cove-bay, **Cala Carbó**, 4km south of Cala Vedella, is a delightfully peaceful place for a day by the beach, and as there are no public transport connections, it never seems to get too packed. There's a lovely little sand and pebble beach, backed by low sandstone cliffs, and tempting, calm seas; the mossy, rounded boulders offshore lend the water a deep jade tone. If you have a snorkel, try exploring the southern shore up to the rocky point at the mouth of the cove, where colourful wrasse and large schools of mirror fish are common. Of the two **restaurants** at the back of the bay, *Balenario* serves snacks, drinks and excellent mixed fish platters, while *Can Vincent*, set in a fine *finca*-style building, has a huge terrace ideal for more formal dining.

To **get to Cala Carbó**, take the main road to the southeast from St Josep and follow the signs to Cala d'Hort; Cala Carbó is clearly signposted on the right. If you're up to a twenty-minute walk, you can also take one of the three daily buses that run from Ibiza Town to Cala Vedella via Sant Josep, and get off at the turnoff for Cala Carbó.

CALA D'HORT

Map 10, B4.

An expansive, cup-shaped beach of coarse sand, pebbles and crystal water, **Cala d'Hort**, 4km south of Cala Carbó along a well-signposted road, is afforded special status by Ibiza's hippies. Boasting one of the most glorious settings in the Balearics, the beach is backed by the imposing, forested hillsides of the Roques Altes peaks and lies directly opposite the startling, vertiginous rock-island of Es Vedrà, source of countless local legends. With no concrete blocks to spoil the coastline, there's a wonderfully isolated feel here, and the remote location, wedged into Ibiza's south-west corner well away from all the main resorts and towns, ensures that things never get too busy. Even in high season you can usually find a quiet spot for your sun lounger and umbrella, and in winter you'll probably have the place to yourself. There are three good, well-spaced fish **restaurants** by the shore – the best is *El Boldado* (see p.231) on the northern lip of the bay, past a string of fishing huts. If you find Cala d'Hort all too captivating and fancy sticking around, try asking at the *El Carmen* restaurant if there's a room for rent – the owners like to keep it quiet, but there's often some simple accommodation available.

Between June and late September only, three daily **buses** on the Ibiza Town–Cala Vedella route (via Sant Josep and Es Cubells) serve Cala d'Hort. The bus stops on the main road above the beach.

Es Vedrà

Map 10, A5.

Rising from the sea like the craggy crest of a semi-submerged volcano, the limestone outcrop of **Es Vedrà** is one of the most startling sights in the western Mediterranean. Despite its height (378m), it's actually only visible once you get within a few kilometres of Cala d'Hort, its ragged, cone-like contours hidden by the high surrounding peaks of Llentrisca, Sa Talaiassa Roques Altes.

The **legends** surrounding Es Vedrà are remarkable – it's said to be both the island of the sirens, where Odysseus was lured from his ship by mermaids in Homer's epic, and the holy island of the Carthaginian love and fertility goddess, Tanit. A reclusive Carmelite priest, Father Palau i Quer, writing about the few weeks he spent on Vedrà in the nineteenth century, reported seeing visions of the Virgin Mary

THE BATTLE OF CALA D'HORT

In 1992, the sparsely populated slopes behind **Cala d'Hort** have been the subject of a bitter battle between **environmentalists** and **developers**, who planned to build a golf course, a 420-bed hotel and a desalination plant smack in the middle of what is one of the island's most spectacular landscapes – an area of unique biodiversity, home to rare Mediterranean orchids and the highly endangered Eleanor's falcon. Supported by powerful local politicians in the Sant Josep municipality and elements within the then-ruling PP party, the scheme outraged Ibiza's environmentalists, who mounted a protracted campaign, successfully paralysing work for years. Though Cala d'Hort had been declared an ANEI (Area of Special Natural Interest), the developers, Calas de Mediterráneo, continued to lobby. The Sant Josep planners maintained their support for the project, and in late 1998 the green light was given to start work on the golf course.

Most Ibizans were appalled, and the issue ignited a wider campaign against rampant overdevelopment, provoking the biggest **demonstration** in the island's history by January 1999, when 12,000 people (one in seven of the population) marched through Ibiza Town in protest at the Cala d'Hort plans. Seasoned political commentators were astounded, and the march is now seen as a seminal event – the day that notoriously apolitical Ibiza woke up, a protest which led ultimately to the ejection of the PP conservatives in the June 1999 elections, after twenty years in power. In August 1999, after Green Party protesters chained themselves to bulldozers at Cala d'Hort, the newly elected Left-Green Pacte coalition finally acted decisively, slapping a veto on any further development. Today, Cala d'Hort is slated for incorporation into a new National Park, and the victory of the environmentalists has had a wider effect, influencing the Balearic government to place moratorium on the building of new golf courses across the Pitiuses.

and satanic rituals. Sailors and scuba divers have reported compasses swinging wildly and gauges malfunctioning as they approach the island, and there have been innumerable reports of UFO sightings around Vedrà. The rock has also played some starring roles in the entertainment world, featuring in the film *South Pacific* as the mysterious island of Bali Hai, and on the cover of Mike Oldfield's album *Tubular Bells II* – the musician lived opposite Vedrà until the late 1990s.

These days, Es Vedrà is inhabited only by wild goats, a unique sub species of the Ibizan wall lizard and a small colony of the endangered Eleanor's falcon; you can often see the birds swooping around the island. Strangely, there are no boat excursions to the uninhabited isle, though boat excursions from Sant Antoni to Cala d'Hort pass close by; for more on these, see p.52.

TORRE DES SAVINAR AND ATLANTIS

Map 10, B5.

Climbing abruptly from the beach at Cala d'Hort, an exhilaratingly scenic road heads east between wooded hills towards Es Cubells. Two kilometres on, a left-hand turnoff leads to **Torre des Savinar**, a defence tower built in 1763 that has also been known as Torre d'en Pirata since Valencian author Vicente Blasco Ibáñez set part of his buccaneer novel, *The Dead Commands*, here. The dirt track from the coast road to the tower is in very bad condition, so unless you have a 4WD it's best to park up after 200m and continue by foot; it's a fifteen-minute walk from here to the tower. As you reach the coast, a *mirador* provides a full-frontal view over the sea to Es Vedrà, and is one of the best places in Ibiza to watch the **sunset**; a small crowd gathers here most evenings. There are even better views once you get to the two-storey tower itself, set 200m above the Mediterranean. You can climb a flight of steps to the upper level, which was completed in 1763, from where there's a jaw-dropping view of Es Vedrà and panoramic vistas across the sea to tabletop-flat Formentera in the east, and the island of Conillera to the west. Immediately beneath the tower, you can also pick out Vedrà's sister island of **Vedranell**, which resembles a sleeping dragon with its snout and spiky backbone protruding from the water.

A little to the east of the tower, you can also see the outlines of **Atlantis**, an ancient shoreside quarry that's something of a sacred site for Ibizan hippies and a place that retains a genuinely magical feel, with an eerie, brutal and unique beauty. It's easy to make out where the colossal chunks of the sandstone rockface were cut out to be shipped to Ibiza Town to build the capital's magnificent Renaissance walls, and many sections of the angular quarry face have been carved with mystic imagery, from blunt-nosed faces akin to Maya gods to swirling abstract shapes, as well as being adorned with stones suspended from the rocks with wire and decades of doodles and engravings. The most remarkable image, a breathtakingly beautiful painting of a Buddha said to have been completed by a Japanese traveller, has given Atlantis its Spanish nickname, "Punta de Buda".

If you decide to tackle the tough forty-minute descent to Atlantis from the tower, bear in mind that many locals are extremely sensitive about the site – treat it with the **respect** that not all visitors have afforded (some insensitive soul spray-painted the route with "London Posse" in the mid-1990s). To **get to Atlantis**, follow the faint path that climbs inland to the north of the tower, passing through thick bush and dwarf pines. After fifteen minutes' walk, the path turns sharply to the east, and it's a steep, twenty-minute descent to the shore.

TORRE DES SAVINAR AND ATLANTIS

The south coast

Ibiza's spectacular **southern coast**, between the headlands of Llentrisca in the west and Cap des Falcó in the east, holds more than a dozen small **beaches**, most linked to the main Ibiza Town–Sant Josep highway by minor roads. None play host to full-scale resorts, and many of the tiny coves have nothing but a seafood restaurant and a few umbrellas to rent. Inland, thick pine forests cover most of the region, and there's just one diminutive village, **Es Cubells**, and the cave of **Cova Santa**, to tempt you away from the sea.

Public transport is very sporadic throughout the area. **Buses** do pass by **Platja Codolar**, **Sa Caleta** and Es Cubells between May and late September, but you'll need your own transport to get to the other beaches – though they are well signposted.

ES CUBELLS AND AROUND

Map 10, D4.

South of Sant Josep, a signposted road weaves around the eastern flank of Sa Talaiassa, past terraces of orange and olive trees, to the southern coast and the tiny cliffside village of **ES CUBELLS**. The settlement owes its place on the map to Father Palau i Quer, the Carmelite priest who visited nearby Es Vedrà. He persuaded the Vatican to fund construction of a chapel here in 1855 on the grounds that the farmers and fishermen of the area lacked a local place of worship. Magnificently positioned above the deep blue Mediterranean, the whitewashed sandstone building, now upgraded to church status, is one of the island's most simple. The tiny garden beside it holds a stone plinth dedicated to Palau i Quer, engraved with an image of Es Vedrà.

Though the church forms the nucleus of today's tiny hamlet, Es Cubells still consists of no more than half a dozen homes, a store and, adjoining the church, *Bar Llumbi*, a small bar and restaurant (May–Oct) where you can get decent grilled fish or a *bocadillo*.

Signposted from the church, the fine **Cala Cubells beach** (Map 10, D5) is 1km and over 100m below the village, via a couple of hairpin turns. It's one of Ibiza's least-visited spots, consisting of a slender strip of grey, tide-polished stones, with a handful of sunbeds and umbrellas and a somewhat overpriced restaurant, *Ses Boques*. If you're looking for an isolated place to get an all-over tan, head to the left past a strip of fishing huts, where three tiny, untouched stony beaches lie below the grey, crumbling cliffs.

CALA LLENTRISCA

Map 10, C5.
South of Es Cubells, the road hugs the eastern slopes of the Llentrisca headland, swooping down for 3km past a small enclave of luxurious modern villas towards the spectacular, isolated cove of **Cala Llentrisca**, cut off from the rest of the island by soaring pine-clad slopes. As no buses serve the beach, you'll need your own transport to visit; however, the road deteriorates the closer it gets, and if you're driving you'll have to park beside the final villa at the end of the road and walk the last five minutes. There's nothing on the pebbly shoreline except a row of seldom-used fishing huts, and very little shade, but there's often a yacht or two moored in the translucent bay waters.

Between May and September, three daily buses pass through Es Cubells on the Ibiza Town–Cala Vedella route.

ES TORRENT AND AROUND

Map 10, E5.

A small sandy cove beach at the foot of a dry river bed, **Es Torrent** is 7km south of Sant Josep but isn't served by public transport; to get there, take the road to Es Cubells, and follow the signposted turnoff that winds down towards the Porroig promontory. Es Torrent's waters are shallow and invitingly turquoise, and offer decent snorkelling around the amber cliffs at the edge of the bay, or a little further out close to the two tiny offshore rocks, Ses Illetes, where the water is a little deeper. Though the beach is lovely, many come here just for the expensive seafood restaurant, *Es Torrent* (see p.232), which is very popular with the yachtie crowd.

Two kilometres southeast of Es Torrent, the road passes **Porroig Bay**, a minute collection of ramshackle fishing huts set below low, eroded cliffs on the western cusp of the low Porroig peninsula. There no reason to stop here, but once you've looped around the prosperous peninsula, dotted with luxury villas and a four-star hotel, and returned to Porroig Bay, you can follow a dirt track that continues northeast for 400m to **Cala Xarcó**, a quiet strip of sand that only Ibizans and the odd yachtie seem to have stumbled upon. There's a little shade from the coastal sabina pines here, a sunbed or two for rent, and the superb, but pricey *Restaurant Es Xarcu*.

If you want to carry on from Xarcó to Cala, it's a couple of minutes' scramble over the cliff behind the restaurant; you can also drive via a precipitous dirt road from the beach; after 200m, take the first right beside some walled villas.

CALA JONDAL

Map 10, F5.

The broad beach of **Cala Jondal**, slap between the

promontories of Porroig and Jondal, is 9km southeast of Sant Josep via a signposted turnoff from the Ibiza Town–Sant Josep highway. A broad, stony seashore at the base of gently sloping terraces planted with fruit trees, Jondal's kilometre-long strip of smooth rounded stones, divided by a dry river bed, doesn't make one of the island's finest swimming spots, but the presence of some of the best beach bars in Ibiza does ensure a certain lively aspect that sets the place apart from other quiet bays hereabouts. Few tourists know about Cala Jondal, which mainly attracts an Ibizan and island-based international crowd, and an innovative home-grown dance and chillout scene has developed here since the mid 1990s. Over on the east side of the bay, the legendary *Jockey Club* (see p.247) is a brilliant beach-bar-cum-club, while the neighbouring *Yemanja* restaurant is renowned for fresh fish and wonderful cava-based sangria. On the other side of the torrent, *Particular* (see p.247) is one of Ibiza's most stylish chillout bars, where local DJs enthral sunbathers with languid, beatless grooves, while on the far west side of the beach *Tropicana* serves excellent fresh fruit juices.

Bear in mind that, as no buses serve Cala Jondal, you'll have to make your way there independently.

SA CALETA AND AROUND

Map 10, F5.

Four kilometres around the coast from Cala Jondal, and reachable by road via the same signposted turnoff from the Sant Josep–Ibiza Town highway, are the ruined remains of **Sa Caleta**, the first Phoenician settlement in Ibiza. Established around 650 BC on a low promontory beside a tiny natural harbour, the small site was only occupied for about fifty years, before the Phoenicians shifted operations to the site of what's now Ibiza Town. Today, a high metal fence surrounds the foundations of the village, which once housed several hundred people, who survived by fishing, hunting and farming wheat as well as running furnaces where iron was smelted for tools. Even though the ruins lack visual impact, the site is a peaceful place to visit, with expansive views over an azure sea towards Platja Codolar and Cap des Falcó.

To the west of the site, a short path leads to Sa Caleta's **beaches**, three tiny adjoining bays occasionally labelled as "Bol Nou" on some maps. The first bay, a 100-metre strip of coarse golden sand, is the busiest spot, and very popular with Ibizan families on weekends – there are some sunbeds and umbrellas to rent here in summer, excellent swimming and snorkelling, and a good, reasonably priced restaurant, *El Rincón del Marino* (May–Oct). The other two bays, both secluded and pebbly, are to the west of the sandy bay, via a path that winds along the shore below Sa Caleta's low sandstone cliffs – both are popular with nudists.

Six daily **buses** pass Sa Caleta, which is on the Ibiza Town–Cala Vedella route, between May and late September only.

PLATJA CODOLAR

Map 10, G6.

East of Sa Caleta, a paved road parallels the ochre-coloured coastal cliffs, heading towards the airport and Sant Jordi. One kilometre along, just as the road heads inland, a sign on the right marked "Chiringuito" signifies the start of **Platja Codolar**, a sweeping pebble beach that stretches for over 3km southeast, swinging alarmingly close to the airport runway and skirting the fringes of the Salines salt pans. Even at the height of summer, there's rarely more than a dozen or so (mainly nude) swimmers and sunbathers here, and the place would be very peaceful were it not for the regular interruption of screaming jet engines revving up on the runway or soaring overhead.

COVA SANTA

Map 10, F4. April–Oct Mon–Sat 9.30am–1.30pm; 400ptas/€ 2.40.
Away from the coastline, the Sant Josep–Ibiza Town highway swings past the signposted turnoff for **Cova Santa** some 5km from Sant Josep. The largest cave in Ibiza, Cova Santa was discovered in the fifteenth century, when local people used it as a hiding place during pirate attacks. It's privately owned these days, and the entry fee includes a reasonably informative guided tour (in English) that takes you, via a staircase, down to the main cavern, replete with the mandatory dripping giant stalactites and stalagmites, and involves some flashy lighting effects.

The far south

Ibiza's most southerly body of land, the promontory that juts into the Mediterranean south of the scruffy settlement of **Sant Jordi**, encompasses an abundance of spectacular landscapes. Lining the coastline are three of the island's finest beaches – the resort of **Platja d'en Bossa** and the back-to-back sands of **Salines beach** and **Es Cavallet**, while the **salt pans** that were the island's only source of wealth until the mass tourism juggernaut revolutionized the economy in the 1960s take up most of the interior.

Regular **buses** buzz up and down the main road from Sant Jordi to Salines beach, while the resort of Platja d'en Bossa enjoys excellent connections with Ibiza Town, including the all-night discobus between June and late September.

SANT JORDI

Map 10, I4.

Dismal-looking and traffic-choked, the small settlement of **SANT JORDI** is trapped in a kind of no-man's land between Ibiza Town and the beaches to the south. Almost lost in the featureless suburban sprawl is the main point of interest, the **Església de Sant Jordi**, 200m north of the roundabout around which the town is centred. It's Ibiza's most fortress-like church, with mighty angled walls gashed with embrasures and topped with full battlements – all security measures to keep out pirates; inside, the austerity of the gingham tiled floor and simple wooden benches seem at odds with the gaudy modern altarpiece, installed in 1990.

The only other reason to visit Sant Jordi is for the Saturday **market**, actually more of a car-boot sale, held in the dustbowl of the **hippodrome**, a former horse-and-buggy race track. It's Ibiza's most quirky affair, far less commercialized than the hippy markets, with a good selection of junk jewellery, trashy clothes, second hand books and furniture to root through. It's open all year and gets going quite early in the day (around 8am), and tails off by about 3pm; there's no entrance charge.

PLATJA D'EN BOSSA

Map 10, I4.

A kilometre east of Sant Jordi, and merging into Figueretes (see p.90) to the north, the conventional, *costa*-style resort of **Platja d'en Bossa** is stretched out along the island's longest beach – a ruler-straight, three-kilometre-long strip of wonderfully fine, pale sand. Lining the beach are a gap-toothed row of lumpish hotel blocks, many abruptly thrown up in the Franco years, others still in various stages of construction, while behind lies an unappealing secondary strip of cafés, restaurants, German bierkellers, British pubs, car rental outlets and supermarkets stuffed with plastic dolphins, lilos and suncreams. Though Platja d'en Bossa is predominantly a family resort, attracting tourists from all over northern Europe, the crop of new **bars** that have sprung up towards the southern end of the resort, close to the club *Space*, now form an embryonic party zone. By far the best-known of these is the beachside club-bar *Bora Bora*, where thousands gather to groove in the high-season months.

For reviews of Platja d'en Bossa's bars and club-bars, see p.262.

Despite the concrete and the tourist tack, Platja d'en Bossa is increasingly popular as a base for savvy, older clubbers who have tired of the San An scene and stay here to take advantage of the location – a few kilometres equidistant from Ibiza Town and the sands at Salines. If you decide to follow suit, you'll find that the main drawback is the lack of decent restaurants, most of which dole out fast food or bland "international" fare. However, you can always escape to restaurant-rich Ibiza Town, connected to Platja d'en Bossa by half-hourly buses and a regular boat service in high season.

SALINES BEACH

Map 10, I7.

A beautiful kilometre-long strip of powdery pale sand backed by pines and dunes, **Salines beach** is Ibiza's most fashionable place to pose. The sands are interspersed with rocks, and well-spaced beach bars dot the shoreline, which mutates from a family-friendly, bucket-and-spade environment close to the *Guaraná* café in the north into the island's

SALINES BEACH

BETWEEN THE BEACHES – A HIKE TO ES CAVALLET

South of Platja d'en Bossa, a shady path follows the coastline along the eastern contours of Puig de Baix to the beach at Es Cavallet. It'll take a little over an hour to complete the four kilometre walk, which traverses unspoiled rocky coves and meanders through thick forest. The route is easy to follow, and not too strenuous, but there are no refreshments on the way.

The path begins at Platja d'en Bossa's southernmost point (Map 10, I5), next to the *Club Med* windsurfing school, and crosses a narrow, rotten-smelling aqueduct that feeds the nearby salt pans with seawater. It then heads for the conical, sixteenth-century **Torre des Carregador**, which sits above the beach to the south on a rocky outcrop and was built to guard the southern approach to Ibiza Town. There are superb views of the Dalt Vila castle and cathedral in Ibiza Town from its base. Past the tower, the path continues around the diminutive semicircular bay of **Cala de sa Sal Rossa** (Red Salt Beach), and passes a ring of fishermen's huts before climbing up the pine-clad hillside ahead. From here onwards, you're always within 50m or so from the sea, climbing up and down undulating slopes thick with thyme and rosemary, and past deserted rocky coves, with La Mola, Formentera's slab-like eastern peninsula, clearly visible for much of the route. Eventually, the path takes you to a paved road that descends to the northern end of **Es Cavallet** beside the *Chiringuito* café-bar, where you can get superb juices and snacks.

To **get back to Platja d'en Bossa**, take an Ibiza Town-bound bus from nearby Salines beach; the route passes close to the northern end of Bossa. If you've parked close to *Club Med*, get off at the Sant Francesc church and walk 1km to Platja d'en Bossa along a dirt road that skirts the northern section of the salt pans.

premier navel-gazing spot around *Sa Trincha* (see p.247) in
the south, where clothing is optional. Beyond *Sa Trincha* are
a succession of tiny sandy coves, enveloped by unusual rock
formations – some were once quarried – that are grabbed
fairly early in the day and jealously guarded as private
beaches by dedicated, and very territorial, sunbathers.
Beyond the coves, the sands give way to a slender rocky
promontory, topped at its end by the **Torre de ses Portes**
defence tower.

Hourly **buses** run to Ibiza Town from a bus stop just
north of Salines beach, close to sorry-looking **La Canal**, a
ramshackle wharf where salt is loaded for export.

ES CAVALLET AND AROUND

Map 10, I6.

A kilometre east of the Salines beach car park, via a delightful signposted road around the sparkling salt pans, are the
honey sands of **Es Cavallet**, the second stunning beach on
this part of the coast. Franco's Guardia Civil fought a futile
battle against nudism here for years, arresting hundreds of
naked hippies before the kilometre-long stretch of sand was
finally designated Ibiza's first naturist beach in 1978. The
northern end of Es Cavallet, close to the *Chiringuito* bar and
car park, attracts a mixed bunch of families and couples, but
the southern half of the beach – and the nicest stretch – is
almost exclusively **gay**, centred around the superb *Chiringay*
bar-café (see p.275). It's a ten-minute stroll over to Salines
beach from *Chiringay*, through sand dunes and wind-twist-
ed sabina pines that double as prime cruising territory.

Punta de ses Portes

Map 10, I7.

A fifteen-minute walk south of Es Cavallet's *Chiringay*

SALINES SALT PANS

Ibiza's spectacular **Ses Salines salt pans** (Ⓦ*www
.insula.org/saltroute/html/body_ibiza.html*) stretch across 1,000
acres, in three separate zones, between Platja Codolar in the
west and the southeastern beaches of Platja d'en Bossa and
Es Cavallet. From the Punic era until the mid-twentieth century
– more than 2000 years – the production of salt was Ibiza's
only real industry and its primary source of wealth, funding the
construction of the city walls and the purchase of arms for
defence, and traded for wheat when harvests failed.

Ibizan salt production began with the **Phoenicians**, who
recognized that the flat land bordering the sea in the extreme
south of the island was perfectly suited to the creation of salt
pans – seawater naturally crystallized here anyway – and that
the dense, clay-based soil made a perfect base for large-
scale production. Roman, Vandal and Visigoth invaders continued to maintain the Phoenician salt pans, but it was the
Moors, experts at hydraulic technology, who developed the
fundamentals of the system of sluice gates, mini-windmills
and water channels that's still in use today. Seawater enters
and leaves the salt pans through narrow stone aqueducts at
Codolar, Es Cavallet and Platja d'en Bossa, with pumps
(rather than the original mill-powered paddles) controlling the
flow and the water levels to ensure that the maximum quanti-
ty of salt residue is collected. The pans must also be flooded
at the right time of year, as too much rainfall prevents crystallization. Approximately 2500 cubic metres of seawater is then
left to evaporate in the relentless summer sun, forming a ten-
centimetre crust of pinky-white powder after three months,

beach bar, Ibiza's most southerly point, **Punta de ses
Portes** is a lonely, rocky spot that's often lashed by winds
and waves. Above the swirling currents and a handful of

which is scooped up and amassed in huge salt hills, then exported from La Canal jetty. Until the late nineteenth century, when a steam engine partially replaced the human workforce, labourers humped the entire cargo to the docks by hand in the terrible heat of August and September; these days, tractors, trucks and conveyor belts perform the hard labour. Around 70,000 tonnes of salt are now exported annually, and mechanization has allowed a few dozen employees to do the work that hundreds previously performed.

As well as producing salt, the pans – one of the first points of call on the migratory route from Africa – also serve as an important habitat for **birds**, and thanks to a 23-year battle by environmentalists against property developers and politicians, Ibiza's salt pans, alongside the salt pans in the important wetlands of Estany des Peix Estany Pudent in Formentera (see pp.185 and 184), are now officially protected as a **natural reserve**; you'll see storks, herons and flamingoes stopping to rest and refuel, as well as over 200 species in permanent residence, from osprey and black-necked grebe to Kentish plover. The salt flats are also rich with endemic plant species such as the pink-flowering molinet, and are regarded as one of the EU's most important wetland habitats. A director and six wardens have been appointed to manage the area and conduct tours, and a visitor centre is due to open at the church in nearby Sant Francesc in 2002. Until then, you're best off viewing them at sunset from the Sant Jordi–La Canal road, around the km3 marker; beware clouds of mosquitoes at dusk and dawn, especially in September.

wave-battered fishing huts is another two-storey, sixteenth-century defence tower, **Torre de ses Portes**, almost a twin of the Torre des Carregador at Platja d'en Bossa, which commands superb views of the chain of tiny islands that reach out to Formentera. One of these, **Illa des Penjats** (Island of the Hanged) was used for executions until the early twentieth century; another, **Illa des Porcs** (Pig Island), was once a pig smugglers' stronghold. Both islands are topped by the lighthouses that guide ships and ferries through the shallow but treacherous Es Freus channel between Ibiza and Formentera.

ES CAVALLET AND AROUND

Formentera

ranquil, easy-going **Formentera** could hardly be more of a contrast to Ibiza, despite being only a thirty-minute ferry ride away. Physically, the island is very flat, consisting of two shelf-like plateaux connected by a narrow central isthmus. It's also very sparsely inhabited, with less than 6,000 people spread thinly over 1000 hectares of rain-starved, sun-baked land and just three tiny, slumberous villages. This isolation and the peaceful, languid pace of life attracts a mellow bunch of visitors: cyclists, hippies, birdwatchers and naturists.

Formentera's unhurried appeal belies a troubled **history**. The struggle of trying to eke out a living from the salt pans and the unforgiving soil, combined with the threat of various invaders and pirate attacks, led the island to be completely abandoned in the late fourteenth century, and it was only repopulated in 1697. This precarious past has ensured that all of Formentera's historic buildings have a defensive calibre: the churches are heavily fortified, and the coastline is studded with watchtowers.

For the first time in its history, Formentera's future prosperity seems secure today. The economy is totally dependent on summer tourism (almost exclusively Germans and Italians), with visitors flocking in for some of Spain's longest, whitest, cleanest and least crowded **beaches**. The authorities have followed a relatively sustainable pattern of tourism development, attracting enough tourists to ensure reasonable levels of affluence without feeling the need to cover their best sandy bays with sprawling concrete resorts, and have devised tight environmental controls to prevent future tourism projects.

The sole resort, **Es Pujols**, is a fairly restrained, small-scale affair, with a lively (but far from raucous) summer bar scene and a couple of small clubs. Formentera's real draw, though, is its magnificent **shoreline** – the clarity and colour of the sea is astonishing, with water turquoise enough to trump any Caribbean holiday brochure. The pick of the beaches are the two back-to-back powdery white sands, **Platja Illetes** and **Platja Llevant**, of the slender Trucador peninsula to the north, and **Platja de Migjorn**, a sweeping six-kilometre sandy crescent that lines much of the island's south coast. Formentera also holds a number of less expansive beaches, including the fine pale sands of **Ses Platgetes**, and the sheltered bay of **Cala Saona**, the island's only cove beach.

Away from shore, the countryside is astonishingly beautiful despite the arid climate, a patchwork of golden wheatfields, vines, carob and fig trees divided by ancient amber-coloured dry-stone walls. It's best explored by bicycling along the "Green Routes" (see p.41), a network of quiet country paths and lanes that connect Formentera's tiny, soporific villages. The island's diminutive capital, **Sant Francesc Xavier**, is the most interesting of these, with a fine spartan church and a smattering of boutiques and bars. The other settlements of **Sant Ferran** and **El Pilar de la Mola** also harbour the odd pocket of cultural and historical interest.

Formentera also boasts some very modest **ancient sites** in the southern Barbària peninsula, as well as the ruined remains of Ca Na Costa near Es Pujols and a Roman fort –

but only the foundations of these buildings remain. Twitchers will find that the **birding** is best at the salt lakes of **Estany Pudent** and **Estany des Peix**, while the wind-lashed extremes of the island – **Cap de Barbària** in the south and **Punta de la Mola** to the east – have a wild, stir-ring feel, with both headlands crowned by lonely light-houses and surrounded by stunning coastal scenery.

Getting around

Most visitors choose to get around Formentera independ-ently, and renting a car or bike is easy, with several rental outlets offering bicycles, scooters, motorbikes and cars. Prices are pretty similar from outlet to outlet, but **Isla Blanca** (☎971 322 559) or **Autos Ca Mari** (☎971 322 921), both on the harbourside, are reliable options.

Formentera has a pretty reasonable **bus** service, with daily services operating a loop around the main settlements of La Savina, Es Pujols, Sant Ferran and Sant Francesc every two hours or so from 9am until 8pm between May and mid-October. Small **boats** also sail up the coast, connect-ing the main port of La Savina with Platja Illetes beach, and on to Espalmador island just north of Formentera.

Reviews of accommodation, restaurants and bars in Formentera start on pp.215, 232 and 248 respectively.

LA SAVINA

Map 11, C3.
Nestled around a small natural harbour in the northwest corner of the island, small, orderly **LA SAVINA** is likely to be your first view of Formentera, as all ferries from Ibiza dock here. It has never been a huge settlement, content to

busy itself with the export of salt and planks of the sabina pine that give the place its name, and it's a still a sleepy place today, only stirring when the Ibiza ferry steams into port. However, the hubbub doesn't last very long, as most passengers make a beeline for the rows of rental scooters and bicycles and make a quick getaway.

Though La Savina is not the most absorbing place in the Pitiuses, the **harbour** is pleasant enough, with a small central marina bristling with yachts from the Spanish mainland and northern Europe. Modern hotel and apartment buildings overlook the marina from the south side of the harbour, housing souvenir shops and cafés at street level that are perfectly placed if you need to while away an hour or so before your ferry departs. If you have an hour or two to kill before your departure, you could easily while away the time at any of these eateries – the stylish *Aigüa* (see p.232) offers the best food and most comfortable surrounds, however.

Just behind the harbour, Formentera's only **tourist information** office (Mon–Fri 10am–2pm & 5–7pm; Sat 10am–2pm; ☎971 322 057) has a good stock of glossy leaflets about the island's history, environment, hotels beaches and Green Routes, and extremely helpful staff. For **accommodation** information, head next door to the Central de Reservas Formentera office (☎971 323 224; ⓦ*www.formenterareservations.com*; see p.206), which has an extensive list of apartments and houses for rent.

ESTANY PUDENT AND ESTANY DES PEIX

Heading southeast out of La Savina, the island's main highway passes an ugly sprawl of roadside warehouses that almost obscure Formentera's two **salt lakes**, the island's main wetland habitats. On the left, appropriately named **Estany Pudent** (Map 11, C3–D4), or "Stinking Pond", is the larger of the two, an oval expanse that apparently smells a lot better now that an irrigation channel has been opened to allow seawater in; however, a rotten aroma still hangs in the air most days. Ringed by scrub bush and an ugly jumble of bungalows, Estany Pudent is not the most aesthetically pleasing place either, but it is popular amongst **birdwatchers**, who come to get a look at common visitors from herons and egrets to black-necked grebes, warblers and even the odd flamingo. Dirt tracks run around the entire circumference of the lake, and you can get to the shoreline via a right-hand turnoff 500m along the main highway from La Savina, which passes through a small patch of salt pans, as well as other turnoffs from the road between Es Pujols and the Trucador peninsula.

Smaller **Estany des Peix** (Map 11, C3–C4), to the right of the highway via a turnoff 1km south of La Savina, has a narrow mouth to the sea, and its shallow waters act as an ideal nursery for young fish. The brackish lagoon is no more picturesque than its neighbour, and not as rich birding territory, but there are plenty of terns and ducks and you may encounter the odd wader.

PUNTA DE SA PEDRERA AND PUNTA DE SA GAVINA

Past the lake, the turnoff from the highway to deteriorates into a dirt track that heads through scrub bush, spiky succulents and prickly pears towards the remote promontories of the northwest coast. Though there are no sights along the way, the route, marked by brown Can Marroig signposts, is popular amongst mountain-bikers, and it's nice for a gentle afternoon stroll, particularly of you time your walk to coincide with sunset. Some 500m from the highway, the track swings west around the southern shore of Estany des Peix, passing a string of loosely dispersed villas, before continuing another 3km northwest through thorny scrub to **Punta de sa Pedrera** (Map 11, B3), a small, thumb-shaped sandstone outcrop, favoured by Formentera's hippies as a isolated place to watch the sun sink into the sea and take in the expansive views across the Mediterranean to Es Vedrà (see p.164). From Punta de sa Pedrera, blue signs marked "kiosko" lead to the east shore of the promontory 100m below, where a the famously testy owner of a dilapidated *chiringuito* sells simple, rather overpriced fried fish; the only refreshments for miles around.

From Pedrera, rough trails following the low coastal cliffs meander 2km to the south through bush and eroded sandstone to **Punta de sa Gavina** (Map 11, B4). Here, a crumbling conical eighteenth-century watchtower, **Torre de sa Gavina**, makes another agreeably quiet spot for sunset watching.

SANT FRANCESC XAVIER

Map 11, C4.

Formentera's tiny capital, **SANT FRANCESC XAVIER**, is a quiet little town 2km southeast of La Savina. The attractive network of pretty, whitewashed streets hold a boutique or two and a couple of historic; Sant Francesc also serves as Formentera's administrative centre, with the police force, health service and local government all based here. Strangely, though, it's not much of a social centre, and though it does have a fair selection of bars Sant Francesc's residents have the reputation of being a somewhat temperate bunch. If you've arrived from the mainland or from Ibiza Town, you'll have to get used to very un-Spanish timekeeping – eating before 10pm and drinking up shortly after 11pm – unless you decamp to the late-night pastures of Es Pujols.

The heart of the town is the **Plaça de la Constitució**, an attractive little square, with a few benches scattered between gnarled olive trunks and sickly-looking palm trees, which is home to Formentera's most notable buildings. Consecrated in 1726, the forbidding, fortified **Església de Sant Francesc Xavier**, sits on the north side of the plaza, its brutally simple, plastered facade embellished only with a tiny window set high in the wall. Until the mid-nineteenth century cannons were mounted on the building's flat roof as an extra line of defence against the ever-present threat of pirate attack, as were the mighty main doors, strengthened with iron panelling. The interior of the church is very sombre and plain, with a single barrel-vaulted nave, six tiny side chapels and a gaudy gold-plated altar. Beside the doorway, the large, alabaster baptismal **font** is its most curious feature, decorated with a crudely executed ox's head. It's thought to date from Vandal times, but no one is quite sure who originally placed it here.

Adjoining the church to the south is the unpretentious, blue-shuttered old government building, while opposite, on the other side of the square, is its attractive replacement, the **Casa de la Constitució**. Built from local sandstone, this modern, two-storey centre of island power is draped with the flags of Formentera, the Balearics, Spain and the EC.

Sant Francesc's bar is reviewed on p.248.

A second chapel, the primitive fourteenth-century **Sa Tanca Vell**, 100m south of the plaza down c/Eivissa, is also worth a quick glance. Barely 5m long by 2m high and topped with a simple barrel-vaulted roof, it was originally constructed in 1362 from rough, and the partly ruined remains were rebuilt in 1697, when Formentera was resettled. Sa Tanca Vell must have been a horrendously claustrophobic place to take Mass or seek refuge from pirates, with just enough space for a congregation of a dozen or so. After the resettlement, it served as the island's only place of worship for thirty years, until the much larger Sant Francesc Xavier was completed. Today the building is fenced in and not open to the public, but you can get a clear enough view of the exterior through the protective railings.

The only other point of interest in Sant Francesc is the modest **Museu Etnològic** (Mon–Sat 10am–1.30pm; 300ptas/€1.80), 100m northwest of the plaza on c/Sant Jaume above a little cultural centre which stages regular free exhibitions by local artists. Housed in two rooms, the museum's collection is not especially interesting unless you have a fascination for highly polished old farming tools and fishing gear, but there are a few curious old photographs of the island, including one from the early twentieth century of a very muddy, desolate-looking Sant Francesc. Outside the museum is the tiny toy-town steam train that used to shunt the island's salt to the docks from the salt pans.

CALA SAONA

Map 11, B5.

South of Sant Francesc, an undulating, ruler-straight main road heads through sunburned fields towards Formentera's southern plateau, the Barbària peninsula. Some 2.5km from the capital, a signposted branch road veers down through rust-red fields of carob and fig and small coppices of aleppo pine to the appealing cove of **Cala Saona**, 3km from the junction. The only cove beach in Formentera (and a fairly busy spot in the summer), Cala Saona boasts temptingly turquoise water, and fine sand that extends 100m back from the coast to the bulky *Hotel Cala Saona*, the bay's only building.

There's some fine cliffside **walking** south of Cala Saona, along coastal paths that meander past sabina pines and sand dunes and offer plenty of quiet, shady spots for a picnic lunch. The sunset views from this section of the coast are stunning, with dramatic views over the Mediterranean to the sphinx-like contours of Es Vedrà and Vedranell, and of the soaring hills of southern Ibiza.

BARBÀRIA PENINSULA

South of the Cala Saona turnoff, the road gradually begins its ascent of Formentera's southern plateau, the **Barbària peninsula**, a sparsely populated, ruggedly scenic region. Along the route are a collection of minor archeological sites (all signposted from the road), but the main attraction is the eerily beautiful lunar-like landscape, capped by a lonely lighthouse and a landmark defence tower. Beautifully located in small arid fields dotted with carob trees and dense patches of pine, which serve as prime habitats for **birdlife**, including flycatchers and the startlingly exotic, zebra-striped hoopoe, **Barbària II** (Map 11, C6) is the first and the largest set of remains, though the fenced-off remnants if this 3800-year-old Bronze Age settlement hardly look impressive. Originally, the site boasted nine simple limestone buildings – bedrooms, workrooms, a kiln and animal quarters – and was occupied for around three hundred years. Another 100m or so south, the second set of remains, **Barbària III**, are of a much smaller Bronze Age site. Excavations have revealed no evidence of human habitation here, and it's likely that the ruins were some kind of storehouse or animal pen used by the inhabitants of Barbària II. The final site, **Barbària I**, is right on the fringe of the last barren section of the peninsula, the Cap de Barbària, beyond a patch of pine forest and an ancient stone wall known as Tanca s'Allà Dins. Consisting of a 3-metre-wide circular formation of upended stone blocks that may have represented a place of worship, the remains are a little more striking, but (sadly), practically nothing is known about their significance. Tiny pottery fragments have been unearthed here, but there's no proof that the site was ever inhabited.

Cap de Barbària

Map 11, B7.

The most isolated, barren region of the Pitiuses, the **Cap de Barbària**, or "Barbary Cape", is named after the North African pirates who passed this way to plunder Formentera. Looking across the bleak, sun-bleached landscape, dotted with tiny green patches of hardy rosemary and thyme, it's hard to imagine that there was a dense pine wood here until the 1930s, when ruined emigrés returning to a jobless Formentera after the American Depression chopped down the trees to make charcoal.

At the end of the road a white-painted lighthouse, the **Far des Barbària**, cuts a lonely figure in this moon-like plateau, standing tall above the swirling, cobalt-blue waters of the Mediterranean. Gulls, shearwaters and peregrine falcons swoop and hover in the sea breezes, and the occasional blast of warm desert wind serves as a reminder that Algeria is closer than Catalunya. If you pick your way 200m south of the lighthouse, you'll find a cave, **Sa Cova Foradada**, which is worth a quick look. You enter by lowering yourself into a small hole in the roof of the modest single chamber; once you're inside you can edge your way to the mouth of the cave, almost 100m above the sea, for a stunning view of the Mediterranean.

In the other direction from the lighthouse, it's a ten-minute walk over to **Torre des Garroveret**, a well-preserved, two-storey eighteenth-century tower that, as Formentera's first line of defence against Barbary pirates, would have been manned night and day in centuries past. Formenterans contend that, on exceptionally clear days, it's possible to see the mountains of North Africa from here, despite the fact that they're 110km away.

SANT FERRAN

Map 11, D4.

Strung out along a busy junction on the main La Savina–La Mola highway, **SANT FERRAN** ("San Fernando" in Castilian), Formentera's second largest town, boasts an abundance of banks, bars, stores and restaurants. With its two main streets plagued by traffic noise and lined with an unsteady-looking sprawl of apartment blocks, your first impression of Sant Ferran may make you want to head straight out again. However, the most attractive part of town, hidden away a couple of streets northeast of the main highway, is well worth investigating, centred around the pleasantly austere village church, **Església de Sant Ferran**. The church was originally built close to the island's salt pans towards the end of the eighteenth century, but poor construction methods and the unsuitability of the sandy terrain meant that the structure soon started to crumble, and in 1883, it was taken down and reconstructed stone by stone in today's location, a process that took six years. Uniquely in the Pitiuses, its simple sandstone facade, topped with a crude belfry, has not been plastered or whitewashed.

Opposite the church is a spacious, paved **plaza**, lined with seats and young palm trees. There's barely a soul to be seen here for most of the year, but during the summer months it becomes a meeting place for young Formenterans and holidaying teenagers, who gather here to gossip and flirt in the balmy high-season heat. The more mature can be found just down the road at the *Fonda Pepe* (see p.248) on c/Mayor, the island's most famous drinking den, or eating at one of the string of restaurants south of the plaza.

ES PUJOLS

Map 11, D4.

Formentera's only dedicated resort, **ES PUJOLS**, 2km north of Sant Ferran, is an attractive, small-scale affair, popular with young Germans and Italians. It's a lively, but not overtly boisterous place, though there is a decent quota of bars and a couple of clubs. Curving off to the northwest, in front of the clump of hotels and apartment blocks, is the reason why virtually everyone is here: the **beach** – two crescents of fine white sand separated by a low rocky coastal shelf and dotted with run-down fishing huts, with beautiful shallow, turquoise water that heats up to tropical temperatures by August. It can get very crowded here in high season, when tan-hungry Italians astride rows of sunbeds pack the sands. There's nothing much to see away from the beach, and most visitors spend the evening wandering along the promenade, selecting a seafront restaurant and browsing the market stalls.

The summer **bar scene** is as lively as you'll get in Formentera, though don't expect cutting-edge tunes – most of the bars use standard-issue Mediterranean holiday-mix tapes. It's not difficult to find the action, mostly centred on c/Espardell just off the promenade and in the streets behind. The hippest spots in town are probably the *Moon Bar*, on the road to Sant Ferran, with live DJ mixing and events; next door is *Tipik*, the better of Es Pujol's two nightclubs.

CA NA COSTA

Map 11, D3.

A kilometre north of Es Pujols, signposted just off the road to the Ses Salines salt pans and overlooking the waters of Estany Pudent, is the fenced-off megalithic tomb of **Ca Na Costa**. The earliest proof of human habitation in

Formentera, the site was first unearthed in 1974 and represents one of the most important archeological finds in the Pitiuses. It consists of a stone circle of upright limestone slabs, up to 2m high, surrounded by concentric circles of smaller stones and standing adjacent to a mass grave where the skeletons of eight men and two women have been found; one of the male specimens, at some 2m tall, is though to have been a sufferer of gigantism. Apart from the tomb itself, the thing that most excites archeologists about the site has been the discovery of flint tools not found anywhere else in the Pitiuses, and extraneous ceramic fragments which indicate that early Formenterans were trading with Mallorca, so suggesting a relatively sophisticated early society with established trade routes.

NORTH TO SES SALINES

Map 11, D4.

One kilometre north of Ca Na Costa along the road that skirts the east coast, a signposted turnoff on the right leads to two neighbouring sandy bays, **Platja de sa Roqueta** and **Platja des Canyers** (Map 11, D3), which both offer good swimming in calm shallow water and hold kiosks selling refreshments. These twin beaches may not be amongst Formentera's most scenic, they are popular with families based in the cluster of hotels behind the sands Continuing north, Formentera's shimmering salt pans, **Ses Salines** (Map 11, D3) swing into view on the right. Though they haven't been in commercial use since 1984, crystallization in the glistening, steely-blue pools process continues nevertheless, with foam-like clusters of salt clinging to the fringes of the low stone walls that divide the pans. For more on Pitiusan salt production, see the box on p.178.

Together with Estany Pudent and Estany des Peix, the salt pans form an important **wetland** zone, attracting gulls, terns, waders and flamingos, the latter encouraged (or perhaps confused) by the presence of two dozen pink concrete impostors. The salt pans and surrounding coastal region of northern Formentera, as well as southern Ibiza and Espalmador, are included within a protected "natural park" in which building is prohibited. Plenty of money has been invested in building wooden walkways and roping off the dunes, but until a new visitor centre opens in Ibiza in 2002, the tourist office is the only place to get more information on the ecosystems contained within the reserve.

TRUCADOR PENINSULA

Map 11, C2–D2.

From the salt pans, a slender finger of low-lying land, the idyllic **Trucador peninsula**, extends north towards the island of Espalmador and to Ibiza. Virtually the entire length of this flat, sandy promontory is blessed with exquisite **beaches** lapped by transparent shallow waters, but mercifully the developers were never let loose here, and Trucador is now included in the Ses Salines Natural Park.

At the base the peninsula, on the west side of the salt pans, several paths lead from a small parking area through dense patches of woodland to a slender, sandy beach, **Es Cavall** (Map 11, C3), sometimes called Cala Savina. You'll find two excellent *chiringuitos*, *Big Sur* and *Tiburón*, and wonderful swimming, as well as more shade than you'll find further up the peninsula. Continuing north along a sandy track you pass a huge old windmill, **Molí des Carregador**, that used to pump seawater into the salt pans – it's now been converted into a mediocre seafood restaurant.

Past the windmill, a sandy dirt track advances north through steep sand dunes, passing a signposted right turn that twists around the northern edge of the salt pans to

Platja Llevant (Map 11, D2), a glorious undeveloped beach that hugs the east coast of the Trucador peninsula. The eye-dazzling stretch of chalk white sand holds the large, popular *Tango* beach restaurant.

North of Platja Llevant, the sandy track eventually ends beside a huge car park, packed with hundreds of scooters and bicycles in high season. Just offshore are two small islets, **Pouet** and **Rodona**, that give the slim stretch of beach its name **Platja Illetes** (Map 11, C2). The sands here are very popular with day-trippers from Ibiza in high season, when you can rent windsurfing equipment from a beachside hut.

You'll have to continue on foot if you want to explore the very narrow final section of the peninsula, barely 30m wide, bordered by blinding white powdery sand that never seem to get too busy. These back-to-back beaches are Formentera's very best, with astonishingly transparent, turquoise-tinged water on both side of the slim, sandy finger of land. A kilometre from the car park, you reach the northerly tip of Formentera, **Es Pas**, or "The Crossing", partially connected to the island of Espalmador. by a 300-metre sandbar. If the sea is not too choppy, you should be able to make it without soaking your belongings.

Regular boats shuttle between La Savina and Espalmador via Illetes beach, between May and October.

Espalmador

Map 11, C1.

A 146-hectare expanse of dunes, sandstone rock and fabulous beaches, **Espalmador** is the largest Pitiusan island after Ibiza and Formentera. It's never been much of a settlement – currently just one large villa is seasonally occupied –

though a small garrison of the Spanish army was stationed here until the early nineteenth century. The one monument, aptly-named **Torre de sa Guardiola**, on the western flank of the island, is a two-storey eighteenth-century defence tower that's clearly visible from the decks of Ibiza-bound ferries.

Most people visit the island for the stunning natural harbour of **s'Alga** on Espalador's southern shore, with its dazzling, shallow water and fine arc of white sand. In summer the sheltered bay bristles with yachts, and is a favoured destination for Ibizan day-trippers. While virtually everyone visits Espalmador on a dedicated sunbathing mission, some take time out to visit the **sulphurous mud pond** a few minutes' walk north of the beach; it's very popular with the day-tripping 18–30 crowd, and if you want to avoid the rush, try to visit very early or late in the day. The entire crust of the four hectare pool has dried out considerably in recent years because of declining rainfall, but even in the height of summer there three or four small ponds of softer mud, that you can climb down to for a good writhe around in sticky gooey bliss.

ALONG THE CENTRAL STRIP: COVA D'EN XERONI

East of Sant Ferran, Formentera's main highway descends towards the **central strip**, a supine isthmus just a kilometre or so wide in places, with glorious beaches occupying its south coast and a largely rocky shoreline to the north. Just off the highway at the 6km marker, there's a signposted turnoff for **Cova d'en Xeroni** (Map 11, D5; May–October 10am–8pm; 500ptas/€3), a large limestone cave consisting of a single, 40m-wide cavern, that was accidentally discovered in the 1970s when the owner of the land started drilling for a well. His son now conducts regular tours of the chamber's spiky crop of stalactites and stalagmites, though only in German, Italian, Spanish or Catalan. The tour has a certain kitsch appeal, as the owners have lit the cavern with 1970s disco lights, but unless you're interested in gawping at vaguely Demis Roussos and Santa Claus-like formations it's not really worth the bother.

The main La Savina–La Mola highway does have cycle lanes, but the parallel Camí Vell is a much less congested, more pleasant way to get around Formentera's central strip.

Platja de Migjorn

Map 11, D5–E6.

Vying with the Trucador beaches for status as Formentera's finest strip of sand, **Platja de Migjorn** (midday beach) is a sublime 6km swath of pale sand washed by gleaming, azure water that extends along the entire south coast of the central strip. Most of it is more or less pristine, with development confined to the extremities; at the western end, **Es Ca Marí** (Map 11, D5), signposted 3km south of Sant Ferran, is a loose scattering of hotel blocks set back from the sand, while at the eastern end, Mar i Land (see p.199) comprises two large hotels. To get to the finest stretch of sand, turn south off the highway around the 8km marker, where a bumpy dirt track passes through wonderfully scenic fields of wheat and fig trees separated by Formentera's signature dry-stone walls. You'll emerge at the sea beside the sand dunes that spread back from the shore and adjacent to *Tipicat* and *Lucky*, two of the best *chiringuitos* in Formentera, both very friendly Italian-run places serving good food and drink. The legendary *Blue Bar* (see p.248), is also a mere 200m walk away through the dunes to the east.

ALONG THE CENTRAL STRIP: COVA D'EN XERONI

Castell Romà de Can Blai

Map 11, E6.

Just south of the highway, around the 10km marker, a signposted turnoff leads to the fenced-in remains of a large Roman fort, **Castell Romà de Can Blai**. The sandstone foundations are all that remain of the structure, originally built to a square format with five towers; a functional, defensive design. Other than the obvious fact that the fort guarded the island's east–west highway and the nearby port, Es Caló de Sant Agustí, very little is known about it.

Es Caló de Sant Agustí and around

Map 11, F6.

Nestled around a rocky niche in the north coast, 2km east of the Castell Romà, the tiny cove of **Es Caló de Sant Agustí** has served as nearby La Mola's fishing port since Roman times. Sitting snug below the cliffs of La Mola, this tiny little harbour of no more than 30m across has never been much grander than it is today, a rocky, semicircular bay ringed by the rails of fishing huts. It's a pretty enough scene, but there's no real reason to stop here other than for Es Caló's two excellent fish restaurants, *Rafalet* (see p.233), where you can dine overlooking the bay and *Pascual*, a little further inland. Other than these, the settlements only other building is the *Hostal Residencia Mar Blau* (see p.216) which makes a superb, tranquil base if you want to linger in the central strip.

The shallow water surrounding Es Caló offers decent **snorkelling**; head for the heavily eroded limestone rocks that ring the bay. However, the meagre scraps of sand don't really constitute a beach; you're better off walking 300m over the rocks (or taking the signposted turnoff from the highway) to the sands at **Ses Platgetes** (Map 11, F5), where a good *kiosko* sells snacks and drinks.

LA MOLA

An intoxicating blend of dense forests and traditionally farmed countryside, the knuckle-shaped tableland of **La Mola**, the island's eastern tip, is the most scenic part of Formentera. La Mola's limestone promontory looks down on the rest of the island from a high point of 202m, and there are stunning views across the ocean from the steep cliffs that have given La Mola's inhabitants protection on three sides since the area was first settled at around 2000 BC.

Getting to La Mola is half the fun. From Es Caló de Sant Agustí the highway dips then begins the long climb up, passing a signposted left turn after 500m for **Camí Romà**, or "Roman Way", a beautiful but steep pathway up to La Mola. Part of the original Roman road across Formentera, Camí Romà is popular with hikers, offering a delightfully shady and traffic-free short cut up the hill. Back on the highway, at the 13km marker, there's a turnoff on the right for the upmarket enclave of **Mar i Land** (also spelled "Maryland"), where two huge hotel complexes spill down a hillside towards the easternmost section of Platja de Migjorn beach. This section of shoreline, known as **Es Arenals** (Map 11, G6), is usually the most crowded spot of the southern coast and, though there are lifeguards on duty here between May and September, take care if you go for a swim, as the currents can be unpredictable.

The highway continues its steep incline past the Mar i Land turnoff, winding through Formentera's largest forest via a series of hairpin bends that will exhaust all but the fittest cyclists. At the 14km marker, the terrace of *El Mirador* restaurant (see p.232) affords a magical vista over the

LA MOLA

199

entire western half of the island, particularly worth taking in at sunset, when the sun sinks into the Mediterranean just beyond the hourglass-like outline of Formentera.

El Pilar de la Mola

Map 11, G6.

The region's solitary village, and something of a social centre for the farmers and hippy stragglers who make up most of the area's population, **EL PILAR DE LA MOLA** is a modest, pleasantly unspoiled settlement of around fifty houses, a handful of stores and a few simple bar-cafés (reviewed on p.248) strung along the main highway. For most of the time, it's a very subdued little place, though there's a flurry of activity on Wednesdays and Sundays in the summer season, when an **art market** (May–late Sept 5–8pm) is held in the village's small central plaza. Much of the jewellery and craftwork is made locally, and tends to be far more imaginative than most of the junk on sale in Ibizan hippy markets; there's usually some live music towards the end of the day, as well. On market days, an extra bus runs across the island, leaving at 5pm from La Savina and passing Sant Francesc, Sant Ferran, and Es Pujols a few minutes later, before arriving in La Mola around 5.30pm; the return service runs along the same route, leaving La Mola at 7pm.

Two hundred metres east of the market plaza is the village church, **Església del Pilar de la Mola**. Built between 1772 and 1784 to a typically Ibizan design, it's the usual minimalist, whitewashed Pitiusan edifice, with a single-arched side porch and a simple belfry.

The only other sights around La Mola are a two ancient **windmills** on the eastern outskirts (another pair are signposted just south of the highway), formerly used for grinding wheat. By the 1960s these windmills had fallen into disuse and became hippy communes – Bob Dylan is said to have lived inside eighteenth-century **Molí Vell** for five months. Though you can't get inside the windmill today, it has been well restored and its wonderfully warped wooden sails are still capable of turning the grindstone.

Far de la Mola

Map 11, H7.

A quick two-kilometre dash from El Pilar de la Mola, through flat farmland planted with hardy-looking vines, to the **Far de la Mola** lighthouse, set in glorious seclusion at Formentera's eastern tip. The whitewashed structure, with a 37 kilometre beam, is something of a local landmark, and was the inspiration for the "lighthouse at the end of the world" in Jules Verne's novel *Journey Around the Solar System* – Verne was obviously taken by the wild isolation of the site, and there's a stone monument to him beside the lighthouse.

Perfectly placed to soak up the oceanic scene, the excellent café-bar here, *Es Puig* (see p.248), is a popular place where islanders come to wait for the first sunrise of the New Year over the Mediterranean.

LISTINGS

Accommodation

Most people visiting Ibiza and Formentera have their **accommodation** included as part of a package holiday, but if you want to make you own arrangements you'll find a wealth of different options, from spectacular rural hotels to simple self-catering apartments and campsites. **Prices** are higher here than elsewhere in Spain, especially in July and August, when demand is so strong that 98 percent of Ibiza and Formentera's accommodation is fully booked. Nightly rates for a standard double room in a top hotel start at 30,000ptas/€180 at this time of year and, even the cheapest twin rooms will set you back around 5000ptas/€36 a night. During the rest of the year, most places also slash prices to around half the peak-season rate and, though you should have no problem finding somewhere to stay, bear in mind that there's less of a choice as many hotels shut down for the winter.

Ibiza Town is by far the most cosmopolitan place to stay, and commands the highest prices; however, rooms in all price bands tend to be small, and it's extremely difficult to find anywhere at all in July and August. Almost all of **Sant Antoni**'s accommodation is block-booked for package holidaymakers, but we've listed a selection of inexpensive options. Elsewhere, there are some spectacular

PRIVATE RENTALS

During the summer, hundreds of privately owned apartments, houses and villas in Ibiza are available to **rent**. The vast majority are unregistered with the tourist board and are sublet unofficially through advertisements in publications such as the *Diario de Ibiza* and *Ibiza Now*, or via notice boards in cafés and bars – the *Croissant Show* and *Chill* (see p.239) in Ibiza Town and *The Ship* (see p.246) in Sant Antoni are the best places to start a search. **Estate agents** such as those listed below operate on a more authorized level, with everything from Sa Penya apartments to vast rural *fincas* available on weekly, monthly and annual contracts.

If you can get a group of people together, renting a **villa** can be a very cost-effective solution to the high-season accommodation squeeze. Bear in mind, though, that, as many places are in remote areas, well away from shops, bars and nightlife, you'll almost certainly need to rent a car (or two) to get around.

Central de Reservas Formentera ⓣ 971 323 224 ⓕ 971 323 241; ⓦ *www.formenterareservations.com*

Ecoibiza ⓣ 971 302 347; ⓦ *www.ecoibiza.com*

Exclusive World ⓣ 01372/463693; ⓦ *www.exclusiveworld.co.uk*

Ibiza Online ⓣ 971 393 400; ⓦ *www.ibiza-online.com /accommodation/index.html*

Ibiza Properties ⓣ 01883/723861; ⓦ *www.ibizaproperties.net*

Loco Motives ⓣ & ⓕ 971 192 166; ⓦ *www.housenation.com/loco-motives.htm*

finca-style country hotels scattered throughout the hilly interior and around the coast, with some tempting off-season bargains available. However, if you want to stay right on the beach, you're best off arranging accommodation as part of a package, as most of the resort accommodation is pre-booked by tour operators. In **Formentera**, demand considerably outstrips supply in peak season, when you'll have to book ahead. Finally, you can also consider **camping** at one of Ibiza's officially designated sites. There are no youth hostels in the Pitiuses.

HOTELS AND APARTMENTS

Spain's fiendishly confusing system of **hotel** and **apartment** categorization is best disregarded at the top end of the scale, but if you're searching for somewhere inexpensive to stay, look out for places designated a *casa de huéspedes* (guesthouse) or a *pensión* (pension). In general, price is a more reliable indicator than category, and you usually get what you pay for. At the bottom end of the scale, very few double rooms in the cheapest *pensiones* (costing 4000–5000ptas/€24–30 a night in high season) have private bathrooms, but almost all have a washbasin; for around 7500ptas/€4.50, you'll get a bit more space plus an en-suite shower or bath, and for 10,000–15,000ptas/€60–90 you can expect extras such as a television or sometimes air conditioning. At the top end of the scale, above 20,000ptas/€120 a night, expect all mod cons, as well as pools, gyms, spas and restaurants on site.

All **tariffs** are officially fixed by the Balearic tourism authorities, and should be clearly displayed in the reception area and on the back of each room door. Normally there are three different rates: low season (Oct–April); mid-season (May–June & mid-Sept to late Sept) and high season (July to mid-Sept). You'll also find that some places impose additional price hikes in mid-August, Easter and New Year. If you're willing to do a bit of bargaining, many proprietors

ACCOMMODATION PRICES

Accommodation listed in this guide has been graded on a scale of ❶ to ❾. These categories show the cost per night of the **cheapest** double room in July and August, and include the seven per cent IVA tax; where more than one category is shown (eg "rooms ❻, suites ❾") the establishment has a selection of accommodation classes. Winter prices are often slashed to half the high-season rate.

❶ under 5000ptas/€30
❷ 5000–7500ptas/€30–45
❸ 7000–10,000ptas/€45–60
❹ 10,000–12,500ptas/€60–75
❺ 12,500–15,000ptas/€75–90
❻ 15,000–20,000ptas/€90–120
❼ 20,000–25,000ptas/€120–150
❽ 25,000–30,000ptas/€150–180
❾ over 30,000ptas/€180

will give you an extra **discount** if things are quiet. Lastly, you should always check if the seven percent **IVA** (value-added tax) is included in the price you're being quoted.

**Unless otherwise stated, all of the properties
listed in this guide are open all year round.**

IBIZA TOWN

Hostal Bimbi
Map 3, A7. c/Ramón Muntaner 55, Figueretes

☎ 971 305 396
℻ 971 305 396
May–Oct
Popular with backpackers, this comfortable family-run *hostal* is just a block from Figueretes

beach and a 10 min walk from the centre of town. The nineteen rooms are all tastefully decorated and spotlessly clean; two have private bathrooms. ❷, with bathroom ❸.

El Corsario
Map 4, F4. c/Poniente 5, Dalt Vila
ⓣ 971 301 248
ⓕ 971 391 953
ⓔ *elcorsario@ctv.es*
Former pirate's den that's now an atmospheric landmark hotel in the heart of Dalt Vila; Dalí and Picasso are said to have stayed in the 1950s. The rooms are quite small for the price, but have plenty of character; some have dramatic harbour views. Avoid the overpriced in-house restaurant. ❻.

Hostal Mar Blau
Map 3, E8. Puig des Molins
ⓣ 971 301 284
May–Oct
Excellent hilltop location, behind the city walls and overlooking Figueretes beach and the Mediterranean, yet just a 5 min walk from the centre of town. All the 28

rooms are simply but appealingly furnished (though kitchenettes lack full cooking facilities), and there's a bar, dining room and sun terrace on site. ❹.

Hostal La Marina
Map 3, K4. c/Barcelona 7, La Marina
ⓣ 971 310 172
ⓔ *hmarina@teleline.es*
Three historic portside houses offering very stylish, good-value accommodation in the heart of the action. Many rooms in the main *La Marina* building overlook the harbour and have wrought-iron beds and mirrors, a/c and satellite TV, while there are cheaper, less well-appointed rooms in the *Aduana* and *Caracoles* buildings close by. Noise can be a problem in the height of summer. ❷, *La Marina* ❺.

Ocean Drive
Map 2, H3. Marina Botafoc
ⓣ 971 661 738
ⓕ 971 312 228
ⓦ *www.oceandrive.de*
Just above the Botafoc marina and close to Talamanca beach,

IBIZA TOWN

Pacha and *El Divino*, this is a favourite amongst DJs and assorted club scenesters. Decor is pure Art Deco, and rates are surprisingly reasonable, especially in low season, but the a/c rooms are small; suites are also available. The restaurant specializes in Basque cooking. ⑦.

Hostal Parque
Map 2, H3. Plaça des Parc 4, New Town
ⓣ971 301 358
ⓕ971 399 095
Quality mid-range hotel in a superb, quiet plaza location. The tastefully decorated, spotless rooms are fairly small, but all have a/c (and heating for winter) and linen bedspreads; many come with wonderful views of the town. Single rooms are especially good value and share access to a rooftop sun terrace. ④.

Hotel Apartamentos El Puerto
Map 3, G1. c/Carles III 24, New Town
ⓣ971 313 812
ⓕ971 317 452
Motel-style block, with

rooms and well-equipped self-catering apartments decorated somewhat soullessly in salmon pink; some have large sun terraces. There's a swimming pool and a reasonable café on site. Rooms ⑥, apartments ⑦.

Apartamentos Roselló
Map 3, F9. c/Juli Cirer i Vela, Puig des Molins
ⓣ & ⓕ971 302 790
Right above the Mediterranean, with spectacular views south, and well away from traffic, hustle and bustle, despite being just a 5 min walk from Figueretes beach and the Ibiza Town bar action. The comfortable, simply decorated apartments have full cooking facilities; some boast wonderful sun terraces. ④.

Sol y Brisa
Map 3, G3. Avgda Bartomeu Vicente Ramón 15, New Town
ⓣ971 310 818
This clean, family-run backpackers' stronghold close to the heart of the town is one of the cheapest pensiones

in the area. The rooms are small and share bathrooms, but are good value nonetheless. **❷**.

La Torre del Canónigo
Map 4, D5. c/Major 8, Dalt Vila
ⓣ971 303 884
ⓕ971 307 843
ⓔ*hotelcanonigo@ctv.es*
Easter–Nov, Christmas & New Year
Magnificently located next to the cathedral, and high above the frenzy of La Marina, this atmospheric place is the first choice for visiting VIPs, but is good value considering the exceptional quality of the suite-sized rooms, which have either harbour or city views, and a/c, satellite TV, video and private jacuzzi. All the public areas are impeccably furnished, and there's a pool. **❾**.

Casa de Huéspedes Vara de Rey
Map 3, H4. Vara de Rey 7, New Town
ⓣ971 301 376
Excellent hostel with friendly management and a useful notice board. Though not the cheapest in town, the scrupulously clean rooms are simply but artistically furnished with seashell-encrusted mirrors and driftwood wardrobes; all share bathrooms. The central location means streetside rooms can be noisy in high season. **❷**.

La Ventana
Map 4, F3. Sa Carrossa 13, Dalt Vila
ⓣ971 390 857
ⓕ971 390 145
Atmospheric hotel just inside Dalt Vila's walls, offering superb service, an excellent restaurant and personal touches that set it apart from more corporate places. Immaculately furnished with antiques and Asian fabrics, rooms are on the small side, but have every modern amenity; some come with four-poster beds and most have great harbour views. Book well ahead. **❽**.

IBIZA TOWN

211

EAST COAST

Hostal Cala Boix
Map 5, E5. Platja Cala Boix
Ⓣ 971 335 224

Superbly situated above stunning Cala Boix beach, the peaceful location and simple, comfortable rooms, with fan and sea or mountain views, represent excellent value. Breakfast is included. ❶.

Can Curreu
Map 5, C5.
Ⓣ & Ⓕ 971 335 280

Small, supremely peaceful rural hotel set in a converted farmhouse high in the hills 1km west of *Las Dalias* bar, and signposted from the Santa Eulària–Sant Carles highway. The spacious doubles are all exceptionally comfortable; most have private patios or terraces and all come with jacuzzi, satellite TV, hi-fi, a/c and heating. The immaculate gardens afford sweeping views, and there's a restaurant, swimming pool, gym and solarium on site. ❽.

Ca's Català
Map 6, E2. c/del Sol,
Santa Eulària
Ⓣ 971 331 006
Ⓕ 971 339 268
Ⓦ *www.cascatala.com*
May–Oct

Stylish, well-run hotel on a quiet street in the heart of Santa Eulària, close to restaurants, shops and beaches and with a gregarious, social atmosphere courtesy of the welcoming English owners. En-suite rooms are comfortable, but not elaborately furnished, and there's a delightful shady courtyard with a small pool and sun terrace. No children. ❸.

Hostal Rey
Map 6, F2. c/Sant Josep 17,
Santa Eulària
Ⓣ 971 330 210
May–Oct

Pleasant, central and spotless place close to the Ajuntament, where the moderately priced rooms are all en suite. Filling, inexpensive breakfasts are served in the downstairs café. ❷.

NORTHWEST

Can Pla Roig
Map 1, H4. Sant Joan
ⓣ & ⓕ 971 333 012
Situated just north of Sant
Joan's church, this Ibiza-
owned guesthouse is one of
the cheapest places in the
island, with an eclectic
selection of simply but
tastefully furnished rooms
with shared or private
bathroom, and a communal
kitchen. ❶.

Can Pujolet
Map 1, F2.
ⓣ 971 805 170
ⓕ 971 805 038
ⓦ http://personal.redestb
.es/ninac
Tranquillity is the main draw
at this luxuriously converted
farmhouse in the hills above
Santa Agnès, reachable via a
signposted turnoff from the
Santa Agnès–Sant Mateu
road. Immaculately furnished
with antiques, rooms come
with a/c and satellite TV;
suites and a self-contained
bungalow are also available,
and there's a glorious

swimming pool and jacuzzi.
Breakfast is included. ❾.

Hostal Cas Mallorquí
Map 5, B1. Portinatx beach
ⓣ 971 320 505
ⓕ 971 320 594
Recently renovated beachside
hotel in quiet Es Portitxol bay
with nine modern,
comfortable rooms; all have
sea views, TV, private
bathrooms, a/c and heating.
There's a reasonable restaurant
downstairs. ❹.

Hacienda Hotel
Map 7, F3. Na Xamena
ⓣ 971 334 500
ⓕ 971 334 514
ⓦ www.hotelhacienda-ibiza.com
May–Oct
Ibiza's only five-star hotel, set
in a spectacular, remote
location in the rugged
northwest cliffs. Rooms have
every conceivable luxury, and
most have terraces with a
jacuzzi aligned for sunset-
watching, and there are two
restaurants, three swimming
pools, a gym and a sauna/spa.
The only drawback – apart
from the prices – is that you're
far from any action. ❾.

SANT ANTONI AND AROUND

Hostal Flores
Map 8, F4. c/de Rossell 26
☏ 971 341 129
May–Oct
Mid-range hotel in the centre of town with 21 fairly large, comfortable rooms, all with private bathrooms, and a popular bar-café downstairs. ❸.

Hostal Residencia Roig
Map 8, F4. c/Progress 44
☏ 971 340 483
Centrally located *hostal*, popular with young British visitors, where the 37 attractive rooms have pine furnishings and private bathrooms. ❷.

Habitaciones Serra
Map 8, F5. c/de Rossell 13
☏ 971 341 326
May–Oct
Run by friendly Ibizan family, this simple guesthouse in a quiet location close to Sant Antoni's church has ten basic, tidy and very inexpensive rooms; all share bathrooms. ❶.

Pike's
Map 1, D3.
☏ 971 342 222
🖷 971 342 312
🌐 www.ibiza-hotels.com/pikes
Signposted off the road to Santa Agnès, this wonderfully idiosyncratic rural hotel with a relaxed, informal atmosphere is the first choice for visiting celebs and A-list DJs. Grouped around the main farmhouse, rooms are individually decorated with stylish fabrics and rugs and equipped with all mod cons. There's a top-class restaurant, a huge swimming pool, a jacuzzi, gym and a floodlit tennis court; all guests are issued with VIP all-access club card. ❾.

THE SOUTH

Hostal Cala Molí
Map 10, B2.
☏ 971 806 002
🖷 971 806 150
May–Oct
Attractive and friendly hotel high in the cliffs 1km south of Cala Molí. Nicely decorated with textile wallhangings, the

seven doubles represent very good value; all overlook the Mediterranean and are ideally positioned for sunset vistas. There's a small pool and a restaurant; breakfast is included. ❹.

Can Jondal
Map 10, F4.
ⓣ & ⓕ 971 187 270
ⓔ *beashab@aol.com*
Quirky rural retreat deep in beautiful countryside above Cala Jondal, the rooms and suites in this French-owned farmhouse hotel are all ethnically bedecked with weavings and art from Mali and Morocco. Holistic pursuits from reflexology to yoga are on offer, and there's a delightful swimming pool. Breakfast is included. ❻.

Hotel Jardins de Palerm
Map 10, E2. Sant Josep
ⓣ 971 800 318
ⓕ 971 800 453
ⓦ *www.jardinsdepalerm.com*
Small luxurious hotel peacefully situated above Sant Josep village, where the stylish rooms have a/c and cable TV. There's a luscious garden, a

decent bar and restaurant, and a beautiful pool. ❼.

FORMENTERA
- -

Hostal Bellavista
Map 11, C3. Passeig de la Marina, La Savina
ⓣ & ⓕ 971 322 255
The forty modern, comfortable rooms in this large, formal hotel next to the marina all have sea views and a/c, and there's a decent harbourside seafood restaurant and terrace bar. ❺.

Pension Bon Sol
Map 11, D4. c/Major 84–90, Sant Ferran
ⓣ 971 328 882
April–Oct
These eight simple but clean and fairly spacious rooms, with shared bathrooms, are just about the cheapest accommodation in Formentera. ❶.

Casitas Ca Marí
Map 11, D5. Es Ca Marí, Platja de Migjorn
ⓣ 971 328 180
May–Oct

FORMENTERA

215

Just a stone's throw from the western end of Formentera's best beach, and set amongst pine trees, these bright, pine-trimmed bungalows all have small terraces and are fully self-catering. ❹.

Hostal Centro
Map 11, C4. Plaça de sa Constitució, Sant Francesc Xavier
☎ 971 322 063
Basic *hostal* set in an aged building across the square from the church, with simply furnished double rooms. The large restaurant, *Plate*, serves reasonable and inexpensive snacks and meals. ❶.

Hostal Residencia Illes Pitiüses
Map 11, D4. Sant Ferran
☎ 971 328 189
ⓕ 971 328 017
ⓔ *hostalillespitiuses @cempresarial.com*
Twenty-six good-value, spacious and comfortable rooms, all with TV, a/c and private bathroom. The highly efficient German management team have lived in Formentera for years and are very helpful; the only minor drawback is the location on a main road; try and book a room at the rear. ❷.

Hostal Residencia Mar Blau
Map 11, F6. Caló de Sant Agustí
☎ & ⓕ 971 327 030
April–Oct
Small, modern hotel next to the fishing harbour, and a short stroll from Ses Platgetes beach, with eight bright, attractive and good-value rooms that have panoramic sea views. The attractive apartments next door, of a similar quality and price, are used as an overflow when the hotel is fully booked. ❹.

Hostal Residencia Mayans
Map 11, D4. Es Pujols
☎ & ⓕ 971 328 724
Pleasant *hostal* in a quiet spot 100m away from the main resort area. The 23 modern, pleasantly decorated rooms, either with sea or island views, all have private

bathrooms, and the terrace café downstairs offers a popular buffet breakfast. **3**.

Pueblo Balear
Map 11, E6. Platja de Migjorn
ⓣ 610 072 368 (mobile)
May–Oct
The stunning location, overlooking the island's best

beach and very close to a couple of excellent *chiringuitos*, is the main attraction here. The nine stylish, self-contained apartments are housed in a superb whitewashed Cubist block; be sure to book well ahead for the summer months. **4**.

CAMPING

There are four **campsites** in Ibiza: two north of Santa Eulària, close to the resort of Es Canar, and two near Sant Antoni, but none at all in Formentera. All the sites open between Easter and late October only and have plenty of shade, a food store and washing facilities; some also have bungalows and cabins to rent. Prices don't vary much between sites; per day, you'll pay a flat fee of around 600ptas/€3.60 to pitch a tent, plus an additional 500ptas/€3 per person.

Though it's illegal to **fly-pitch** in the Pitiuses (the coastal dunes are particularly fragile areas), many people ignore the law and camp illegally in remote areas where they are unlikely to be caught. If you follow suit, make absolutely sure that any fires you light are well contained and are completely extinguished before you leave – thousands of acres of woods are lost to forest fires every year.

CAMPSITES

Camping Cala Bassa
Map 9, C6.
ⓣ 971 344 599

Beautiful site close to busy Cala Bassa beach, with full facilities, including a restaurant. Regular buses and boats run to and from Sant Antoni in the daytime, but you'll need your own transport or a taxi at night.

Camping Cala Nova
Map 5, D6.

☎971 331 774

Very well-equipped site 100m from Cala Nova beach and a short walk from Es Canar. Attractive, self-contained log cabins sleeping either four (6700ptas/€40.26) or six (8800ptas/€52.88), plus mobile homes that sleep four (8400ptas/€50.48) are also available.

Camping Sant Antoni
Map 9, H4.

☎617 835 845 (mobile)

Pleasant shady spot just a 5 min walk from the Egg, though it can get noisy. One-

bedroom bungalows are also available, costing 6400ptas/€38.46 with a bathroom, or 3400ptas/€20.43 without; discounts are available for stays of more than two weeks.

Camping Vacaciones Platja Es Canar
Map 9, D6.

☎971 332 117

Popular with families, this facility-rich site close to the beach in the resort of Es Canar has a pool, a laundry and a bar/restaurant. Bungalows and caravans, both sleeping four, are also available; both cost 8600ptas/€51.68.

Eating

biza boasts a huge variety of **places to eat** in all price
ranges, from hole-in-the wall takeaways through to
cafés, *tapas* bars and restaurants serving everything from
sushi and curry to pizza, as well as Ibizan and Spanish dishes. There's much less choice in **Formentera** and, though
there are some decent seafood restaurants and a crop of
good, informal *chiringuitos*, there's little in the way of global
dining. Nevertheless, there are plenty of excellent places to
eat on both islands, and the listings below represent the best
options at all ends of the price scale. Bear in mind, though,
that at many places the splendour of the setting – from a
converted chapel or farmhouse to an elegant harbourside
terrace – may not be reflected in the food, particularly at
the upper end of the scale.

Pitiusan **cuisine** is relatively unsophisticated in compari-
son to other parts of Europe, with many smart-looking
restaurants seemingly stuck in a 1970s timewarp – you'll
regularly come across period pieces like steak and
Roquefort sauce, prawn cocktail, Black Forest gateau and
tiramisu. In the **resorts**, where most establishments are
geared to churning out big portions of somewhat bland,
international food to diners they'll probably never see again,
you may be disappointed. However, if you head for village
and backstreet bars, you can tuck into the chunks of fish,

SOME COMMON CASTILIAN AND CATALAN FOOD TERMS

	English	Catalan	Castilian
Basics			
	Bread	*Pa*	*Pan*
	Butter	*Mantega*	*Mantequilla*
	Cheese	*Formatge*	*Queso*
	Eggs	*Ous*	*Huevos*
	Oil	*Oli*	*Aceite*
	Pepper	*Pebre*	*Pimienta*
	Salt	*Sal*	*Sal*
	Sugar	*Sucre*	*Azúcar*
	Vinegar	*Vinagre*	*Vinagre*
	Garlic	*All*	*Ajo*
	Rice	*Arròs*	*Arroz*
	Fruit	*Fruita*	*Fruta*
	Vegetables	*Verdures*	*Verduras*
In the restaurant	Menu	*Menú*	*Carta*
	Bottle	*Ampolla*	*Botella*
	Glass	*Got*	*Vaso*
	Fork	*Forquilla*	*Tenedor*
	Knife	*Ganivet*	*Cuchillo*
	Spoon	*Cullera*	*Cuchara*
	Table	*Taula*	*Mesa*
	The bill	*El compte*	*La cuenta*

meat or vegetables, cooked in a sauce or served with a dollop of salad, that make up the **tapas** menu. **Vegetarian** options are not plentiful in formal restaurants, but you'll find that many *tapas* are meat-free, and there's usually some fish on the menu. If you don't eat meat or fish, you may have to resort to ordering a couple of starters in restaurants, or eating *bocadillos* or *tostadas* alongside the usual pizzas, pasta and salads.

Breakfast is usually a fairly light affair, often taken in the nearest bar or café. Standards don't vary that much, and even in the roughest-looking joints you can count on an excellent *café con leche* (milky coffee), *café solo* (a thick espresso-like shot of coffee) or a freshly squeezed orange juice (*zumo de naranja*). The classic accompaniment is a *tostada*: half a baguette, toasted on one side, dribbled with olive oil and topped with either chopped tomato (*tomate*), ham (*jamón*) or cheese (*queso*). In the high-season heat, many locals are content on a *bocadillo* (sandwich) – usually with ham, cheese, egg (*huevo*) or tuna (*atún*) – for **lunch**, though if you're up for something more substantial, keep an eye out for excellent-value *menú del día* (set lunch) deals, which typically include three courses and half a bottle of wine per person.

Dinner is usually taken very late in the summer, between 9pm and 11.30pm; in Ibiza Town and some country eateries, it's common to start ordering after midnight. Most restaurants concentrate on grilled meats and fish, usually served with a small portion of seasonal vegetables and potatoes, though there's often a local speciality on offer (see box on p.222). If you just fancy a pizza or bacon and eggs, you won't have to look too far in the resorts, and there is a good crop of Asian restaurants if you yearn for something spicy – though the Chinese restaurants are all pretty dire and worth avoiding.

**Almost every restaurant will give you a basket
of bread and thick, rich *all i oli* (garlic mayonnaise)
to dip into before you order.**

EATING

IBIZAN AND FORMENTERAN CUISINE

Traditional **Pitiusan cuisine** is quite distinct from the Spanish-European food that you'll encounter in most local restaurants, but you can often find a regional speciality or two on most menus. Many local dishes are very hearty and filling (and tend to be bit heavy in the summer months), concentrating on dense meat stews, fish broths and rice dishes. Perhaps the most famous **meat** dish is *sofrit pagès* (country stew), a formidable carnivore's delight of lamb and chicken (often with rabbit, as well), potatoes, garlic, parsley and lashings of lard and oil. As in many parts of rural Spain, the pig is most important source of protein, with the annual *matanza* (killing) providing the basis for a winter larder of delicious pork-based products. Tasty *tapas* of Ibizan *butifarra* (blood sausage akin to black pudding) and *sobrassada* (spiced sausage) are available in most bars.

Fish (*peix*) and **seafood** (*marisc*) are the other main sources of protein: red mullet (*moll*), sardines (*sardines*), wrasse (*raor*), lobster (*llagosta*), squid (*calamar*), cuttlefish (*sèpia*) and octopus (*polp*) are usually grilled, barbecued or pan-fried or added to stews. Local fish dishes include *bullit de peix*, a flavoursome fish broth made with skate, and *guisat de peix*, a delicious stew seasoned with cinnamon and saffron. Dried fish has always been a Formenteran speciality, with skate and tunny commonly used to inject flavour to broths or as a salad garnish. Salt cod (*bacallà*) is another important culinary favourite, and is usually cooked with onions, peppers, garlic, nutmeg and pine nuts to form the rich *bacallà amb salsa* (cod with sauce).

Rice (*arròs*) is another Pitiusan staple, used to make many paella-like local dishes such as the fragrant *arròs sec*, with meat, fish, seafood and saffron and lemon, and *arròs amb* *peix*, with cuttlefish, parsley and peppers. You may also come across *arròs amb caragols* (rice cooked with snails), heavily seasoned with thyme, basil and fennel, and *arròs amb col* (rice with cabbage).

Among the various **vegetarian** options, look out for the traditional **salad** (*enciam*) of tomato, onion, green pepper and garlic, which can be fantastically flavoursome and is far superior to the bland but more common Spanish *ensalada*, made with iceberg lettuce and tomato topped with sweetcorn and raw onion. As many vegetarian dishes are cooked with lard or bacon, you should check if the food is *"sin carne"* (without meat) before ordering. Staple concoctions include thick, wholesome *olla fresca* (bean and potato hotpot) and *cuinat* (chard, bean and sweet-pea casserole). Spanish omelette or tortilla, locally known as *truita*, is usually meat-free. If you're in the Pitiuses in autumn, don't miss the vivid orange *cèpe* and *pebrasso* (milk) mushrooms, especially delicious when pan-fried with garlic butter and served with chopped flat-leaf parsley; you'll find them served in restaurants across both islands.

Local **snacks** include the *coca*, a kind of pastry pizza-pie topped with tomato, onion and roasted peppers, which can also be fruit-based, using apricots or cherries. Dry, flaky spiral **pastries** dusted with icing sugar, *ensaimadas* are very common across the Balearics and are often given as presents. Dry *ensaimada* pieces are also mixed with eggs, milk, cinnamon and lemon rind and baked to become a *greixonera* cake. At fiestas, you're sure to come across *bunyols* and *orelletes* (little ears) which are both humble, doughnut-like pastry fritters flavoured with anise. *Flaó* is by far the best Balearic **dessert**, a wonderful crumbly flan made with pastry, eggs, fresh cheese, plenty of sugar and topped with mint.

IBIZA TOWN

El Bistro

Map 4, F3. Sa Carrossa 15, Dalt Vila

☎ 971 393 203

Easter–Oct daily 1–4pm & 7.30pm–1am. Moderate
Classy French-Mediterranean place inside Dalt Vila's walls on restaurant-rich Sa Carrossa; food is served on the pavement terrace or intimate dining room. Good value, flavoursome cooking, majoring on grilled meats (try the ribs), some interesting,

well-priced wines and professional service.

La Brasa

Map 3, H4. c/Pere Sala 3, La Marina

☎ 971 301 202

Daily noon–4pm & 7.30pm–12.30am. Moderate–expensive
Elegant place with a delightful garden terrace for relaxed summer eating, and a wonderfully atmospheric indoor dining room with a log fire for winter. The Mediterranean meat- and fish-based menu is a fairly simple affair, with some

DINING PRICES

Each restaurant listed in this guide has been categorized according to the following grades: budget (under 2500ptas/€15), inexpensive (2500–3500ptas/€15–21), moderate (3500–5000ptas/€21–30) and expensive (above 5000ptas/€30) per person. These ratings relate to the price for a starter, main course and dessert, and include half a bottle of house wine. *Tapas* prices vary a lot less, typically costing around 250–400ptas/€1.50–3.00 per portion depending on your choices. Wine is much cheaper than in northern Europe, with house wines starting at around 750ptas/€4.50; a bottle of Rioja is almost always available for under 2000ptas/€12.

seasonal specialities. Service manages to be both relaxed and efficient.

Bar Flotante

Map 2, H3. Talamanca beach
⊤971 190 466
Daily noon–11pm. Budget
Simple café-restaurant at the southern end of Talamanca beach, with a large terrace right next to the waves. Fish and seafood are especially good: huge portions of sardines, hake and cod are grilled or fried and served with chips and salad.

Macao

Map 3, N5. Plaça de sa Riba, Sa Penya
⊤971 314 707
Daily: May–Oct 1–4pm & 7.30pm–1am; Nov–April 7.30–11.30pm.
Inexpensive–moderate
Italian restaurant with a commanding position at the extreme eastern end of the harbour, serving succulent grilled meats, well-prepared fish, and particularly good fresh pasta – try the pumpkin-stuffed ravioli. Decent wine

list with some interesting Italian options.

Pasajeros

Map 3, L4. 1st Floor, c/Vicent Soler, La Marina (no phone)
May–Sept daily 7.30pm–12.30am. Budget
Tucked away on a tiny side street off c/Barcelona, this cramped, canteen-like diner serves some of the tastiest, best-value food in town: excellent, imaginative salads, filling main courses, plenty of vegetarian options and inexpensive wines. Plenty of club workers get their weekly vitamin intake here, so a good place to find out what's going on.

El Pirata

Map 3, L4. c/Garijo 10, La Marina (no phone)
May–Sept 8pm–1am. Budget
Authentic, Italian-owned pizza house, set in the heart of the port area, where you can munch on vast thin-crust pizza on a harbourfront pavement terrace. There's also a hole-in-the-wall takeaway window to the rear, on c/d'Enmig.

IBIZA TOWN

Sake Bar
Map 3, K5. c/Santa Llúcia 5, Sa Penya
℡ 971 192 598
May–Sept daily 8pm–1am. Inexpensive–moderate
Zany, candlelit Japanese diner serving fresh sushi, sashimi, tempura and teriyaki in a delightfully intimate, plaza-like outdoor setting just above the *Dôme* bar. Hot or cold sake is the perfect accompaniment, but decent-value wines and beers (including Kirin) are also available.

Sa Torreta
Map 4, D2. Plaça de Vila, Dalt Vila
℡ 971 300 411
May–Sept daily 1–3.30pm & 7.30pm–1am. Expensive
Superbly positioned inside the walls, the cuisine at *Sa Torreta* is a little more accomplished than the other options along atmospheric Plaça de Vila. The French-style menu has good fish and seafood options, plus a tempting dessert list.

Restaurant Victoria
Map 3, I3. c/Riambau 1, La Marina
℡ 971 310 622
Daily 12.30–3.30pm & 7.30–11pm. Budget
Old-fashioned Spanish *comedor* (canteen), established in 1946, with simple furnishings, a good selection of traditional, well-prepared food and plenty of decent, inexpensive wines.

AROUND IBIZA TOWN

El Comedor
Map 1, E6. Avgda Cap Martinet, Jesús
℡ 971 314 252
Tues–Sat 1–3.30pm & 8pm–midnight. Moderate
Pseudo-rustic decor and appropriately hearty, large and competitively priced Spanish food served with vegetables – try the grilled squid. Service is direct rather than deferential.

El Clodenis
Map 1, E4. Plaça de s'Església, Sant Rafel
℡ 971 198 545
April–Oct daily 12.30–3.30pm &

8pm–1am. Expensive
A good place for a splurge, offering an appropriately immoderate wine list, a wonderful Provençal menu that's one of the island's best, and a sublime setting opposite the whitewashed village church in Sant Rafel; book ahead for a terrace table.

EAST COAST

Restaurant Cala Mastella
Map 5, E5. Cala Mastella
May–Oct 12.30–3.30pm. Moderate
Set in a tiny inlet just around the rocks on the north side of a pretty cove, this is one of Ibiza's best-kept secrets. Feast on epic *guixat de peix* (two courses: fish and potato stew, followed by shellfish and rice) and grilled squid at long wooden tables right by the water's edge. Simple dessert and wine list.

Es Caló
Map 5, E3. Cala de Sant Vicent
ⓣ 971 320 140
May–Oct daily 12.30–3.30pm &

7pm–midnight. Moderate
At the northern end of the beach, *Es Caló* is the finest restaurant in the area, with comfortable rattan seating and lots of modern art in the large terrace overlooking the bay. The menu majors in Ibizan and Spanish specialities such as *buillet de peix*, and there's a nightly barbecue and an extensive wine list.

Restaurant La Noria
Map 5, E5. Cala Boix
ⓣ 971 335 397
Daily 12.30–4pm & 8pm–midnight. Moderate
High above Cala Boix beach, with spectacular views over the ocean and well-spaced tables scattered below the clifftop pines. Of the excellent seafood specialities, paella, *calderata de langosta* (lobster broth) and *guisado de pescado* (fish stew) are particularly recommended.

Restaurant Salvadó
Map 5, F5. Pou des Lleó
ⓣ 971 187 879
Daily 1–3.30pm & 7.30–11.30pm. Inexpensive–moderate

Overlooking an undeveloped fishing bay, *Salvadó* has a first-class reputation for serving some of the freshest fish in the east; paella and *bullit de peix* are especially good, and the service is friendly.

Taberna Andaluza

Map 6, G2. c/Sant Vicent 51, Santa Eulària
Ⓣ 971 336 772
May–Oct daily 12.30–3.30pm & 7pm–midnight. Inexpensive
Simple taverna on Santa Eulària's main restaurant strip, with delicious *tapas* – try the baked squid or meatballs – plus wonderful country bread with *all i oli*, and friendly service from a dynamic señora and her family.

NORTHWEST

Amalur

Map 1, E5. Ibiza Town–Sant Miquel road
Ⓣ 971 314 554
Daily 12–4pm & 8pm–12.30am. Expensive
One of the finest restaurants in the island, serving beautifully prepared and presented Basque cooking in a tasteful terrace setting, 9km north of Ibiza Town. As fish and seafood are the basis of Basque cuisine, you're best off sticking to the exquisite red mullet, swordfish, tuna and shellfish.

Bambuddha Grove

Map 1, F5. Ibiza Town–Sant Joan road
Ⓣ 971 197 510
Ⓦ *www.bambuddha.com*
May–Oct daily 7.30pm–1am; Nov–April Thurs–Sun 7pm–midnight.
Inexpensive–moderate
Stunning pyramid-roofed dining area built from reed, rush and bamboo, and a successful Thai-based menu; duck and green chicken curries, pad Thai noodles and salads are a little light on the chilli, but are authentically seasoned with fresh herbs, and served with perfect jasmine rice. Candlelit tables overlook lush gardens, and there's a funky bar area with DJs.

Es Caliu

Map 1, F5. Ibiza Town–Sant Joan road
ⓣ971 325 075
Sept–June daily 1–4pm & 8pm–midnight; July & Aug 8pm–midnight. Moderate
A carnivorous feeding-frenzy *par excellence*, this country restaurant serves up grilled meat (and nothing else) to an almost exclusively Ibizan clientele. Decor is appropriately rustic, with whitewashed walls bedecked with the odd stag's head and stuffed fox, and there's a pleasant terrace for the summer months. Book ahead on Sundays.

Cilantro

Map 1, F4. Santa Gertrudis
ⓣ971 197 387
May–Oct daily 1–4pm & 8pm–12.30am. Moderate
Delightful garden restaurant just south of the village church serving a varied, reasonably priced pan-Asian *tapas* menu – Vietnamese spring rolls, Persian-style pilau rice, Thai-spiced fish – plus warm service and a decent wine list.

Es Pins

Map 1, G5. Ibiza Town–Sant Joan road
ⓣ971 325 034
1–4pm & 7.30–11.30pm; closed Wed. Inexpensive
Very simple, inexpensive Ibizan restaurant, with log-cabin-like decor, solid, functional wooden tables and chairs and a spartan menu of island specialities such as *sofrit pagès* and grilled meats. Three-course set-menu lunches are excellent value.

SANT ANTONI AND AROUND

- -

Can Pujol

Map 9, E5. c/des Caló, Sant Antoni bay
ⓣ971 341 407
1–3.30pm & 7.30pm–midnight; closed Wed. Moderate–expensive
Excellent seafood restaurant, located just east of Port des Torrent, with a prime location right on the beach and hypnotic views over the Mediterranean. Lobster is competitively priced (choose

your own from the tank), there's superb paella and fish is grilled to perfection.

Sa Capella
Map 9, H3. Sant Antoni–Santa Agnès road
☎ 971 340 057
April–Oct 1–4pm & 8pm–1am.
Expensive

Set in an eighteenth-century chapel just off the Sant Antoni–Santa Agnès road, and well patronized by the DJ elite and assorted island celebs, the evocative setting is more of a draw than the rather overpriced Mediterranean menu.

El Chiringuito
Map 9, F3. Cala Gracioneta
☎ 971 348 338
May–Oct daily 12.30–4pm & 8pm–12.30am. Moderate

Sublime setting right by the water's edge of this sandy cove 2km north of Sant Antoni – it's especially pretty at night, when the restaurant owners float candles in the bay's sheltered waters. The straightforward menu includes swordfish steaks, paella and delicious

barbecued meats, and there's a decent wine list.

Kasbah
Map 8, B2. Caló des Moro
☎ 971 348 364
May–Oct daily 10am–11pm.
Inexpensive–moderate

At the far north of the San An bay, with an excellent sunset view, this superb new addition to the local scene has an elevated terrace setting, an irrepressibly friendly vibe and a lethal cocktail list. The fresh, inventive menu is exceptional (try the tuna fish cakes or herby chicken salad), and there's peaceful daytime chilling too, with sunbeds on the beach below.

Es Rebost de Can Prats
Map 8, F4. c/Cervantes 4, Sant Antoni
☎ 971 346 252
Daily 12.30–3.30pm & 7.30pm–midnight; closed Feb.
Moderate

Very traditional family-owned Ibizan restaurant in a late nineteenth-century house, with pleasingly old-fashioned decor and warm service. Plenty of interesting dishes to sample, including pork rice, *calamars farcits* (stuffed squid) and *guisado de pescado*, plus daily specials like hake in green sauce.

Casa Thai
Map 8, I13. Avgda Dr Fleming 34, Sant Antoni
☏ 971 344 038
May–Oct daily 11am–11pm. Budget

Brilliant, inexpensive Thai diner with Bangkok-style, neon-lit outdoor seating adjacent to the fume-filled highway, serving an authentic selection of curries, stir-fries and noodle dishes, all served up at a furious pace. The set menu – three courses plus a drink – is great value.

SOUTH
- - - - - - - - - - - - - - - - - - - -

El Boldado
Map 10, B4. Cala d'Hort
☏ 626 494 537 (mobile)
Daily 1–4pm & 7.30–11.30pm. Moderate

Prime position opposite Es Vedrà, this is a stunning location for meal at sunset, with a reasonably priced

seafood menu – try the paella-esque *arroz marinera* or *guisado de pescado*. The restaurant is a 5 min walk west of the beach, and you can also drive there via a signposted sideroad just northwest of Cala d'Hort.

Can Berri Vell
Map 10, E1. Plaça Major, Sant Agustí
☏ 971 344 321
Sept–June Thurs–Sat 12.30–3.30pm & 8pm–midnight; open daily (same hours) July & Aug. Inexpensive–moderate

Atmospheric farmhouse setting, with a warren of rooms and a large dining terrace with views over the village church and the southern hills. The setting is the real draw, but the simple menu is a very well-priced affair, with plenty of grilled meats and a few vegetarian options.

El Destino
Map 10, E2. c/Atalaya 15, Sant Josep
☏ 971 800 341
Mon–Sat 7.30pm–midnight. Inexpensive

Wonderfully peaceful setting, just off the village plaza opposite the church, with a small outdoor terrace and a comfortable dining room. Healthy, modestly priced menu with plenty of choice for vegetarians – try the couscous. Book ahead on summer nights.

La Sal

Map 10, H5. Sant Francesc
☎ 971 395 793
April–Oct daily 8pm–1am. Moderate
Opposite this tiny hamlet's church, *La Sal* has an atmospheric dining room and a spacious terrace plus funky, chilled background tunes, and a varied Italian/European menu that includes excellent pasta, lobster and grilled meats.

Es Torrent

Map 10, H5. Es Torrent beach
☎ 971 187 402
May–Sept daily 12.30–4.30pm & 7.30–11.30pm. Moderate
Simple-looking place with a wonderful shoreside setting and fine, well-presented fish and seafood. As there's no menu, the proprietor guides you through the daily specials; there's always fresh lobster and a good choice of fresh fish.

FORMENTERA

Aigüa

Map 11, C3. La Savina
☎ 971 323 322
April–Oct daily 1–4pm & 7pm–midnight. Moderate
Very modish harbourside bar/restaurant that's a regular venue for chillout events, with stylish, comfortable seating, a large terrace overlooking the marina, and a modern menu with an ambitious lineup of Spanish and European dishes and some interesting salads, plus a decent *menú del día*.

El Mirador

Map 11, F6. La Savina–La Mola road
☎ 971 327 037
April–Oct daily 1–4pm & 7–11pm. Inexpensive–moderate
Jaw-dropping views over the island from the terrace and an inexpensive Spanish menu – with good portions of grilled meats and fish dishes – make this one of the most popular restaurants in Formentera.

Book ahead in July and August for a table with a sunset view.

Es Pla
Map 11, B5. Cala Saona road
ⓣ971 322 903
May–Sept daily 7–11.30pm.
Inexpensive–moderate
The best pizzas in Formentera, straight from a wood-fired oven, plus an extensive, inspiring selection of Italian dishes. The setting is wonderfully rustic, with a large dining room and a delightful garden terrace – perfect for summer eating.

Restaurant Rafalet
Map 11, F6. Caló de Sant Agustí
ⓣ971 327 077
May–Sept daily 1–4pm & 7–11.30pm. Moderate
Right on the water's edge, this is one of the finest seafood restaurants in the Pitiuses, with a comprehensive menu of Spanish and Balearic dishes. The paella and *bollit de peix* are tremendous and filling house specialities – for something lighter, try the perfectly grilled squid, sole or prawns.

FORMENTERA

Bars and Cafés

Founded on Spanish sociability, and fuelled by a substantial resident crew of dedicated party people, Ibiza's dynamic high-season **bar scene** is excessive, outrageous and runs around the clock, a summer-long marathon of bacchanalian excess. The action is mostly concentrated in Ibiza Town and Sant Antoni – both wildly different in character and clientele – but there are also idyllic beach bars, club-bars, locals' locals, Internet cafés and bohemian hideaways scattered throughout the island. Slumberous **Formentera** is much more restrained, with just a handful of good, no-nonsense village bars, some excellent chillout *chiringuitos* and a small but lively summer scene based in the resort of Es Pujols.

Ibiza Town offers an astounding choice of wildly cosmopolitan drinking dens. Beatnik bars sprung up here in the 1960s after the first wave of travellers descended, but the scene is much more diverse these days. In the La Marina port quarter, many bars offer fine harbourfront views, and a ringside seat for the outrageous club parades that are such a feature of Ibizan nights. Sa Penya, just to the east, has much more of a sleazy, underground feel, full of cavern-like bass bunkers catering to straight, gay and mixed crowds. Up above, Dalt Vila is a lot quieter, but there are some classy joints on Sa Carrossa, while over in the New

Town Plaça des Parc and Vara de Rey are perfect for an outdoor beer or a coffee, night and day.

Sant Antoni is very different, but almost as busy in the barmy, balmy summer season. The scene is younger, far less urbane and almost exclusively geared to suit the tastes of the legions of British clubbers who fill the streets in high season. The hooligan mentality that so characterized the resort in the 1970s and 1980s still survives to a certain degree in the notorious West End, but there's also the **Sunset Strip**, where a dozen or so stylishly designed bars have sprung up in the wake of the success of *Café del Mar*, where the hugely influential DJ and producer José Padilla created the sunset-bar concept, playing ambient soundscapes to the setting sun during his seminal residency. In addition, many bars around Sant Antoni's revitalized harbourfront now flaunt sunbeds and hammocks for commodious daytime chilling, as well as terraces for sunset-watching and dancefloors for the pre-club wind-up.

Away from the towns, each village has its own bar-café or two, where good-value *tapas* or more substantial meals are always available. Even the most basic place will have a decent bottle of Rioja or Navarra, and a barrel of *vi pagès* – Santa Gertrudis, in particular, has a number of excellent, atmospheric establishments. Reflecting the area's longstanding association with all things esoteric, **northern Ibiza**'s bars have a distinctly bohemian flavour, with Sant Carles's *Las Dalias*, or *Anita's* in Sant Joan, being the best-known examples of the dual hippy Ibizan identity. If you're after more of a clubby flavour, **southern Ibiza** is the place: *km5*, *Bora Bora* and *Jockey Club* all put on live DJ sets; most are free, at those that do charge door fees are minimal. Finally, **Formentera** holds the finest chillout bars in the Pitiuses – perfect for dreamy days by the sea and inspirational ambient music.

However, the vitality of the bar scene is compromised considerably by the sheer **expense** of it all: drinking in

Ibiza can be stratospherically costly in high season, with prices that send hundreds of fuming backpackers aboard the first ferry out of the island. Harbourside La Marina is an especially easy place to get stung – here, dozens of very ordinary, anonymous-looking bars exist by charging unknowing punters far over the odds for a drink. The terrace bars on c/Barcelona, which employ posses of pony-tailed geezer-greeters, are particularly dangerous territory, but in the summer anywhere stylish or well located in the capital or in Sant Antoni charges around 500ptas/€3 for a small beer and up to 1200ptas/€7 for a spirit and mixer. During the low season, though, even the most clatteringly chic bars slash their prices – but you'll still pay a little more than in mainland Spain. Thankfully, prices are much more reasonable in the smaller resorts and in village bars all year round.

Gay bars are reviewed on p.274.

The drinks may be expensive, but the happening bars of Ibiza Town and San An are the places to ask about club **guest passes**, where snippets of gossip and inside island information are exchanged alongside the powders and pills that fuel the Ibizan night.

There's much less of a distinction between **cafés** and bars here than in most parts of the world. Almost every café in the island serves alcohol, and of course virtually every bar will serve you a creamy *café con leche*, a *café solo* or one of the hundred or so different varieties of coffee available in Spain.

ALCOHOLIC DRINKS

Wine (*vino* in Castilian, *vi* in Catalan) is generally inexpensive, with a bottle of house plonk rarely costing more than 1000ptas/€6, and a decent Rioja or Navarra around

DRINKS

	English	Catalan	Castilian
Alcohol			
	Beer	*Cervesa*	*Cerveza*
	Wine	*Vi*	*Vino*
Hot drinks			
	Coffee	*Café*	*Café*
	Espresso	*Café sol*	*Café solo*
	White coffee	*Café amb llet*	*Café con leche*
	Tea	*Te*	*Té*
Soft drinks			
	Water	*Aigua*	*Agua*
	Mineral water	*Aigua mineral*	*Agua mineral*
	(sparkling)	*(amb gas)*	*(con gas)*
	(still)	*(sense gas)*	*(sin gas)*
	Milk	*Llet*	*Leche*
	Juice	*Suc*	*Zumo*

2000ptas/€12. Available only in village bars, the local wine, *vi pagès*, is pretty rough and potent, but very cheap, at around 100ptas/€0.60 a glass. Sparkling wine (*cava*) is excellent, costing around 2500ptas/€15; Cordorníu and Freixenet are the most reliable brands. Many restaurants and bars offer customers a *chupito* (shot) of liquor as a digestif – often a glass of *hierbas*, a very sweet local spirit flavoured with thyme and other herbs. Spanish **cerveza** (lager beer) is generally good. The two most popular brands are San Miguel and Estrella. Equally refreshing, though often deceptively strong, is **sangría**, a wine-and-fruit punch that's really delicious when made with *cava* and a shot of Cointreau. The most popular **mixed drinks** include *vodka*

ALCOHOLIC DRINKS

237

limón (vodka and Fanta lemonade), *vodka tónica* (vodka tonic) and *cuba libre* (rum and coke with lime) though you can also get any combination you'd normally drink at home.

All the usual fizzy soft drinks and juices are available, and you'll find **mineral water** (*agua mineral*) – sold in bottles of either sparkling (*con gas*) or still (*sin gas*) – to be inexpensive and infinitely preferable to tap water.

IBIZA TOWN

Bar Zuka
Map 3, M5. c/de la Verge 75, Sa Penya
April–Oct daily 9pm–4am
The most stylish place in Ibiza Town, bar none. Wonderfully artistic design unites giant antique mirrors, a stately fireplace (with logs burning in winter) and a gingham-tiled floor, and the formidable sound system is worked to great effect by guest and resident DJs including Andy Wilson, Leftfield's Paul Daley and co-owner Nancy Noise. Service is superb, and it's a good place to get island info.

Base Bar
Map 3, M4. c/Garijo 15–16, La Marina
May–Oct daily 9pm–3am
Friendly and welcoming, this attitude-free place, run by a veteran Ibizan party-hard crew, is a gathering point for a glamorous, sociable bunch of clubbers, dance-industry faces and well-seasoned rave scenesters, and serves as a local information station. A superb port location with a substantial terrace and a small, marine-green interior, plus live DJ sets from residents including Colin Peters, plus support from John and Sahara.

Sa Botiga
Map 3, F3. Avgda d'Ignaci Wallis 14, New Town
Daily noon–midnight
With rattan chairs,

monochrome photographs, sandstone walls, a beamed roof and a palm-shaded patio out back, this is the area's most elegant bar-café, perfect for delicious *tapas* or a more substantial bite from the well-priced *menú del día*. Most people come for a civilized coffee, but there's also draught Guinness and some decent wines.

Bulldog

Map 3, I1. Avgda Santa Eulària 11, New Town

Daily 11am–3am

This Ibizan franchise of the legendary Amsterdam coffee shop enjoys a prime spot facing the port area, with an air-conditioned interior and a big pavement terrace. There's always a character or two at the bar, which becomes a focus for Ibiza's north European expat community in winter. All the major football games are shown on multiple TVs, and the service is the best in town.

Can Pou Bar

Map 3, I3. c/Lluís Tur i Palau 19, La Marina

Daily noon–2am

With a prime position by the harbourside and a quirky, disparate clientele of Ibizan artists, writers, intellectuals and the odd drunk, this is one of the few bars to retain its character all year round. Music is a mere minor distraction, as island politics are discussed and black tobacco puffed. Tasty *bocadillos* are available on request.

Chill

Map 3, C5. Via Púnica 49, New Town

ⓦ *www.chillibiza.com*

Mon–Sat 10am–midnight, Sun 5pm–midnight

Ibiza's best Internet café, and a popular hangout in its own right, with funky decor and excellent food and drink: Greek salads, bagels and brownies as well as huge frothy coffees, herbal teas, fresh juices, beers, wine and spirits. Good notice board, as well.

Croissant Show

Map 3, J4. Plaça Constitució, La Marina

Daily: April–June & Oct 6am–2am; July–Sept open 24hr.

Superb site under the main gateway to Dalt Vila, and a reputation for some of the finest patisserie in town. There's a steady daytime trade, but it's often most lively around dawn, when the club community stagger to the pavement tables to perform a postmortem on the night's action. Service can be defiantly negligent, so not the best place for a speedy refuel.

Grial
Map 2, E1. Avgda 8 de d'Agost 11
June–Sept daily 8pm–4am; Oct–May Tues–Sun 9.30pm–4am
Very funky, pub-like bar with pool, darts and live DJ grooves that attracts a hip, gregarious bunch of island-based regulars. With *Pacha* almost next door and *El Divino* just around the corner, it's a popular pre-club meeting point all year round.

Madagascar
Map 3, H4. Plaça des Parc, New Town
Daily 9am–midnight
Classy bar-café on delightful Plaça des Parc that's stylish

rather than self-consciously chic. Comfortable rattan furnishings, an outdoor terrace and jazz set a tasteful tone. Wonderful juices, shakes and a limited food menu, but most people are here for the finest *café con leche* in Ibiza.

Montesol
Map 3, H3. Vara de Rey, New Town
Daily 8am–midnight
Unchallenged as the epicentre of Ibizan high society, and popular with the perma-tanned, coiffured, Gucci-toting crowd. Punctilious service from immaculately attired waiters, and prices are far from outrageous considering the location and reputation. *The* place to be seen, or a rather tired old joke, depending on your generation.

Nación Tierra
Map 3, K4. c/des Passadís 10, Sa Penya
May–Oct daily 9pm–3am
Tiny, groovy bar that draws a sociable, predominantly Spanish crowd, who come for the lovely *caipiriñas* and *mojitos*

and the eclectic Latin sounds.
The outside tables make an
ideal perch to peruse the club
parades.

Noctámbula

Map 3, K4. c/des Passadís 18,
Sa Penya

May–Oct daily 9pm–3am

Brilliant Italian-owned funky
bunker with DJs mixing
chunky house and garage.
The lower-level bar is almost
organic in design, with
sculptured aquamarine walls,
plenty of nooks and crannies
and a party fever in the air,
and there's a comfy chillout
zone upstairs.

Rock Bar

Map 3, M4. c/Garijo 14, La
Marina

May–Oct daily 9pm–3am

Ibizan institution, next to the
Base Bar, run by one of the
best-known faces of the local
scene. Boasts a stylish cream
interior, DJ decks and a
capacious terrace and, as it's
popular with club promoters,
it's a good place to start if
you're in search of a guest
pass.

Sunset Café

Map 3, G4. Plaça des Parc,
New Town

Daily 9am–2am

Stylish pre-club bar that
effortlessly functions as a
daytime café as well, ideal for
a late breakfast of fresh juice
and epic *tostadas* (try *jamón
serrano* and tomato). Arresting
decor successfully combines
animal prints, velvets and
neo-industrial fixtures to
wicked effect, while the
musical vibes evolve from
chilled daytime trip-hop and
nu-jazz into live DJ sets in the
evenings.

Teatro Pereira

Map 3, I4. c/Comte Roselló,
New Town

Daily; closed 9am–5am

Set in what was the foyer of a
nineteenth-century theatre,
this is Ibiza Town's premier
live music venue by night, and
a stylish café in daylight hours,
with good creamy coffee,
juices and *bocadillos*. The
night-time jazz and blues is
soaked up by a sociable
middle-aged crowd; entrance
is free but drinks are
expensive.

IBIZA TOWN

La Tierra
Map 3, L4. Passatge Trinitat 4, off c/Barcelona, La Marina
Daily 9pm–3am

Steeped in hippy folklore, this gorgeous little bar is one of the town's most historic drinking dens, the scene of major "happenings" back in the 1960s. There's less patchouli oil around these days, but the ambience remains vibrant, carried by an eclectic mix of hard-drinking Ibizans and an international crowd of clubbers. Musically, things are funky rather than bangin', and there are regular (but not nightly) live DJ sets.

AROUND IBIZA TOWN

Alternativa
Map 1, E6. Jesús
Daily 8pm–5am

Probably the closest thing to an Ibizan pub in the whole island, with four rooms, a pool table and a dartboard – but not a football shirt in sight. After midnight, DJs spin house, funk and even Spanish rock to an eclectic, sociable crowd of clubbers, bikers and island headcases.

Bon Lloc
Map 1, E6. Jesús
Daily 7am–midnight

Untainted village bar rammed in the early mornings with brandy-and-*café solo* downing, Ducados-puffing Ibizan workers kickstarting their day in inimitably Spanish style. Later on, it's ideal for an inexpensive *tapa* or two, with more substantial meals also available. Huge historic monochrome photographs adorn the walls and there's a good, information-rich notice board.

Croissanteria Jesús
Map 1, E6. Jesús
Daily 7am–3pm

Excellent breakfast café, with a big pavement terrace and a cheery interior. Choose between wholemeal toast, flaky butter-rich croissants, muesli, fresh juices, eggs and ham, or opt for the set breakfast menu.

Café del Mar, Sant Antoni, Ibiza

Amnesia, Ibiza

Citrus orchard, Ibiza

Es Vedrà, Ibiza

Formentera

Salt pans, La Savina, Formentera

Formentera

Barbària peninsula, Formentera

Manumission Motel
Map 1, E6. Ibiza Town–Santa
Eulària road
May–Oct 10pm–4am
Bizarre, wobbly-looking,
dirty-pink building in the
sub-industrial no-man's land
north of Ibiza Town, with a
richly deserved reputation as
the island's premier temple of
sin. In-house entertainment
includes strip and sex shows
and observation of the
resident wildlife (house
guests have included Derek
Dahlarge and Howard
Marks). Live mixes in the
basement bar from regulars
including Alfredo, plus a
substantial rooftop chillout
terrace overlooking Dalt
Vila.

EAST COAST
- - - - - - - - - - - - - - - - - - - -

Anita's
Map 5, D5. Sant Carles
Daily noon–1am
Highly atmospheric village
inn, just north of the
church, once *the* gathering
point for northern Ibiza's
hippies and travellers, and
now attracting a mixed

bunch of local characters.
Superb *tapas* – munch away
in the snug bar or the vine-
shaded patio.

Café Guaraná
Map 6, G5. Port Esportiu,
Santa Eulària
May–Oct daily 10pm–6am;
Nov–April Sat & Sun 9am–4pm
The funkiest bar in Santa
Eulària and the sole venue for
pre-club parties in the north
of the island, with US garage-
geared musical mixes from
residents and all the main
Ibiza-based DJs.

Las Dalias
Map 5, C5. Santa Eulària–Sant
Carles road
Daily 8am–2.30am
Brilliant bar with a large main
room, a good-sized garden
terrace and a schizoid
clientele of farmers and
hippies. Hosts the weekly
Namaste evening on
Wednesdays, an Indian-
themed night with live music
and vegetarian curries, plus
assorted rock and jazz events
and a quirky Saturday market
(see p.268).

EAST COAST

243

NORTHWEST

Bar Costa
Map 1, F4. Santa Gertrudis
Daily 8am–1am
Richly atmospheric village bar, with a cavernous interior, a monumental hearth, and a great outdoor terrace. Racks of *jamón serrano* garnish the ceiling, giving a delightful sweet-spicy aroma, the walls are covered in paintings (donated by artists to clear their bar bills) and the place is alive with both local and neo-Ibizan characters. There's a decent full menu – but many prefer to stick to the delicious *tostadas*.

Bar Es Canto
Map 1, F4. Santa Gertrudis
Daily 7am–4pm
Balearic bar *par excellence*, patronized by an incongruous clientele of disparate characters who come to devour the jumbo *tostadas* and *bocadillos*, and savour the wines, including Riojas and *vi pagès*. Fair prices and a raucous atmosphere, especially early in the morning, when the bar catches the sun.

Cafeteria Es Pi Ver
Map 7, G6. Sant Miquel
Daily 7am–midnight
Uncontrived village bar – the 1970s Formica and fake wood decor isn't gunning for listed status approval, but the atmosphere is warm and welcoming. Decent *tapas*, country wine and beers.

Can Cosmi
Map 1, E2. Santa Agnès
Daily noon–3pm & 6–11pm
Famous for serving Ibiza's finest tortilla, *Can Cosmi* is also a great local bar, with a convivial atmosphere, plenty of local characters, moderate prices and good service. The elevated, ramshackle terrace is ideal for summer quaffing.

Eco Centre
Map 1, H4. Sant Joan
Mon–Sat 11am–9pm
Part ethnic bazaar, part Internet café, where northern Ibiza's New Age crew gather to surf, snack and generally wallow around in pre-punk nostalgia. There's a notice board covered with info on rebirth groups, spiritual awakenings and the like.

SANT ANTONI AND AROUND

- -

Bar M

Map 8, H8. Avgda Dr Fleming
May–Oct daily 9am–3am
Just south of the Egg, this spectacular purple, silver and lime-green beach bar, owned by the *Manumission* team, is an essential pre-club venue, with a hot tub, propulsive live mixes from resident DJs, and a packed outdoor terrace. Good food too, from sandwiches to healthy breakfasts.

Café del Mar

Map 8, B5. Sunset Strip
April–Oct daily 10am–2am
The original sunset bar, widely credited with initiating the globally influential Ibiza chillout music scene. Resident DJs maintain José Padilla's dreamy sunset soundscapes and raise the tempo as the night progresses with soulful house grooves. Perhaps the greatest disappointment is the bar itself – it's set beneath an unlovely concrete apartment block, and the garish decor is on the trashier side of

bubblegum kool. Buy the CD and get the T-shirt in the store at the back.

Café Mambo

Map 8, B5. Sunset Strip
May–Oct daily 10am–2am
Funky music-geared bar where DJs mix everything from trip-hop to easy listening until sunset, when dreamy ambient soundscapes rule, before increasing the pressure and mutating the mix into seamless house grooves. Hosts innumerable pre-club parties with big-name guest DJs, and has a stylish, canopy-shaded, double-deck bar terrace with sun loungers for the UV-heads.

Itaca

Map 8, I9. Avgda Dr Fleming
May–Oct daily noon–3am
Imposing Neoclassical, temple-like design and in pole position next to s'Arenal beach promenade overlooking the Sant Antoni bay. With live mixing and guest DJ slots, the infectious party vibe ensures it's used by many promoters as a pre-club venue.

SANT ANTONI AND AROUND

Kanya

Map 8, B2. Caló des Moro

May–Oct daily 10am–4pm

Superlative orange-and-blue creation that boasts its own pool and sun terrace for blissful daytime chilling, and a restaurant for seaside dining. It's the only Sunset Strip bar with an after-midnight dance licence, and the quality house music draws a funky bunch of Ibizan and British clubbers. Drinks are expensive but there's no admission charge.

Kumharas

Map 9, F5. c/Lugo, Sant Antoni bay

April–Oct daily 11am–3am

A radically different take on the standard sunset-bar formula. The emphasis here is non-commercial and influenced by the travels of the Ibizan owner: a pan-Asian food menu, a "no party anthems" psychedelic-trance and ambient music policy, and plenty of weird and wonderful active art and sculpture. Surrounded by concrete and far from the town centre, the location lacks inspiration, however.

Savannah

Map 8, B6. Sunset Strip

May–Oct daily 10am–2am

Triple-deck bar, towards the southern end of the Sunset Strip, with an extensive terrace, sun loungers and a backroom Internet café. Placid daytime chillout tunes from resident DJ and Balearic house mixes after sundown unleashed by guests from the UK and USA.

The Ship

Map 8, F5. Plaça de s'Era d'en Manyà

April–Oct daily 10am–3am

Home from home for legions of English workers that functions as a pub-cum-information station, with notice boards full of apartment rentals and jobs, Internet access plus British ale.

THE SOUTH

Bar Can Bernat Vinye

Map 10, E2. Sant Josep

Daily 7am–midnight

Scruffy, smoky locals' local in Sant Josep village, where

conversation usually centres on the rainfall, the harvest and who's making the most money from lucrative house rentals. Tables spill into the delightful plaza outside in summer, and inexpensive *tapas* and gutsy *vi pagès* are on offer.

Jockey Club
Map 10, F5. Cala Jondal
April–Sept daily 11am–6am
Chilled beach café by day, and club-bar by night, popular with island scenesters and Ibiza Town's groove-smitten crew who dance under the stars to fearsomely funky, tribal club mixes; local DJs generate a real fiesta vibe in the high-season months, but the dancefloor action doesn't really get going until after 1am. Free (or very minimal) entrance charge for the night events.

km5
Map 10, G4. Ibiza Town–Sant Josep road
Oct–May Wed, Fri & Sat 11pm–4am; June–September daily 10pm–4am
Former brothel that's now one of the best bars in the island,

with a decidedly clubby feel – live DJs, a small dancefloor and a funky crowd – all in the heart of the countryside 5km from Ibiza Town. There's a huge, verdant garden, with lantern-lit, well-spaced tables, and great food: free-range chicken, steaks and a good vegetarian selection. A brilliant boogie option if funds are running low.

Particular
Map 10, F5. Cala Jondal
May–Oct daily 11am–10pm
Very cool beachside bar spread over a large, shady plot with fine (if a little pricey) food – fresh fish, salads and barbecued meat – plus sumptuous smoothies and blended juices. Sunbeds and fluid, largely beatless chillout sounds from live DJs make this a wonderful place to kick back.

Sa Trincha
Map 10, I7. Salines beach
Daily: April–Oct 11am–9pm; Nov–March 11am–6pm
The definitive Ibizan *chiringuito*, set at the southern end of the hippest beach on

THE SOUTH

the island. Mellow, textural sounds from resident DJs and a neo-Noah's Ark of beautiful Balearic wildlife – dancers, freaks, clubberati, models and slacking Europeople – to observe. Service can be appallingly slow – not that the stoned regulars seem to care.

FORMENTERA

Blue Bar
Map 11, E6. Platja Migjorn
℡ 971 187 011
April–Oct daily 11am–3am
Blissful location in the centre of Formentera's best beach and inspirational, beat-free ambient soundscapes make this the best chillout bar in the Pitiuses. The wooden-decked terrace with lounge-around cushions is an exceptional place to stargaze and sunbathe, and there's table football and pinball machines inside. There's also a simple evening menu (book a table in advance), but be prepared to wait for your food.

Café Martinal
Map 11, C4. c/Archiduc Salvador 18, Sant Francesc
Daily 8am–9pm
In the heart of the capital, this is by far the most popular breakfast café in Formentera, with a cornucopia of healthy set menus that include fresh juices, yoghurt and muesli.

Fonda Pepe
Map 11, D4. Sant Ferran
Daily: June–Sept noon–1am;
Oct–May noon–midnight
Legendary drinking den, established in 1953, that's steeped in hippy history and was once *the* happening bar in Formentera. Nostalgia reigns supreme in the bar, with photos and doodles from the 1960s on the walls. Bustling in summer, when the slender terrace is packed with (mainly German) visitors.

Moon Bar
Map 11, D4. Es Pujols–Sant Ferran road
May–Oct noon–3am
Stylish bar on the outskirts of Es Pujols, with a huge terrace, modish lighting, and soul,

funk and melodic house sounds from island-based and visiting DJs.

Es Puig

Map 11, H6. Punta de la Mola
May–Oct 9am–9pm; Nov–April 9am–6pm

The bar at the end of the world, right next to the Far de la Mola lighthouse, and famous for its legendary *platos de jamón y queso* – huge portions of local and Menorcan cheese, and piles of cured ham and salami. It's also *the* place to wait for the first sunrise of the New Year, when the bar stays open all night.

Tipicat

Map 11, E6. Platja Migjorn
May–Oct noon–9pm

Groovy *chiringuito* in the dunes with panoramic views over Platja Migjorn, dope downbeat tunes, plus yummy Italian food. Try the very special *caipiriñas*.

FORMENTERA

Clubs

It is a short hop from Majorca to Ibiza, but one that should be made with more than some trepidation. I fear for my life every time I board a plane bound for that terrible place, wondering whether my will and constitution will be strong enough to hold out in the face of such provocation.

Robert Elms, *Spain*

Though the hype is monumental, few would contest Ibiza's status as the **clubbing** capital of the world, consistently delivering pure, hedonistic carnage. Home to seven of the planet's most celebrated clubs, plus scores of minor venues, the Ibizan scene is potent enough to break new tunes and influence dancefloors and airwaves from Tokyo to Argentina. There's simply nowhere else that has the same dependence upon, and commitment to, club culture and dance music – all the greatest house DJs have played here, and all the big players return year after year to move a uniquely enthusiastic crowd. At the peak of the summer season, the spirit and atmosphere in the clubs can approach almost devotional intensity, and the leading DJs attain almost iconic status.

The mayhem starts in mid-June with the spectacular opening parties that mark the start of the clubbing season, and continues incessantly, 24 hours a day, until the last of the closing parties in early October. During these months, there's a club or a club-bar open at any time of the day or night – many seasoned campaigners prefer a good night's sleep before an all-day session, caning it on the terrace at *Space* or by the beach at *Bora Bora*, rather than the more conventional night on the tiles. By contrast, though, there's little to get excited about in generally mellow **Formentera**, though you'll find a couple of small venues in the resort of Es Pujols.

As the engine room of the island economy, clubbing in Ibiza is an overtly commercial business. Giant promotional billboards for *Cream* and *Gatecrasher* on the airport road hail your arrival in Europe's club central, armies of *ticketeros* comb the streets and beaches dispensing flyers, and poster teams plaster every spare lamppost and shop window with lineups for upcoming club nights. The most flamboyant displays of the island's endemic club culture, however, are the **club parades**: exuberant processions of banner-wielding stilt-walkers, silver spacemen, red devils and horny dwarfs employed by promoters to advertise their club nights and drum up interest by patrolling the bars of Ibiza Town's port area and Sant Antoni's Sunset Strip.

Partly because of the money at stake, few club promoters are willing to take risks when booking DJs, and in terms of **music** the mix can get a little monotonous. Sunny party anthems and slamming trance cuts form the main dishes, with little sonic experimentation in evidence – drum 'n' bass, hip-hop and R&B remain very peripheral on Ibizan dancefloors. Since the late 1990s, **UK garage** has emerged as an alternative to the dominant four-four house beat, though in Ibiza the two-step garage style is still championed largely by a small number of British rather than

CLUBS

CLUB SURVIVAL

Clubbing in Ibiza is an inordinately **expensive** affair; entrance charges average at 5000ptas/€30, and can cost anything up to 8000ptas/€48 at *Pacha* and *Privilege*; average entry fees to the smaller venues listed on p.264 is lower, however, at around 2000ptas/€12. If you are planning to go to the large clubs, it pays to seek out **advance tickets**, available in the hip bars of Sant Antoni and Ibiza Town, which typically save you 1000ptas/€6 (and include a free drink), or try to blag a guest pass if you can from bar staff. **Drinking** is equally exorbitant – soft drinks cost around 1000ptas/€6, and a spirit with a mixer will set you back anything up to 2500ptas/€15 – not surprisingly, most people get livened up somewhere else before they get to a club. Unless you can stomach drinking tap water (which won't poison you, but tastes foul), you'll also have to pay about 1000ptas/€6 for bottled water; in the summer heat, with hundreds of thousands of clubbers popping pills and dancing all night (and all day), the dangers of dehydration are all too obvious; if you are planning to take ecstasy, ensure you're carrying enough cash to maintain a steady fluid intake.

Bear in mind that the big seven clubs will pay your taxi fare from anywhere in the island, provided that four people purchase an entrance ticket, and that you can return home inexpensively via the Discobus service (see p.38).

island-based DJs. The **chillout** scene, concentrated in bars rather than clubs, is Ibiza's most creative musical genre, fusing nu-jazz, ambient, dub, Latin and Afro beats.

We've organized the club listings by venue rather than by night, as the action can change from month to month. Big promoters such as Ministry of Sound and Manumission usually set up camp at a specific venue for the season, but bust-ups happen and nights fail, so before you set out it's best checking the **club listings** and DJ lineups set out in special Ibiza editions of *Ministry*, *The Islander*, *Mixmag* or the best of the lot, *DJ Magazine* (see Basics, p.26), which are regularly updated. Alternatively, check the clubs' own **Web sites** or visit Ⓦ *www.worldpop.com*, which has daily updates on the summer club scene.

THE BIG SEVEN

Amnesia

Map 1, E5. Ibiza Town–Sant Antoni road

Ⓦ *www.amnesiaibiza.com*
May–Sept; 5000 capacity
Musically, *Amnesia* is the most influential club in Ibiza, responsible for igniting the whole British acid-house explosion and the resultant global clubbing revolution. In the mid-1980s, whilst *Pacha* and the *Ku* were catering to playboys and medallion men, and the Sant Antoni clubs were lost in a swirling sea of Stock, Aitken and Waterman-produced Europap, seminal events were happening at *Amnesia*, where resident DJ Alfredo was busy creating the infamous Balearic Beat sound (see p.306).

A lowly farmhouse thirty years ago, *Amnesia* became a hangout for hippies in the 1970s, home to LSD-fuelled parties with a soundtrack that ranged from prog-rock to reggae and funk. After being completely eclipsed by the *Ku* over the road in the early 1980s, *Amnesia* reinvented itself as Ibiza's first after-hours club, opening at 5am – and successfully enticing the *Ku* crowd with an eclectic mix based on British electronic pop sounds.

In 1985, Alfredo unleashed a haul of dark hi-energy, minimal proto-house tunes and electro Italian club hits he'd collected over the winter, and *Amnesia* quickly became the most fashionable club on the island. Its reputation continued to grow over the next few years, but by 1990 new noise pollution laws led

THE BIG SEVEN

DRUGS

To the majority of the British media, Ibiza and drugs go together like fish'n'chips or rock'n'roll. First dubbed "ecstasy island" by *The Sun* newspaper in 1989, Ibiza's reputation as the Med's premier stimulant-soaked holiday horror-show remains unchallenged. To some extent, the accolade is justified – perhaps half the Ibizan economy is dependent upon "techno tourism", and ecstasy is so integral to the clubbing scene that removing it from the equation would remove the reason why many people want to visit Ibiza in the first place.

Nonetheless, ecstasy, cocaine, heroin, speed and acid are all **illegal**, and you could be looking at a jail term if caught with any of these substances. For more on drugs and drug laws in Ibiza, see Basics, p.35. If you are arrested for possession of drugs, inform the British Consulate (☎971 301 818), who have a list of English-speaking lawyers. All other nationalities should contact the relevant embassy in Madrid: US ☎91 587 2200; Canada ☎91 431 4300; Ireland ☎91 576 3500; Australia ☎91 579 0428; New Zealand ☎91 523 0226.

to open-air clubbing being banned. *Amnesia*'s owners were forced to construct a roof over the club. The demise of alfresco partying, combined with a brutal, techno-based musical direction unsuited to the holiday atmosphere of the island, meant that *Amnesia* lost its way for a while in the early 1990s. Things improved by the middle of the decade, when the first wave of British clubs, especially Liverpool's *Cream*, together with the club's own *espuma* foam parties, injected fresh passion and new punters. By Millennium Eve, *Amnesia* was, once again, *the* Ibizan club to be in, throwing a free party that was the talk of the island.

Amnesia remains a great club today, but the vast, dark warehouse-like main room would benefit from an overhaul. The huge dancefloor is ideally suited to trance and hard, intense house – an environment that *Cream* DJs Seb Fontaine and ex-resident Paul Oakenfold have exploited perfectly. On the right night, *Amnesia* can feel more like a live gig than a nightclub, with a cast of thousands facing the DJ stage and punching the air to trance anthems. You'll find bars scattered around the main floor, and an extensive VIP balcony above, as well as several podiums. In contrast to the main room, the terrace, on the other side of the club, is crowned by an elegant atrium, and its bar areas are beautified by lush greenery. There's a dancefloor here, too, but the musical policy deliberately concentrates upon less intense US house and Balearic rhythms.

Eden

Map 8, I6. c/Salvador Espiriu, Sant Antoni

Ⓦ www.edenibiza.com

May–Oct; 4000 capacity

Though it's now Ibiza's most modern venue, *Eden* (formerly the *Star Club*, then *Kaoos*) was considered a bit of a joke for years – a disco throwback where all the leading DJs refused to play. However, serious investment by *Mambo*'s Javier and his crew in 1999 and 2000 resulted in state-of-the-art sound and visual systems, a new industrial-decor refit and multiple new rooms, stages, bars and podiums. BBC Radio One's Dave Pearce and Judge Jules were positioned as Saturday and Sunday residents, and boosted by massive support for *Gatecrasher* and the *Retro* house night, *Eden* had assumed local supremacy by the end of the 2000 season.

Approaching Sant Antoni from the Ibiza Town highway, you can't miss *Eden*'s unmistakable electric-blue domes and minarets. If the exterior looks to the east for

THE BIG SEVEN

inspiration, it's pure, Occidental minimalist design inside, however. With its doors flanked by twin steel serpents, the wild lobby sets the tone, leading to the huge, elongated main room with its great domed roof. On the right is a chillout zone, topped by another elegant cupola, while left of the entrance the spacious back room is home to alternative sounds. The entire indoor arena is ringed by a curvy, Gaudí-esque steel balcony, which forms the substantial upper-level gallery, housing the VIP zone, VJ booths and more bars. The final party piece is the adjacent *Garden of Eden*, a stylish open-air bar-café that doubles as an after-hours morning venue.

El Divino

Map 2, F2. New Harbour
Ⓦ *www.ibiza-online
.com/ElDivino/index2.html*
Easter–Oct and some winter
weekends; 1000 capacity
Jutting into the Ibiza Town harbour, with water on three sides, *El Divino* boasts the most enviable location in

Ibiza, and this mustard-coloured, temple-like place vies with *Pacha* as the ultimate destination for the seriously solvent. The stained-glass lobby, embellished with the half-sun/half-moon club logo, leads almost directly onto the dancefloor, while a series of arched windows reveals a panoramic vision of the floodlit old town beyond the port waters. Beyond the windows and to the left is the VIP terrace, complete with sumptuous, well-spaced sofas. The opulent restaurant, a formal but not outrageously expensive affair, occupies the right side of the terrace.

The club cannot claim to be especially musically influential, but it has always attracted a cosmopolitan crowd, with Euro-celebs, Gulf sheiks and the odd Russian mobster all mingling with the mainly Spanish and Italian masses. Built in 1993, *El Divino* was expanded and revamped in 1999, when the sound system was upgraded and the entrance area improved to allow better circulation. Naples-based club

Angles of Love and Birmingham's *Miss Moneypenny's* have been the most successful nights in the last few years, always packing the club with a glam, label-conscious crowd. Though lively and sociable, *El Divino*'s patrons tend to be a little more restrained than the pilled-up, histrionic Ibiza-virgins elsewhere.

Pacha

Map 2, F1. Avgda 8 de Agost, Ibiza Town

ⓦ *www.pacha.com*

Open all year; 3000 capacity

When Ibizans are asked to describe the island's favourite club, the *grande dame* of the scene, the answer is usually simply, "*Pacha* is *Pacha*". Ibiza's most urbane, classy club, all the ingredients seems to be right here: faultless decor, a decidedly international clientele, professional staff and the island's best dancers. *Pacha*'s origins lie in the elegant Catalunyan beach resort of Sitgès, where founder Ricardo Urgell first purchased a decrepit house in 1966,

turning it into a nightclub because he wanted to "earn enough money to live like a pacha". Entrance was 150ptas, the cloakroom was 10ptas, the music was the Stones and the Doors, and the go-go dancers were from Martinique. Today, there are more than twenty *Pachas* around the world, spread from Brazil to Japan.

Pacha Ibiza opened in 1973 in a farmhouse on the edge of the capital, and to this day the whitewashed exterior of the old *finca*, framed by floodlit palm trees, creates a real sense of occasion. To the left of the tastefully tiled entrance area is the restaurant and the salsa room, Pachacha, while ahead is the beautiful main room, with its four bars, sunken dancefloor, stages, podiums and roped-off VIP enclosure. To the left of the main room, a flight of stairs leads to El Cielo (also known as the Funky Room for its musical policy) while to the right is dark techno/hard-house zone, Zenith. Finally, reachable via Zenith or the Funky Room, the elegant, expansive terrace, spread around several layers, is

THE BIG SEVEN

a wonderfully sociable, open-air affair, with cushioned seating, three bars and vistas of the city skyline.

The one Ibizan club that's open all year round, *Pacha* has such cachet that it's not dependent on outside promoters to bring in the crowds, and the owners have free pick over who they want to work with. Over the years, the most successful partners – *Made in Italy*, *Ministry of Sound* and *Renaissance* – have all concentrated on uplifting, vocal-rich house rather than slamming techno or trance, music that suits the sophisticated regular crowd, who are by far the most diverse in the island, with fifty-year-olds salsa-stepping in Pachacha, a multiracial crowd soaking up the funk in El Cielo and a disparate mix of still-swinging playboys and young Ibizans filling the main room.

Es Paradis

Map 8, I7. c/Salvador Espiriu, Sant Antoni

ⓦ *www.esparadisibiza.com*

May–Oct; 3000 capacity

Aesthetically, *Es Paradis* is one of the most stunning clubs in the Mediterranean. Perfectly proportioned, its square foundation is topped by a beautiful glass pyramid, the venue's retractable roof, which dominates the skyline of Sant Antoni bay. Named in full as *Es Paradis Terranial* (Paradise on Earth), it's the second oldest of the big seven Ibizan clubs, having celebrated its 25th anniversary in 2000 with the opening of a second interior room and a new lower-level bar. More than anything, the structure is a testament to the vision and endeavour of owner and founder Pepe Aguirre, a perfectionist who oversees every little detail, including employing a full-time gardener to maintain the luscious greenery.

Like *Pacha*, *Amnesia* and *Privilege*, the origins of *Es Paradis* are humble. It started out as a simple outdoor venue, and grew organically until 1990, when its 120-tonne pyramidal roof proved to be the most innovative and successful solution to the island's new noise regulations. This set the club up for a consistently successful decade, with water parties (when the whole dancefloor is flooded) and *Clockwork Orange* nights ensuring that the place was consistently packed; despite Sant Antoni's less-than-glamorous, beer-boy profile, *Es Paradis* retained credibility.

The layout is straightforward, with an imposing lobby framed by Doric-style columns leading to a blindingly white arena filled with neo-Greco columns, marble flooring and verdant foliage, while ten bars, one in front of a giant tropical fish tank, podium dancers and awesome sound and light systems compete to impress. Encircling the entire building, the upper balcony gives a brilliant perspective of the dancefloor, and holds a new room with alternative sounds that's converted into an art gallery outside the peak season months.

With the transformed *Eden* now established over the road, the first years of the Millennium are going to be a testing time for *Es Paradis*. The scene is changing quickly, and Sant Antoni-based clubbers are now much more eager to explore nights at other venues away from the resort; there's also the issue of the flash Neoclassical environs, decor which sits slightly awkwardly with the stripped, minimalist trance and hard-house crew. Expect further links with the UK garage massive, as the sexy, label-conscious two-step scene seems perfectly matched with the *Es Paradis* environment.

Privilege

Map 1, E5. Ibiza–Sant Antoni road
Ⓦ*www. privilege-ibiza.com*
Open May–Sept; 10,000 capacity

Listed in *The Guinness Book of Records* as the biggest club in the world, *Privilege* is also home to Ibiza's biggest night – *Manumission*. For ten years (when it was called *Ku*) it was also the most beautiful club in the island, but the 1990 noise pollution laws led to an ugly roof being built over the

THE BIG SEVEN

MANUMISSION

Probably the predominant club night in Ibiza, and certainly the most successful of all the British promoters, the biggest Balearic story of the last ten years has been the **Manumission** phenomenon (Ⓦ www.manumission.com). Not content with packing the 10,000-capacity *Privilege* every Monday, *Manumission* has spawned a decadent empire that includes Ibiza Town's opprobrious *Manumission Motel*, Sant Antoni's *Bar M*, the *Vida Loca* boutique, a *Manumission* movie and even clubbers' holidays.

Manumission is, in effect, two brothers, Andy and Mike McKay, and their partners Dawn and Claire. In addition, a revolving ensemble of colluding artists – dildo-wielding strippers, performing dwarfs, lesbian nurses and fluffy pink bunnies – all collude in a Malcolm McLaren-style publicity drive to shock and revolt the British and Ibizan media, and get *Manumission* talked about. The greatest PR stunt of all was undoubtedly the **live sex shows**, starring Mike and Claire, which crowned the club night until the end of the 1998 season. The British tabloids were sent into foaming fury of indignation and revulsion, thus ensuring that *Manumission* was the one night on the island that the clubber couldn't miss.

Having started out as a gay event in the dingy *Equinox* club in Manchester in January 1994, *Manumission* (Latin for "freedom from slavery") helped put the fun back into

whole, vast alfresco affair, transforming the pleasure zone into a (somewhat flawed) pleasure dome.

Ku originated in mainland Spain's most fashionable resort – San Sebastián in the Basque country – where three local businessmen and a Brazilian built a *discoteca* (also called *Ku*) that became the natural home for the nation's clubbing crème. The founders visited Ibiza in 1978, bought a clubbing in a city wracked by gangster feuds and police inaction, and after three months they were locking out 500 people. Then the gangsters targeted *Manumission*, dousing Andy with petrol and threatening to set him alight. The brothers blew their takings on a holiday in Ibiza, liked what they found, and stayed. *Manumission*'s first foray here was to host a night in *Ku*'s *Coco Loco* bar at the start of the 1994 season. Within a few weeks, they had taken over the main body of the club and were pulling in 6000 punters a night. The formula has remained the same, with stunning parades, floorshows, extravagant costumes, acrobats and stilt-walkers all supported by a mean flyering and promotional team.

These days, a night out at *Manumission* is still one of Ibiza's great experiences. The atmosphere tends to be more voyeuristic and theatrical than participatory, with the night built around the show rather than being driven by the DJ, a ploy *Manumission* have long used to avoid paying for the industry's most expensive turntable technicians. Given that the hip international crowd have largely ceased to attend, and that efforts to work with London's seminal gay club *Trade* have not been a raging success, it will be interesting to see how the "family" promote *Manumission* in the next few years. With increased competition from the likes of *Eden*, and other strong nights booked in a revitalized *Privilege* itself, the creative team will have to work hard to ensure *Manumission*'s continuing pre-eminence.

bar/restaurant called *Club Rafael*, and for the next ten years set about creating the most extravagant, luxurious club in the world – *Ku* – named after a Polynesian goddess of love.

The sheer scale and splendour of *Ku* was breathtaking. There were seven bars, numerous dancefloors, phenomenal sound and light systems (the laser shows could be seen in

MANUMISSION

Valencia), a swimming pool and a top-class restaurant, as well as huge terraces planted with pine and palm trees. Cocaine spoons and champagne cocktails were *de rigueur*, and there was no shortage of celebrities: Freddie Mercury sang *Barcelona* here with Montserrat Caballé; James Brown performed; and Grace Jones danced naked in the rain during a thunderstorm.

After construction of the roof in 1990, though, *Ku* suffered badly from underinvestment, and has been usurped by the glamour of *Pacha* and the innovation over the road at *Amnesia*. The name change to *Privilege* in 1995 did little to change its fortunes, and it wasn't until the arrival of *Manumission* in 1994 that *Privilege*'s comeback began. The 2000 season was the club's most successful for a decade, with *Manumission* enjoying another solid summer, and *Renaissance* shifting over from *Pacha* to fill the venue with an outstanding combination of live acts and a world-class DJ lineup.

On the right night, *Privilege* is an unforgettable experience. As you enter, the sheer scale of the venue becomes apparent, with a vast main dancefloor straight ahead and the DJ plinth above the swimming pool. Behind is a stage for live acts, while two large bar areas – the revamped, pink *Coco Loco* and a double-deck back room – are to the right. Fourteen further bars and a café are scattered around, two VIP zones are on the upper levels, and there's even a DJ in the toilets. The vast, metal-framed open-air dome above the café serves as the club's chillout zone.

Space

Map 10, I4. Platja d'en Bossa
Ⓦ *www.space-ibiza.com*
May–Oct; 3000 capacity
A vast cream-coloured minimalist bunker just off Platja d'en Bossa beach, *Space* was built in 1996 and is essentially a day venue, kicking off after sunrise when regular clubs are closing – recently, though, the owners have also been trying to

establish nocturnal events. *Space* is also used as a post-party venue by many of the biggest promoters, including *Manumission* and *Gatecrasher*, for a true – and often very messy – test of stamina. This carry-on-clubbing scene tends to attract a very hardcore crowd, and perhaps the most cosmopolitan mix in Ibiza.

Since the start of the 1990s, Sunday at *Space* has been one of *the* most fashionable places to be seen, an Ibizan institution that draws an eclectic crowd of Balearic-based clubberati, international party freaks and assorted island headcases. In 1999 the party fever intensified as London's self-styled superclub *Home* took over the promotion of the Sunday session. The formidable roster of global DJs helped to create the island's most fearsome session, beginning at 8am and only closing at dawn on Monday after 22 hours of pure mayhem. Inevitably, the increased popularity of the Sunday session altered the nature of the crowd to a degree, and Saturdays have now started to assume the Sunday status, with many of the old crowd returning to dance to the island-based DJ lineup.

Space is divided into two parts: a dark, cavernous, bunker-like interior, and a wonderful open-air terrace with peach- and purple-painted sandstone walls. Ibiza legend has it that the whole terrace scene was kicked off by DJ Alex P, who took his decks outside to play in the sunshine in the early 1990s. Daytime terrace sessions often get going slowly, as punters drift in from other clubs, refuelling on cappuccinos and croissants and exchanging gossip around the sweeping mahogany bar. Steadily, the stepped sandstone tiers around the terrace fill up, the DJ mix intensifies and the dancefloor gets moving. On Sundays the floor can be rammed by

Daytime *Space* sessions aren't much fun without sunglasses.

midday, with the Balearic fever continuing until the early evening, when many head for the *Bora Bora* beach bar over the road. The terrace closes around midnight and the action shifts to the dark, more moody interior, an ideal setting for pounding beats, where minimal lighting helps to reduce the somewhat sobering impact of the no-design decor: a brackish melange of 1980s disco tack and holiday-camp-style furnishings. Welcome additions in recent years are a new toilet block – to reduce the notorious queues – and a new café at the back.

OTHER CLUBS

Besides the big seven clubs listed above, a number of other minor venues compete for dancing feet. At northern end of Platja d'en Bossa, bunker-on-the-beach **Konga** (Map 1, D6) is the best on the east side of the island – a 500-capacity day club that many big promoters have used for after-hours affairs. On the same beach, the tacky **Kiss** (Map 1, D6) club is prime wet-T-shirt territory, popular with German holidaymakers and definitely best avoided. Further south on the Salines road, bar-cum-club **DC 10** (Map 10, I5), with a sunny terrace and a dark clubby interior, has hosted some brilliant, truly Balearic events, mainly with local DJs, and was one of the success stories of the 2000 season, attracting a very hardcore party crowd for its Monday day sessions. Its future is less assured, as the venue has always been plagued by licensing problems.

Over on the west side, the **Summun** club (Map 9, G5), 3km west of the Egg in Sant Antoni bay, is the best of the town's bad bunch, a well-established venue with popular UK garage nights. The dire **Extasis** (Map 8, H6) club, right by the Egg, is well worth sidestepping. In the heart of Sant Antoni's West End (Map 8, F5–F6), centred on c/Santa Agnès, you'll find an infamous strip of **disco–bars**. All the venues (*Koppas*, *Play 2*, *Kremlin*, *Nightlife*, *Gorm's Garage*) and probably the most popular venue, the *Simple Art Club* open between 11pm and 6am and draw a very youthful, raucous British crowd. There's very little dance-floor action in tranquil **Formentera**, but there are two small clubs in Es Pujols (Map 11, D4) – *Tipik* and *Magoo*. Both are only open in summer and stick to fairly main-stream dance sounds.

Shopping

biza has an eclectic **shopping** scene, reflecting the style-conscious nature of the island. This is a place where locals and visitors really get dressed up – though there's much less preening and consumer choice in Formentera. **Ibiza Town**'s La Marina quarter is *the* place to head for all things hip, with dozens of clothing stores and boutiques selling clubbing gear and funky accessories. This area is the heartland of Ibiza's **Ad Lib** fashion enclave, a globally influential bohemian style, originally characterized by long white flowing fabrics, that evolved in the island during the 1960s. The hippy-chic look continues to define today's Ad Lib style, and the tag is still used to promote the *Moda Ad Lib* fashion shows, some of the best-attended in Spain.

Ibiza and Formentera's foremost indigenous **arts and crafts** traditions – basketry, tapestry and ceramics – are all struggling to survive in the age of mass tourism. Sant Rafel (see p.92) is a good place to head for ceramics, while tiny basketry stores full of broad-rimmed Ibizan hats and *espardeny*es (grass sandals) still exist in La Marina amongst the chic boutiques. There are several **galleries** scattered around the island – Ibiza's luminous light and stunning countryside have attracted artists since the early 1900s, and there are hundreds of resident painters and sculptors. In central Ibiza, Es Molí in Santa Gertrudis, and the *Bambuddha Grove* restaurant (see p.228), always have some interesting exhibitions by local artists, while in Santa Eulària try Galeria Cascais on the harbourfront below the *Hotel Tres Torres*. In Ibiza Town, Van der Voort in Dalt Vila's Plaça de Vila is the island's most exclusive, and Galería Altamira at Avgda Espanya 29 is also worth a browse. For **antiques**, try L'Occasione at c/de la Verge 47 in Sa Penya, Ibiza Town, or the excellent **auction** house, Casi Todo, in Santa Gertrudis (see p.135).

You'll find auction dates and full gallery and exhibition listings in the monthly magazine *Ibiza Now*, available from most newsagents.

CLOTHING SHOPS

Ambulance
Map 3, H3. Avgda Bartolmeu Vicent Ramón 5, New Town, Ibiza Town
Funky menswear retailer, with a good stock of streetwear labels (including G Star and Stussy), plus a limited range of beach and club gear.

Envy
Map 3, I4. c/de Montgrí 22, La Marina, Ibiza Town
Quirky, groovy, girly and highly individualistic clubwear and accessories at this friendly, affordable boutique.

Amaya
Map 8, F5. Plaça de s'Església, Sant Antoni
Large store with inexpensive trendy clothing and party-time accessories.

Cuatro
Map 8, G5. c/Ramón i Cayal 4, Sant Antoni
Select men's gear, including Stussy and Freshline, and no-attitude service.

La Vida Loca
Map 8, F4. c/Bartomeu Vicent Ramón 15, Sant Antoni
☏971 347 438
Manumission-owned wardrobe outlet with vast costume range available to rent (deposit needed) and for sale.

CHAPTER ELEVEN

La Artesana
Map 11, D4. c/d'Espardell, Es
Pujols, Formentera

Moderately priced surf and
skate wear and an in-store
tattoo parlour.

RECORDS AND CDS

If you can't get that tune out of your head, you can probably pick it up at one of the recommended vinyl and CD
specialists listed below.

DJ Beat
Map 3, K3. Plaça de la Tertulia,
Ibiza Town

Pacha Records
Map 3, I3. c/Lluís Tur i Palau
20, Ibiza Town

Megamusic
Map 8, F6. c/Santa Agnès,
Sant Antoni

Plastic Fantastic
Map 8, F6. c/Sant Antoni 15,
Sant Antoni

MARKETS

If you're after meat, cheese, fresh fruit or veg, head for the
produce **markets** in Ibiza Town (see p.63) and Santa
Eulària (see p.101). Souvenirs, sarongs, tie-dyed garb and
jewellery are the mainstay of the **hippy markets** held in all
of the main resorts, though most of the stock is pretty
pedestrian. There's nothing spontaneous about these hippy
markets, either; all are widely promoted, with opening
hours and directions available at the tourist offices, and
excursions to Es Canar's mammoth Wednesday extravagan-
za (see p.105) offered by most hotels. The best of a bad
bunch is the market at *Las Dalias* (see p.243), near Sant
Carles, a smaller-scale event with some quirky stalls selling
quality crafts amongst the general tat. For a different
flavour, check out the **specialized markets**: the car-boot-
style at Hippodrome (see p.174), organic produce at Can

Sort (see p.121) and the Mercat d'Art (art market) in Formentera for interesting jewellery and hand-made souvenirs (see p.200).

Festivals

While Ibiza and Formentera cannot claim to host particularly extravagant **festivals**, the parade of annual celebrations forms an important part of the social calendar and presents the chance for grand family get-togethers. Every single settlement holds an annual *festa* to celebrate the patron saint of the community, and all of them follow a similar pattern: religious services and cultural celebrations in the church or village square, usually Ibizan *ball pagès* (folk dancing) and often a display from another region of Spain, plus some live music of the soft-rock variety. Bonfires are lit, *torradas* (barbecues) spit and sizzle, traditional snacks like *bunyols* and *orelletes* are prepared, and there's always plenty of alcohol to lubricate proceedings. Some of the bigger events, such as the Sant Bartomeu celebrations in Sant Antoni on August 24 and the *Anar a Maig* in Santa Eulària, involve spectacular firework displays. We've listed the highlights in the festival calendar below; full lists of each village *festa* are available from the tourist board (see p.60).

"Molts anys i bons" ("Many years and good ones")
is the customary Pitiusan festival toast.

WATER WORSHIP

Throughout the Pitiusan countryside, but particularly in Ibiza, **water-worshipping** ceremonies (*xacotes pageses*) are performed at springs (*fonts*) and wells (*pous*) to give thanks for water in islands that are perpetually plagued by droughts. Thought to be Carthaginian in origin, the festival-like ceremonies involve much singing, dancing and general celebration. In recent years the culture department of the Consell Insular has began a restoration programme of Ibiza's historic wells, which are then opened with a fanfare of media publicity with speeches and the like, but in isolated spots (unadvertised) traditional events continue away from the cameras and reporters. For details of the better-known ceremonies, contact the tourist board.

FESTIVAL HIGHLIGHTS CALENDAR

February/March
Carnaval. Towns and villages in both islands live it up during the week before Lent with marches, fancy-dress parades and classical music concerts.

March
Semana Santa (Holy Week) is widely observed, with thousands assembling to watch the Good Friday religious processions through Dalt Vila in Ibiza Town and up to the Puig de Missa in Santa Eulària.

May
Anar a Maig. Large *festa* held on the first Sunday in the month in Santa Eulària, with processions of horse-drawn carts, classical music, a flower festival and a big firework display for the finale.

June
Nit de Sant Joan. Midsummer Night (June 23) features huge bonfires and effigy-burning in Sant Joan,

Ibiza, and throughout the Pitiuses.

July

Día de Verge de Carmen. The patron saint of seafarers and fishermen is honoured on July 15 and 16 throughout the islands, with parades and the blessing of boats; celebrations are particularly large in Ibiza Town and La Savina, Formentera.

Festa de Sant Jaume. Formentera's patron saint is celebrated all over the island on July 25.

August

Festa de Sant Ciriac. August 8 sees a small ceremony at the Capella Sant Ciriac in Dalt Vila (Map 4, C5) to commemorate the Catalan conquest of Ibiza in 1235, followed by a procession through the town and a mass watermelon fight in Es Soto below the Dalt Vila walls.

Día de Sant Bartomeu. Huge harbourside fireworks display in Sant Antoni on August 24, plus the usual concerts and dancing.

December

Wine festival in Sant Mateu, Ibiza over the first weekend in December.

Christmas (*Nadal*). Candlelit services throughout the Pitiuses on December 25.

New Year (*Cap d'Any*). Big parties in clubs and on Vara de Rey, Ibiza Town, where revellers celebrate the New Year in the traditional manner by eating twelve grapes as the clock strikes midnight.

Gay Ibiza

One of Europe's leading **gay** destinations, Ibiza's scene centres around twenty bars, a club, a network of gay-owned restaurants and a couple of lovely beaches. However, though queer visitors have been made welcome here since the late 1960s, the island remains an essentially **male** destination. There's no real **lesbian** scene as such, but plenty of gay women do choose to holiday in cosmopolitan, liberal Ibiza Town nonetheless.

For more on Sa Penya, Figueretes and Es Cavallet, see pp.64, 90 and 177 respectively.

With numerous scene-oriented bars, restaurants and boutiques, the **Sa Penya** area of Ibiza Town has become something of a gay village, with the island's only dedicated gay club, *Anfora*, a short hop away inside the Dalt Vila walls. A compact beach resort fifteen minutes' walk southwest of the capital, **Figueretes**, which also attracts plenty of families and straight couples, is the other main centre. Grouped around the seafront are four or five gay bar-cafés, while many of the hotels and apartments in the resort have a predominantly homosexual clientele. Same-sex couples are very unlikely to experience any hostility on Figueretes beach, but many prefer to head 4km south for the glorious

GAY-FRIENDLY ACCOMMODATION

The vast majority of gay visitors choose to stay in Ibiza Town or Figueretes and, while you're extremely unlikely to encounter any prejudice in Ibiza, the apartments and hotels listed below are especially gay-friendly.

La Torre del Canónigo	see p.211.
Hostal La Marina	see p.209.
Ocean Drive	see p.209.
Apartamentos Roselló	see p.210.
La Ventana	see p.211.
Hostal Parque	see p.210.
Hostal Mar Blau	see p.208.
Hotel Apartamentos El Puerto	see p.210.

sands of nudist Es Cavallet, or to the tiny sandy beach below the *Apartamentos Roselló* between Ibiza Town and Figueretes, where partners can canoodle in peace. Salines beach (see p.175) is also a favourite hangout – the most popular section is to the south of the *Sa Trincha* bar.

BARS AND CAFÉS

The heart of the gay **bar scene** is the c/de la Verge, a wild, 400-metre-long lane that meanders through the Sa Penya area of Ibiza Town that's lined with over a dozen atmospheric, cave-like bars, each with its own pavement terrace. Just to the south, c/d'Alfons XII has another crop of funky drinking dens, while inside the city walls you'll find a couple of classy places on Sa Carrossa, below the Baluard de Santa Lúcia, itself a popular night-time cruising zone. In Figueretes, the scene is more scattered and less chic, but popular places include the lesbian-run *Monroe's*, and

BARS AND CAFÉS

Magnus, which has a big terrace beside the main beachside promenade.

Angelo

Map 3, K5. c/d'Alfons XII 11, Sa Penya, Ibiza Town
May–Sept daily 10pm–3am
Squaring up to *Dôme* on c/d'Alfons XII, and competing with it as the hippest gay bar in the neighbourhood, *Angelo*'s commands pole position for the club parades, but beware the vertiginous bar prices.

Capricho

Map 3, L4. c/de la Verge 42, Sa Penya, Ibiza Town
Easter–Nov daily 9pm–3am
It's tricky to single the most happening bar on gay Ibiza's main drag, but the ever-popular *Capricho* is always one of the busiest, with a classy interior, beautiful bar boys and perhaps the most gregarious street terrace in town.

Chiringay

Map 10, I7. Es Cavallet beach
April–Oct daily 10am–8pm
Superb beachside bar-café, with a wonderful selection of

juices, fruit smoothies, healthy snacks and full meals. Spread over wooden decks, all the tables have views over the sea, and there's mellow chilled sounds and a resident masseur.

Dôme

Map 3, K5. c/d'Alfons XII 5, Sa Penya, Ibiza Town
May–Oct daily 10pm–3am
The most beautiful bar staff, the most expensive drinks, and perhaps the town's best location, in the plaza-like environs of c/d'Alfons XII. As the final destination of most of the club parades, the atmosphere on the terrace outside reaches fever pitch by 1am during the summer.

GC

Map 3, L4. c/de la Verge 32, Sa Penya, Ibiza Town
May–Oct daily 10pm–3am
Party central for the leather and rubber crowd and the scenes of legendary Friday-night underwear parties, with

BARS AND CAFÉS

275

a stylish bar zone and an intimate, sociable back room.

and passé really, but try telling the regulars that.

Monroe's
Map 3, A7. c/Ramón Mutaner, Figueretes
May–Oct daily 7pm–3am
Run by a larger-than-life British lesbian couple, and featured in the nauseous *Ibiza Uncovered* TV series, this temple of kitsch to Hollywood's celluloid goddess, with Marilyn memorabilia on every wall, is one of the most popular bars in Figueretes. All rather tacky

La Muralla
Map 4, G4. Sa Carrossa 3, Dalt Vila, Ibiza Town
Easter–Nov daily 10pm–3am
Set right next to the Dalt Vila walls, this is the island's most elegant gay bar, and one of the friendliest, with artwork on the sandstone walls and a wonderful mahogany bar. The long, narrow terrace outside is wonderful for an amiable evening drink.

CLUBS

Though *Anfora* is the only gay club in Ibiza, *Pacha*, *Privilege*, *Amnesia*, *Space* and *El Divino* all attract a mixed crowd, and all regularly promote gay nights. London's *Trade* frequently team up with *Manumission* and take over the back room at *Privilege*, and the regular *Scandal* nights at *Pacha*, and *La Troya Asesina* at *Amnesia*, are also worth looking out for. Bear in mind that the Sant Antoni club scene is, by nature, very heterosexual.

Anfora
Map 4, G4. c/Sant Carles, Dalt Vila, Ibiza Town
May–Oct, plus Easter and New Year
500 capacity

Set inside a natural cave in the heart of Dalt Vila, spectacular and stylish *Anfora* attracts a very international, mixed-age crowd, but you may find the sounds a little outdated – resident DJs tend to mix driving house music with camp anthems. Downstairs, there's a gingham-tiled dancefloor, a central bar and a stage (usually used for drag acts), while upstairs the very dark darkroom screens hardcore movies.

CLUBS

Directory

AIRLINES Iberia is the only airline with an office in Ibiza, at Passeig Vara de Rey 15, Ibiza Town ☏ 971 300 614 – outside office hours call ☏ 902 400 500. For Air Europa and Go, call ☏ 902 401 501; for Spanair, call ☏ 902 131 415.

AIRPORT INFORMATION ☏ 971 809 000.

ELECTRICITY The current is 220 volts AC, with the standard European two-pin plug. UK appliances function fine with an adaptor, but North American appliances will also need a transformer.

EMERGENCIES Call ☏ 112 for police, ambulance or fire brigade.

INTERNET In Ibiza Town, try *Chill* (see p.239), or *CIE* at Avgda d'Ignasi Wallis 39 (daily 10am–10pm). In Sant Antoni, try *E-Station*, Avgda Dr Fleming 1 (daily 10am–midnight), or *Café Ebob* (May–Oct daily 11am–11pm), at c/Sant Antoni 15. There are no designated Internet cafés in Formentera, but *PO BOX* on the main east–west highway in Sant Ferran (Mon–Sat 10am–2pm & 5–8pm) has a couple of terminals.

LAUNDRY All resort hotels have laundry facilities. Otherwise, try Wash & Dry, Avgda Espanya 53, Ibiza Town, where you can surf the Web while you wait for your wash, or Pernia Izquierdo, c/Isidor Macabich 34, Santa Eulària.

PHARMACIES Farmacia Juan Tur Viñas, c/d'Antoni 1, Ibiza Town ☏ 971 310 326; Farmacia Villangomez Mari, c/Ample 12, Sant Antoni ☏ 971 340 891; Farmacia Antich Torres, c/Sant Jaume 50, Santa Eulària ☏ 971 330 097; Farmacia Torres

Quetglas, c/Santa Maria, Sant Francesc, Formentera ⓣ971 328 004.

PHOTOGRAPHY The following photographic shops stock regular, monochrome and slide film; Fotocentro, c/Aragó 70, Ibiza Town; Foto Toni, c/de la Soledat 6, Sant Antoni; Foto San Francisco, Plaça de s'Església, Sant Francesc, Formentera.

SUPERMARKETS Ibiza's biggest and best supermarket is SYP, situated just outside Ibiza Town on the inner ring road, Carreterra Santa Eulària (Mon–Sat 9am–10pm, Sun 10am–8pm). In Formentera there's a smaller branch, on Urbanizacíon Sa Senieta, Sant Francesc (Mon–Sat 9am–8pm).

TIME Ibiza and Formentera follow CET (Central European Time), which is 1hr ahead of the UK, 6hr ahead of Eastern Standard Time and 9hr ahead of Pacific Standard Time. Spain also adopts daylight-saving

time in winter: clocks go forward in the last week in September and in the last week of March.

TIPPING It's not essential to tip in cafés and bars, but many locals leave some change when they get their bill; in restaurants, ten percent is sufficient.

TRAVEL AGENTS The following companies can arrange excursions and help with booking flights: Viajes Urbis, Avgda 8 d'Agost, Edificio Bristol, Ibiza Town ⓣ 971 314 412 ⓔ *urbisibz@juniper.es*; Viajes Martours, c/Miramar 7, Sant Antoni ⓣ971 340 294 ⓔ *info@viajesmartour.com*; Viajes Tagomago, Plaça d'Isidor Macabich 28, Santa Eulària ⓣ 971 330 385; Ultramar Express, Avgda Mediterránea 13, La Savina, Formentera ⓣ971 322 136.

YOGA Contact Jivana Ashram, Apartado de Corrreos 157, Sant Antoni, E07820 Ibiza ⓣ 971 342 494.

CONTEXTS

A brief history of Ibiza and Formentera

Until very recently, it was thought that the Pitiuses were first inhabited in around 1900 BC, just before the Bronze Age. However, in 1994, the carbon dating of sheep and goat bones found at s'Avenc des Pouàs cave near Santa Agnès seems to prove that Ibiza was first settled much earlier, around 4500 BC, by **Neolithic** people from the Iberian mainland. Little is yet known about them beyond the fact that they were pastoralists who brought their livestock with them, as the only mammals on the island before their arrival were bats. It's assumed that they probably remained close to the shore, living in natural caves and gradually establishing new settlements across the Pitiuses. The earliest sign of human habitation in **Formentera** is the cluster of important sites in the Barbària peninsula, which date from around 1850 BC, where family groups raised cattle, fished and grew crops.

Just to the north, at **Ca Na Costa**, an impressive megalith-ic burial chamber also dates from the same era, where stone and bone tools, buttons and beads have been unearthed.

Axe heads, arrow tips and other metal utensils first began to be used in both islands at around 1600 BC. As no metal deposits had been discovered locally, the implements would have been imported from elsewhere in the Mediterranean, and were probably produced by the sophisticated Talayotic people, who had by that time established themselves throughout Mallorca and Menorca; though they never col-onized the Pitiuses, they are thought to have exported goods to the south. By the late Bronze Age, around 800 BC, copper, lead and tin tools, and pottery from Mallorca and Menorca, were being traded with the people of Ibiza and Formentera. More settlements had spread across both Pitiusan islands by this time, including hilltop sites at Punta Jondal and Puig Rodó in southern Ibiza, and Sa Cala and La Savina in Formentera.

The Phoenicians

Though the Greeks passed Ibiza and Formentera in the ninth century BC, they never settled in either island. The first colonizers from the east were **Phoenicians**, skilled seafarers and merchants who originated in the Levant (modern-day Lebanon) and had established ports and trad-ing passages throughout the Mediterranean by 800 BC. They arrived in Ibiza around 650 BC, attracted to the island by its strategic position for their main east–west and north–south trade routes between North Africa, the Iberian mainland, Sardinia and western Sicily.

The Phoenicians first settled in **Sa Caleta** (see p.171), above the low cliffs on the south coast of Ibiza, where they established a village of several hundred people, who survived mainly by hunting and fishing. Just fifty years later they abandoned Sa Caleta for the safer hilltop site and sheltered harbour of today's Ibiza Town. They named the new settlement **Ibosim** (Island of Bes), after Bes, a primary god of dance, usually depicted as a bearded dwarf with a huge phallus. His link with Ibiza is almost certainly derived from his role as a protector against snakes – Ibiza lacks any poisonous creatures.

It's impossible to draw a line between Ibiza's Phoenician and Carthaginian periods as the city of Carthage was founded and settled by Phoenicians, and the lack of wars or treaties provide historians with no obvious crossover date. But by the mid-sixth century BC, Carthage had eclipsed the Levantine Phoenician cities of Sidon and Tyre in influence and wealth, assumed dominance over established trading routes, and was unquestionably the most powerful settlement in the western Mediterranean. **Punic**, derived from the Greek word for Phoenician, is usually used to describe the Phoenician–Carthaginian settlements of southern Spain, Corsica, Sardinia and Sicily.

The Punic era

During the **Punic era** (550–146 BC) Ibiza became a pivotal part of the Carthaginian empire (Formentera, though, was never settled). The imposing capital of Ibosim boasted a temple to the god Eshmun, a god of healing, atop the peak of today's Dalt Vila, and a "fine port, great walls as well as a considerable number of admirably built houses", according to the Roman chronicler Diodorus Siculus. The Carthaginians established Ibiza's salt pans (see p.178), and the economy centred around the trading of salt, plus silver and lead mined from s'Argentera in the north of the island.

Wheat, olives, figs and fruit were farmed, and pottery was produced on an industrial scale from workshops around Ibosim and exported all over the Mediterranean. Above all, however, Ibiza became rich on the export of a precious purple **dye** extracted from the tiny sea snail *murex brandaris* and used to tint the togas of Roman noblemen.

In addition to its status as trading settlement, Ibiza also came to be regarded as something of a spiritual nerve centre for the Carthaginian empire, a holy place sacred to Tanit, the goddess of love, death and fertility who was the most revered of all the Punic deities. She was worshipped at various sites throughout Ibiza, but is particularly associated with the **Cova des Cuieram**, and with **Illa Plana** on the Botafoc peninsula. Tanit's status as goddess of death was the origin of her association with Ibiza – as the island harbours no poisonous creatures (a main Carthaginian prerequisite for a burial site), it assumed religious significance for the Carthaginians as the most acclaimed burial site in the Mediterranean. They believed that burial in Ibiza would facilitate a fast-track route to the afterlife, and the wealthy would pay in advance to have their bodies transported to the **Puig des Molins** cemetery, which holds over three thousand tombs.

The Romans

The walled city of Ibosim, despite a three-day bombardment by the Roman general Cneus Cornelius Scipio in 217 BC, remained under Carthaginian control until the final Punic war. After the defeat and destruction of Carthage by Rome in 146 BC, Ibiza made a pact with the victors and obtained confederate status, the greatest degree of autonomy possible under Roman law. For the next two hundred years Ibiza maintained a dual Roman/Carthaginian identity. Coinage continued to be minted locally, but with Roman emblems on one side and Carthaginian gods Bes or

Eshmun on the other, while Punic temples and cemeteries were preserved alongside Roman ones.

This was an extremely prosperous period for most Ibizans. The economy continued to flourish, based on the export of salt, pottery and *garum* (a fish sauce prized by the Romans), and all sectors were boosted by the introduction of slave labour and by new technology that revitalized agriculture. Colossal olive presses and millstones made from volcanic rock were introduced, aqueducts were constructed and fish farms established near the modern resort of s'Argamassa, where tuna was salted and dried for export. Hundreds of settlers and slaves moved to near-deserted **Formentera**, where innovative Roman techniques also boosted fishery and agriculture with great success, and by 70 AD the island's population under Roman rule had grown to over three thousand, a figure that was not reached again until the early 1970s.

This prosperity peaked soon after Roman law was extended to all Hispanic lands in 74 AD, and Ibiza was downgraded to mere municipal status. All traces of Punic identity were gradually erased – Ibosim was renamed **Ebusus**, and the temple to Eshmun was rebuilt and dedicated to Mercury. The economy soon began to suffer as well, as the Romans centralized agricultural production in North Africa under the *latifundia* system, importing vast numbers of slaves to tend their crops. Production of olive oil, *garum*, wine and pottery diminished in Ibiza and Formentera, where there could never be equivalent economies of scale. Swathes of land were abandoned and the population fell; by the end of the fourth century, as the overstretched Roman empire had begun to crumble, Ibiza was little more than a minor trading post, still exporting salt and some lead, but dependent upon extracting taxes from merchant ships for most of her wealth.

THE ROMANS

Vandals and Byzantines

More than five hundred years of Roman domination ended when the **Vandals**, a warrior tribe that originated in central Asia, swept through mainland Spain in the early fifth century, conquering the Pitiuses in 455 AD before establishing their main settlement in the same spot as the former Carthage. Very little is known about Vandal rule in Ibiza, which lasted for just eighty years, but it was clearly a time of great tension, with religious issues causing most of the instability. The Vandals became Christians during their long migration west, adopting the Arian belief in the concept that Christ and God were two distinct figures rather than elements of the Trinity alongside the Holy Ghost. To the Catholic **Byzantines**, the main challengers to the Vandals for hegemony in the region, this was deemed heretical (though the Romans had been driven out of Ibiza, a Catholic presence remained in the island). Despite a treaty drawn up in 476 AD between the two competing powers, the Vandal king Henrich executed Ophilio, the Catholic bishop of Ibiza, in 483 AD, and there were further martyrs from both faiths across the region. Tensions ensued for another fifty years before the great Byzantine general Belisarius conquered the Vandal power base at Carthage in 533, and the Balearic islands two years later, driving out Arian Christianity for good. Despite attaining control over the Pitiuses, which were of very peripheral interest, the Byzantines did not colonize the islands, and it's assumed a primitive form of Christianity, combined with Punic forms of worship, would have continued to be practised.

The Moors

The **Moors** first made contact with the Balearics when they pillaged Mallorca in 707 AD; however, they didn't gain formal control over the islands until the beginning of the tenth century. Almost no records from the eight and ninth centuries have survived; the islands certainly had very little protection, as they were periodically ravaged by Viking and Norman raiders. For two centuries Moorish influence amounted to not much more than the periodic collection of taxes. This epoch of great instability was brought to an end in 902, when the Emir of Córdoba conquered the Balearics.

Moorish rule revitalized Ibiza and Formentera, introducing new names (**Yebisah** for Ibiza and Faramantira for Formentera), a new language (Arabic) and a new religion (Islam), though in remote locations a form of Christianity was still clandestinely practised. New and specialized technologies, above all the implementation of innovative irrigation systems, rejuvenated the agricultural sector, enabling crops like rice and sugar cane to be grown in the arid Pitiusan terrain and helping to produce two harvests a year in the fields of **Ses Feixes** (see box on p.86) around the harbour of Yebisah Medina, today's Ibiza Town.

For two hundred years, Moorish Ibiza, under tolerant *walis* (governors), was generally prosperous and stable; however, troubles erupted when control of the Balearics passed to the **Almortadha** dynasty of governors in 1085. The Almortadha pursued an aggressive foreign policy, raiding towns in mainland Spain and persecuting Christians from bases in the Balearics, thus provoking a massive invasion of Ibiza in 1114 by tens of thousands of troops from five hundred Pisan and Catalan ships – an action supported by the Pope as a mini-crusade. Though the invading forces massacred most of the island's Muslim population and ended Almortadha control, they didn't take control of the islands, thus opening the door for the next Moorish rulers, the more benign **Almoravids**, and the final dynasty, the **Almohads**.

THE MOORS

The Catalan conquest

The key to the **Catalan conquest** of the Pitiuses was the unification of the kingdoms of Aragón and Catalunya under Jaume I, which gave the Christian king the political and military strength to contemplate hitherto unfeasible dreams of empire expansion. Mallorca was taken in 1229, Menorca in 1232, and in 1235, Jaume I combined forces with the Crown Prince of Portugal, the Count of Roussillon and Count Guillem of Montgrí to attack Yebisah. The invaders took the citadel on August 8, 1235 after a long siege, possibly entering through an entrance inside the tiny chapel of Sant Ciriac in Dalt Vila (see p.73).

Initially, Catalan rule was very positive for Ibiza (now renamed Eivissa) and Formentera. The islands received a rather progressive charter of freedom, the **Carta de Franquicias**, which guaranteed freedom of commerce, no military service, an independent judiciary and free legal services for all citizens. Crucially, profits from the sale of salt, the foundation of the islands' economies, were to be retained locally. In 1299, King Jaume II allowed the islands even greater freedom by creating the Universitat, a system of democratic self-government.

These progressive measures, together with the promise of land and a house, were essential to entice reluctant farm workers from the mainland to the islands, not an easy task in the thirteenth century, when the expense and difficulty of transport must have made the Pitiuses seem like the other side of the globe. Under the Catalans, Pitiusan society underwent radical change that shaped the contemporary scene; Catalan was introduced as the main language, and Catholicism became the official religion. The invaders divided Ibiza into five *quartons* – Eivissa, Sant Jordi, Santa Eulària, Sant Miquel and Sant Antoni – and built a chapel in each region to help get Christianity established in rural areas.

Plague and pirates

The optimism of the late thirteenth century was to be fairly short-lived, however. Bubonic **plague** (dubbed the Black Death) first spread to Ibiza from the devastated cities of the mainland in 1348. The already sparse population was cut to just five hundred people by the beginning of the fourteenth century, while Formentera was left utterly uninhabited – the threat of disease, combined with the threat of pirate attacks, ensured that it wasn't resettled until 1697.

Plague returned to Ibiza in the fifteenth century, but a more serious outbreak occurred in 1652, when one in six of the by-now 7000-strong population perished. To compound matters further, the outbreak occurred during the summer months when salt (the primary source of income) was being gathered; Ibiza was deemed a contaminated port by the salt merchants, and famine inevitably followed.

Pirates were another constant menace. Between the fourteenth and late fifteenth centuries the attacks were sporadic, as Moors seeking slaves pillaged their old colony from bases just a day's sail away in North Africa. The onslaughts multiplied from the start of the sixteenth century, as Turkish buccaneers bombarded the capital with cannon fire, reducing the city's fortified walls to rubble. Complete reconstruction ensued (see box on p.68), and following the destruction of Santa Eulària in 1545 the fortifications around the Puig de Missa hill were also upgraded. The first defence tower, Torre de Sal Rossa, was built as part of a network that soon spanned the entire Pitiusan coastline; the towers were constantly manned so that fires could be lit to signify the first sign of an enemy ship.

Castilian control

Following the 1702–14 war of Spanish Succession, the victorious **Castilians** assumed control of the Pitiuses and, in a familiar pattern, imposed their language (Castilian Spanish) and the name Ibiza. The island suffered for backing the losers in the Civil War: the salt pans were claimed by the new Spanish state, and the Universitat replaced by a Castilian municipal administration with very limited power. The Pitiuses became even more of a backwater and gradually settled back into provincial stupor. Pirate attacks presented less of a threat in the eighteenth and nineteenth centuries thanks to the efforts of the **corsairs**, but though the population grew slowly life remained desperately poor for most.

The Catholic **Church** was the other dominant power in Spain, and targeted considerable funds to attempt to restructure Ibizan and Formenteran society around village churches, which they constructed across the islands. Work quickly began on new chapels at Sant Francesc, Formentera in 1724, and in Sant Joan, Sant Josep and Sant Francesc in Ibiza. Later in the century, Abad y Lasierra was appointed as the islands' first Catholic bishop since Vandal times, and Ibiza Town's Santa Maria church was consecrated as a cathedral in 1782. The new bishop quickly authorized the establishment of a dozen new parishes (including Sant Mateu, Santa Agnès and Sant Agustí) but the populace were unwilling to move to these new villages, preferring the independence of the country-side.

Ibiza and Formentera remained very peripheral corners of Spain in the early nineteenth century, with a stagnant economy and few employment opportunities. Even the option of becoming a corsair was all but ruled out after the French claimed Algeria as a colony in 1830 and began to subdue piracy. Thousands of young men emigrated to Florida, South America and Cuba, especially from Formentera, which became known as "s'illa des ses dones" (the island of women). The salt pans were sold to a private

CORSAIRS

Nautical vigilantes authorized by the Catalan (and later Spanish) Crown to attack and plunder enemy ships, Pitiusan **corsairs** (or privateers) were issued registration certificates as far back as 1356, when the Ibizan-born Pere Bernat defended the Pitiusan coast from Moorish attack. Under the terms of the registration they were entitled to keep four-fifths of the booty they captured, with the remainder going to the Crown. However, the corsairs were not a force to be reckoned with until the seventeenth century when, following devastating pirate assaults throughout the sixteenth century, Ibizan corsairs began to regain the initiative, successfully counterattacking Moorish ships and reclaiming stolen booty from Barbary coast ports. They steadily gained a fearsome reputation in the western Mediterranean as skilled and courageous seamen, and Ibiza's security situation improved, enabling the resettlement of Formentera in 1697.

A corsair would have been one of the main career choices for a young male Ibizan in the late seventeenth to mid-nineteenth centuries. **Antoni Riquer** (1773–1846), born in Ibiza Town's La Marina quarter, is one of the most celebrated sons – he's said to have overpowered over a hundred enemy ships, including a much stronger Gibraltarian craft, the *Felicity*, in Ibiza Town harbour in 1806, a struggle witnessed by most of the town's population. Evidently, they were impressed enough to name a square, Plaça d'Antoni Riquer, after him; it lies in La Marina on the Passeig Marítim harbourfront (see p.61), opposite a stone monument to the corsair profession.

company (for over a million pesetas, then a colossal sum) by the Spanish state in 1871 in a desperate measure to raise some revenue, and conditions for salt workers worsened under private ownership.

Isolation and civil war

Ibiza only began to recover towards the end of the nineteenth century, when the introduction of regular ferry services to and from the mainland helped ease the island's isolation, and even brought the odd curious adventurer from northern Europe – the first tourists. The initial bohemian travellers (including Raoul Haussmann, the artist and Dadaist photographer) were joined by artists and writers escaping the march of Fascism across Europe, and represented Ibiza's first proto-hippies. Though the economic impact of these visitors would have barely touched the island economy, any hopes of an embryonic tourist industry were snuffed out by the **Spanish Civil War** (1936–39). In one of the very darkest chapters of Ibizan history, a previously largely apolitical island became bitterly divided on Nationalist and Republican lines. Atrocities were committed on both sides, but Catalan Anarchists, briefly in control of the island after the expulsion of Franco's Nationalist forces, committed the worst act, slaughtering over a hundred Nationalist prisoners inside the Dalt Vila castle before fleeing the island. Republicans were hunted down in the Nationalist backlash that ensued; hundreds fled to the hills, and those who were not executed or imprisoned were dispatched to a concentration camp in La Savina, Formentera, where dozens died from malnutrition. The wounds of the Civil War remain something of a taboo subject in Ibiza, and many local historians still refuse to tackle the matter for fear of stirring up issues that split families over sixty years ago.

Artists and tourists

Ibiza's transformation from isolated backwater in the aftermath of the Civil War into one of the globe's most fashionable tourist destinations has been startlingly swift. By the mid-1950s, two decades after the end of the Civil War, a trickle of bohemian travellers had begun to return to the island. Based at the *Hotel El Corsario* in Ibiza Town (see p.209), a scene developed around the "Grupo Ibiza '59", a collection of artists including Bechtold and Neubauer, and architects including Erwin Boner and Josep Llúis Sert, who worked closely with Le Corbusier.

Sant Antoni was also embarking on the wobbly path from fishing port to resort town during the 1950s, when hotels and Costa-style paraphernalia – including the prerequisite bullring that's alien to Catalan culture – sprung up around the town's bay. By the early 1960s, Spain's Franco-directed tourism drive was transforming the whole island, with beach after beach earmarked for development, and the first hotels in Formentera constructed at Es Pujols. By 1965, Ibiza was importing 30,000 tonnes of cement a year, and an army of building workers, waiters and maids from the mainland arrived, swelling the population by 43 percent during the course of the 1960s.

Beatniks and hippies

Though the roots of the Pitiusan **hippy scene** can be traced right back to the first wave of travellers in the early twentieth century, things really took off in the late 1950s when young beatniks first reached Ibiza. The attraction was simple: a beautiful island just off the overland trail to Morocco, with an established community of artists and Spanish leftists (Ibiza was remote enough from Franco's Madrid power base for dissidents to feel reasonably secure), cheap living costs and a famously tolerant population. At first the action was concentrated around bars such as *Dominos* in La Marina, and on Figueretes beach, where a small jazz scene developed. Word spread quickly through the travellers' grapevine, and in the mid- to late 1960s, visitor numbers were swollen by American draft-dodgers avoiding the call to fight in Vietnam.

Dubbed *peluts* (hairies) by the locals, Ibiza was quickly adopted as a class A Mediterranean hangout, with Formentera achieving at least a B+ (Bob Dylan lived there for a time and Pink Floyd recorded the soundtrack to their film *More* on the island). Though Ibiza Town was the main focus of the scene in the early 1960s, Sant Carles, Sant Joan and La Mola later became the main hippy artistic centres, and remain so today. The hippies brought character (and plenty of drugs) to an isolated corner of Europe, putting Ibiza on the map and helping forge its modern identity as a tolerant, hedonistic island. The legendary parties of the 1960s and 1970s initiated the club scene; *Pacha*, *Amnesia* and *Ku* (now *Privilege*) originally had a distinctly hippy identity. Today the word "hippy" maintains a certain cachet in the Pitiuses long absent in most parts of Europe, and the islands' hippy heritage is now used as a stratagem to entice visitors to the island in the tourist authorities' promotional literature.

Ibiza and Formentera today

Following the return of democracy in 1976 after Franco's death, Ibizan **politics** were dominated by the conservative **Partido Popular** (PP) for over two decades. However in 1999, the left-leaning **Pacte Progressista** coalition, fronted by the charismatic and urbane Pilar Costa, was elected as leaders of the island government largely as a result of their opposition to Partido Popular-supported construction and development proposals, including a plan to build a golf course at Cala d'Hort (see p.163). Under the PP, the political agenda had been massively biased towards unbridled tourist development, as blocks-on-the-beach were thrown up around the coastline with little or no regard for environmental considerations. Local people registered their objections to this rampant development with their ballot papers, and since the 1999 victory environmental issues have remained in the forefront of Ibizan politics. Ironically, a flood of new building projects started almost immediately after the election, as desperate developers sought to push through mothballed projects before new building legislation could be set in place, often using licences issued back in the 1980s. Finally, a year after the election, and a bust-up between Costa and her Green Party environment minister over the speed of change, comprehensive new construction laws outlawed new coastal projects and left fourteen large tourism developments paralysed.

The other hot issue is one of **cultural identity**, as the Pitiusan authorities attempt the difficult task of maintaining the islands' Balearic/Catalan heritage. **Language** is a very divisive subject, as the local government steadily adopt a much more stringent attitude to the promotion of Catalan, a rather heated issue considering that only 38 percent of Ibiza's population (a little more in Formentera) speak the local Eivissenc Catalan dialect. Partly a legacy of Franco years, when it was banned, this is mostly due to the presence of thousands of Castilian speakers who migrated in the boom years of tourism. The ruling that all teachers must now speak Catalan has resulted in recruitment shortages, and proposals that Catalan should become the main language of education in the islands troubles many Spanish-speaking parents, whose children already have to struggle with English, and often German, classes.

Tourism remains the linchpin of the Ibizan and Formenteran economies, and it's estimated that over eighty percent of the working population now earn their living indirectly or directly from the sector. The industry is very seasonal in the Pitiuses, however; even though the official season is May to October, the islands only really fill up for three months, between mid-June and mid-September. Unlike Mallorca, which has established a strong winter season, most of the Pitiusan resorts shut down completely for the other nine months of the year. Unemployment rates soar in winter, when many locals leave to work in the Canaries or other parts of Europe. Pitiusan tourism is also dangerously dependent on the British market (almost fifty percent of all visitors are from the UK), and on young clubbers, with little sign of the "Third Age" tourists or cultural travellers visiting in the numbers that the island government would like. In the first few years of the twenty-first century, however, as young people continue to flock to Ibiza to experience the unique party scene, there seems to be no sign of the Balearic bubble bursting.

IBIZA AND FORMENTERA TODAY

Wildlife and the environment

The Balearics were separated by sea from mainland Spain around five million years ago, when the mountainous barrier between Gibraltar and Morocco that acted as a dam between the Atlantic and the dry Mediterranean area burst. In effect, the islands are continuations of mountains that start on the mainland south of Valencia, and are mainly made of limestone and red sandstone, plus a little basaltic (volcanic) rock.

The name "Pitiuses" is thought to derive from the ancient Greek for pine tree, *pitus*, and **pine forests** still cover large swathes of **Ibiza**. These consist mostly of Aleppo pine – distinguished by its bright-green spines, silvery twigs and ruddy brown cones – but also of sabina pine near the coast, and some Italian stone pine in the hills. By the coast there are many varieties of **palm tree**, including one endemic species, *phoenix dactylifera*. Other trees include olive, carob, almond and a rich variety of fruit trees: fig, apricot, citrus, apple, pear, plum, peach and pomegranate.

WILD FLOWERS

One of the delights of the Pitiusan countryside is the astonishing array of **wild flowers**, partly a result of the fact that pesticides and fertilizers are not widely used, and fields are regularly left fallow. The best time of year is spring, when orchids, cornflowers, white rock roses and vast fields of poppies bloom, but there's always something to see, even in the summer, when the incessant heat stunts most plant growth. In the shady torrents, you'll see wild oleander and the delicate creamy travellers' joy flower, while sea daffodils and thistles thrive near the coast.

With the first rains in late September, the pale-pink Mediterranean heath flowers open and herbs and grasses abound. In December, keep an eye out for the brown bee orchid, and lavender and rosemary flower as early as January.

Formentera is ravaged by the cool, dry *tramóntana* wind from the north, and the hot *xaloc* that blows from the Sahara, giving the island's limited vegetation a contorted, wind-blown appearance – the trunk of the **sabina** pine is often twisted and bent double by the force of the wind. There's nowhere else in the Balearics that has the same density of these hardy trees, much valued for construction purposes: the wood is extremely durable and ideal for support beams and window frames because of its highly resinous nature. The fact that the island's main port – La Savina – is named after it is a measure of the tree's importance on the island. The deciduous **fig** tree, with its large lobed leaves, is another common Formenteran species, its huge branches nearly always propped up by massive scaffold-like supports added by farmers.

Mammals

Other than bats, there were no **mammals** at all in the
Pitiuses before the arrival of the first humans around 4600
BC. The first settlers brought sheep and goats with them
from the mainland, and by 1900 BC cattle and pigs were
being kept in both islands. Though settlers brought more
mammals over the centuries, there's not a great diversity
today, partly because of hunting, which remains a popular
pastime. The pine marten, for example, is a popular quarry
and has been on the brink of extinction for the last few
decades.

The largest mammal in the Pitiuses is the rare, cat-like
genet, possibly introduced by the Carthaginians. Light
brown in colour with a long bushy, ringed tail, it's an
extremely shy nocturnal species and hunts mice and other
rodents. A much more common sight is the Ibizan hound,
ca eivissenc. It, too, is thought to have been introduced
from North Africa: images of the same breed are depicted
in the tombs of the Middle Kingdom in Egypt (2050–1800
BC). The skinny, rusty brown-and-white hound is a
bizarre-looking beast – all ears and limbs – is perfectly
adapted to its environment, and is a superb hunter of the
islands' plentiful populations of **rabbits** and **hares**.
Squirrels, weasels, mice and rats and the North African subspecies of the hedgehog are also found, while Formentera is
home to a vary rare subspecies of rodent, called the **garden
dormouse** (*eliomys quercinus*).

Reptiles and insects

The dryness of the terrain and the distance from the main-
land means there are few **reptiles** and amphibians in the
Pitiuses. By far the most commonly found reptile is the
Ibizan wall lizard, which is unique to the islands and has

evolved into several distinct subspecies. In Ibiza, the lizard averages 10cm in length and is coloured brown and vivid green, with flecks of blue. The Formenteran variant is slightly larger, and coloured more garishly: an almost electric blue and luminous green. Many of the smaller islands that make up the Pitiuses, including Espalmador, Espardell and Tagomago, also have their own native subspecies, the most spectacular of which is the **Es Vedrà lizard**, an ultramarine colour, with yellow stripes. Despite the dry conditions, the **Iberian frog**, or marsh frog, is reasonably widespread.

The Pitiuses are rich in **insect** life, reflecting the relative lack of pesticides used in the fields. Of the beetles, the staghorn is the largest, but there are also scarab, scarred melolontha and bupredid varieties. Butterflies are plentiful, most exotically the spectacular twin-tailed pacha, which can reach 10cm across, but also the swallowtail, the clouded yellow, Bath white, Lang's short-tailed blue, painted lady and cleopatra. Dramatic hawk moths such as the death's head, hummingbird and oleander are infrequently seen, while the European mantis is more common. Dragonflies and damselflies are best spotted in marshland areas.

Birds

In contrast to the paucity of mammal species, the Pitiuses are home to a rich variety of **birds** and are a crucial migratory base for numerous species. Not surprisingly, there's a wealth of **marine birds** on the islands. Of the **gulls**, the most common is the large Mediterranean herring gull, easily identifiable by its yellow beak. On the west coast of Ibiza it's even possible to see the rarest gull in the world, Audouin's Gull (*larus audouinii*), recognizable by its red beak and olive-green feet. Other winter visitors are the lesser black-backed gull, the black-headed gull, the little gull, and the Mediterranean gull. Seven species of **tern** visit the Pitiuses in autumn and spring, and cormorants and shags are common. Offshore, puffins and razorbills are sometimes seen on isolated rocks, well away from ports and people. Finally, the dull-looking greeny-brown Balearic shearwater, known locally as the **virot**, can still be seen gliding around the capes of Formentera, despite having been hunted until relatively recently.

A wide variety of **marsh birds** reside in southern Ibiza, particularly in the environs of the salt pans and close to Ibiza Town at Ses Feixes. In the rich wetlands, little white egrets, only 50cm or so in height, with thin black bills and yellow feet, are fairly common. Formentera attracts fewer marsh birds, though several species of heron visit both islands, as do bitterns and, less frequently, the white stork, spoonbill, ibis and crane. By far the most exotic wetland bird seen is the European **flamingo**, which, after an absence of a decade or so, is again breeding on the islands, especially in the Ibizan salt pans: over five hundred were counted in the area in October 2000 and over sixty in Formentera.

Other visitors to the salt pans are various species of **waders**, including the black-winged stilt, with its unmistakable red legs. Redshank and greenshank, lapwing, curlews, godwits and five species of plover can also be spotted, plus visiting shoreline and salt-pan waders. Woodcock, snipe and stone curlew favour the freshwater marshes.

Compared with the vultures, red kite, and osprey of Mallorca and Menorca there are few large **birds of prey** on the Pitiuses. Of those that are found, the most spectacular is **Eleanor's falcon**, an elegant predator of migrant birds such as swifts, which resides in Ibiza between April and November. Es Vedrà has the largest colony in the Balearics, but others are frequently seen on the northwest coast near Sant Mateu. The supremely acrobatic, slightly

BIRDS

larger **peregrine falcon** is a rare sight now, much persecuted by pigeon fanciers. Kestrels, marsh harriers and sparrowhawks are more common, plus honey buzzards in Formentera, and the occasional booted eagle in Ibiza. **Owls** include fair numbers of barn owls, spotted even around Ibiza Town, where they prey on sparrows and mice. Other residents are the scops owl and the short-eared owl; the latter unique in that it hunts in daylight – it can occasionally be seen in marshland areas like Ses Feixes.

Of the vast order of **passerines**, usually simplified to mean **perching birds**, most of the usual European species are represented. Some of the more unusual species include the Kentish plover, thekla lark, crossbill, the Sardinian and Marmora's warbler and the blue rock thrush. Some of the most exotic European birds are quite common in the Pitiuses, including the spectacular crested and zebra-winged **hoopoe**, the turquoise-and-yellow **bee-eater**, the kingfisher and the large blue-green **roller**.

Green politics

Until recently, Ibiza's record of **environmental protection** was pretty poor. After decades of rampant development of the island's coastline, Green issues have been forced to the top of the political agenda, and urbanization issues now rival tourism for column inches in the local press. The **Green Party** (Els Verds) formed part of the victorious Pacte Progressista alliance that won the 1999 local elections, and despite a very public squabble with the dominant Socialists a year after the historic victory, which saw the Green environment minister Joan Buades leave the coalition, they remain a force to be reckoned with in Ibizan politics.

The issue that ignited Green consciousness in Ibiza was a proposal to develop housing the near-pristine hills around the **salt pans**, in the extreme southeast of the island. Developers were repulsed in 1977 by a planning commission, but others returned in 1990 with a proposal to build over six hundred villas. A vigorous and ultimately successful "Salvem Ses Salines" campaign was launched by the Green activists GEN and Friends of the Earth to save a unique part of Ibizan heritage. They managed to secure ANEI (Natural Area of Special Interest) status, and later achieved international recognition. Today, the region is recognized by the EU as one of Europe's most important wetland habitats, and is due to be listed by UNESCO as part of Ibiza's World Heritage Status award.

The battle over **Cala d'Hort**, a sublime slice of Ibiza coastline, became the focus of the next main Green issue and second big test case between developers and environmentalists. It's fair to say that the proposals to build a golf course marked a turning point in modern Ibizan history, provoking the largest demonstration the island had ever seen and helping oust the Partido Popular conservatives from power.

Elected with a mandate to introduce tough new building restrictions, the Pacte took over a year to draw up legislation, which was immediately contested by the powerful construction industry lobby. The Norma Territorial Cautelar law introduced in 2000 was sweeping, however, banning new development within 500m of the coast, cancelling building licences and introducing new quality requirements. Hoteliers, tour operators, media and local public opinion were supportive of the new legislation and, though many environmentalists thought it didn't go far enough, the general consensus was that a good start had been made to limit further unsustainable development.

GREEN POLITICS

The Balearic Beat

Born under the stars in Ibiza, Balearic Beat was Alfredo's baby. Paul Oakenfold and Danny Rampling kidnapped it and raised it indoors in cold, grey London.

Jane Bussmann, *Once in a Lifetime*

An all-embracing musical style developed by the island's resident DJs in the 1980s, Ibiza's home-grown **Balearic Beat** became a pivotal part of the UK's acid-house revolution. Above all it's a positive, optimistic blend, founded in electronica, but fused with afro, Latin and funk charisma and certainly not locked to a four-four thud or two-step shuffle. Though Ibiza's globally renowned clubs may seem like the obvious place to get a flavour of the local music scene, you'll find that these days a lot of the really creative, Balearic action now happens well away from the clubs in the island's secluded beach bars and funky cafés.

The term "Balearic Beat" was first coined in the mid-to late 1980s by visiting English DJs such as Paul Oakenfold and Danny Rampling, to describe the music played by **Alfredo** – a former Argentinian journalist, and a fugitive from his country's military junta – whose eclectic mixes at *Amnesia* fused Chicago house, Italian club-disco, indie and Europop together with a smattering of James Brown and reggae. Many of the big tunes were extended mixes of Woodentops or Cure records considered to be deeply uncool by London's clubberati and music press, but in Ibiza if it worked then it was used: Fleetwood Mac's *Big Love* and Chris Rea's *Josephine* became Balearic classics, played alongside slamming early house and techno.

The other vital ingredient that precipitated this spirit of open-mindedness, unleashing collective euphoria across Balearic and British dancefloors, was **Ecstasy**, which captured the tribe of young Londoners, who brought tales of the scene back to the UK. An early effort by Paul Oakenfold in 1986 to recreate the Ibizan vibe in London had failed – the capital's dancefloors were polarized into soul, rave groove and indie camps at the time and the Balearic concept of a musical masala proved tricky to translate – but this synchronization of ecstasy and house music blew the roof off clubland. However, though Balearic classics played an important part in the UK clubbing revolution that ensued, it was the ferocious energy of **acid-house** that the UK rave masses really latched on to.

The eclecticism that defined the Balearic Beat is disturbingly rare on the main Ibizan dancefloors today. Alfredo still pursues a diverse, cross-cultural musical direction, even dropping a little UK garage into his devastating sets at *Manumission* and *Space*, and the spirit survives in other isolated corners of Ibizan clubland such as *Pacha*'s Funky Room, but in general, DJs don't tend to diverge from the four-four house beat these days. As many of the biggest club nights are booked by overseas promoters who pay big bucks to import their own DJs, few will take risks or drop the beats-per-minute count. British DJs like John Kelly and Scott Bond have successfully championed the **trance** sound, but after the Brits have all left at the end of the season Ibiza reverts back to what works best in the island: positive (sometimes verging on the fluffy) US garage and uplifting house.

In terms of sheer musical experimentation, today's **chill-out** scene is a much broader church, with DJs adopting a freestyle approach in the best Balearic tradition. When blended by the don of the genre, José Padilla (who pioneered the chillout concept at the *Café del Mar*), Jonathan Grey or Phil Mison, chillout can include ambient moments, British–Asian fusion, Bristolian breakbeats, Jamaican dub, jazzy drum 'n' bass and a slice of flamenco. In the Balearic sunshine, the only common denominator is that the music must share a positive, engaging feel.

All things considered, the Ibizan scene looks healthy today, with musician-cum-producer Lennart Krarup releasing cut after cut of blissful Balearic electronica on his Ibizarre label, Alfredo continuing to champion diverse beats and move feet, José Padilla still coming up with the goods and a battery of other island-based DJ talent (including Andy Wilson, DJ Gee, David Morales, Reche and Java) providing depth and support.

Discography

The select discography below is unashamedly biased towards the chillout side of the Balearic sound, though there are some rave favourites, and some of the very best hard- and deep-house mixes. If you're after a really Balearic flavour, you're best off avoiding almost anything labelled "Ibiza" or "sunset" – tags used by record companies to sell cheesy dance hit compilations or duff sets of downbeat tunes. However, we've listed a few notable exceptions below.

A Man Called Adam, *Duende* (Other). The quintessential Balearic band's second album of sensitive, uplifting songs includes *Estelle*, *Easter Song* and *All My Favourite People*.

Afterlife, *Simplicity Two Thousand* (Hed Kandi). Balearic music of real substance from long-term Ibizaphiles, featuring the mellifluous vocals of Rachel Lloyd. The double-CD pack includes a compendium of mixes from Deep and Wide, Spoon Wizard and Chris Coco.

Basement Jaxx and other artists, *Atlantic Jaxx* (XL). One of the strongest compilations of the last ten years, with an eruptive samba flavour throughout and moments of pure house magic that include plenty of Ibizan anthems. Basement Jaxx's solo album, *Remedy*, is another Balearic-style masterpiece blending samba-house with ragga and even ska.

Primal Scream, *Screamadelica* (Creation). Unequalled indie-dance collaboration, tweaked to perfection by producer Andy Weatherall, which captures the euphoria (and comedown) of the early 1990s and still sounds startlingly fresh and relevant.

Various, *Ambient Ibiza* volumes 1–4 (Ibizarre). Beautiful, cinematic home-grown sounds created by Lennart Krarup, one of the most influential figures in the local scene, plus Ibizan collaborators.

Various, *Back to Love* volumes 1 & 2 (Hed Kandi). All the seminal late 1980s rave anthems, plus some rare groove tunes, all beautiful packaged and presented. Volume one includes Joe Smooth's *Promised Land*, Ten City's *That's The Way Love Is* and Ritchie Havens' *Going Back to My Roots*, while volume two serves up more club classics from Rhythm is Rhythm, Lil Louis and Soul II Soul.

Various, *Back to Mine* (DMC). Fantastically diverse, consistent series with no fillers or duff tracks. All the imaginative mixes – by Nick Warren, Dave Seaman, Danny Tenaglia, Groove Armada and Faithless – are seamlessly blended and fizzle with emotion and atmosphere.

DISCOGRAPHY

Various, *Beach House* (Hed Kandi). Quality deep-house selections from one of the UK's most consistent labels, with full-length versions of classic cuts by Blue Six, Bossa Nostra and Sven van Hees.

Various, *Bora Bora I & II* (React). Propulsive hard-house soundtracks of the best beach fiesta in the island supplied by Ibiza resident DJ Gee.

Various, *Café del Mar* volumes 1–4 (React) & 5–7 (Manifesto). Definitive chillout series, with the first six compiled by ex-resident José Padilla, and the seventh by Bruno Lepretre. All are worthy purchases, but volume two (with heavy ambient atmospherics from Salt Tank and classy flamenco from Paco de Lucía) and volume six (with Talvin Singh, Nitin Sawhney and Kid Loco) are absolutely essential.

Various, *Cam del Mar* (Pagan). Despite the corny title, this is an excellent compilation, put together by Rob da Bank, which concentrates on beatless, dreamy ambient soundscapes.

Various, *Chillout* volumes 1–3 (Avex). Complied by ex-*Muzik*

editor Ben Turner and mixed by former *Café del Mar* resident Phil Mison, these captivating mixed CDs contain a blissful blend of rhythm and melody from the mid-1990s; no fillers, just sublime, emotive electronic music.

Various, *Classic Balearic 1* (Mastercuts). Balearic gems from the rave days from artists including Sueño Latino, Electribe 101, Chris Rea and A Man Called Adam.

Various, *Global Underground* (Boxed). This series of double mix CDs are simply the very finest of their genre. Of the twenty or so pumping hard-house and trance mixes from the world's best DJs, the Paul Oakenfold, Sasha, Dave Seaman and Danny Tenaglia blends are the cream of the crop.

Various, *The House that Trax Built* and *Chicago Trax Volume 1* (Trax). Compilations of the seminal Chicago house tunes of the 1980s (including Adonis's *No Way Back* and Phuture's *Can You Feel It?*) that Alfredo played at *Amnesia*, as well as Marshall Jefferson's *Move Your Body* and

Jamie Principle's *Your Love* and *Baby Wants to Ride*.

Various, *Mixmag* series (DMC). Excellent series; highlights are Dimitri from Paris's *Deluxe House of Funk*, which unleashes a lavish blend of funk-house soaked with Latin and jazzy undertones, and Tom Middleton's *A Jedi Night's Out*, an outstanding melange from ambient to filtered tech-funk.

Various, *Perceptions of Pacha* (Pacha). Terry Farley and Pete Heller have been hugely influential figures since the early days of house music, and this excellent mix reflects the soulful deep-house style they champion.

Various, *Real Ibiza* volumes 1–3 (React). The odd New Age warble notwithstanding, these are solid, good-value compilations in mixed or unmixed format. Volumes two and three are the strongest selections, with key contributions from Ibizarre, Afterlife, Mellow and José Padilla.

Various, *Soundcolours* volumes 1–3 (X-Treme). Three wonderful mixes from Phil Mison, seamlessly blending Latin, funk and house tunes in the best Balearic tradition. The first volume includes a rare Latin house masterpiece by Rey de Copas, and the second the obscure, brilliant Bossa track *Nights over Manaus* by Boozoo Bajau.

Various, *Undiscovered Ibiza 1 & 2* (Pinnacle). Emotional electronic moments selected by Pacha resident DJ Pippi, with cogent tracks from Patrice, Oversoul and Afterlife.

Various, *Warehouse Raves* 1 & 2 (Rumour). The first volume includes a collection of formative Balearic music, with 1988 anthem *Let Me Love You for Tonight* by Kariya and Rhythim is Rhythim's timeless *Strings of Life*. Volume two is another strong offering; highlights include Gil Scott Heron's *The Bottle* and the inspirational *Dreams* by Adonte.

DISCOGRAPHY

Language

U ntil the early 1960s, when there was a mass influx of Castilian Spanish speakers to the islands, **Eivissenc**, the local dialect of **Catalan**, was the main language of the Pitiuses. Catalan had continued to be spoken after the Civil War, despite the efforts of Franco, who banned the language in the media and schools across Catalan-speaking areas of eastern Spain.

However, although Catalan is still the dominant tongue in rural areas and small villages, **Castilian Spanish** is more common in the towns, and because virtually everyone *can* speak it Spanish has become the islands' lingua franca. Only 38 percent of Ibizan residents (a few more in Formentera) now speak Catalan, a situation the government is trying to reverse by pushing through a programme of Catalanization. Most street signs are now in Catalan, and it is soon likely to become the main medium of education in schools and colleges.

English-speaking visitors to Ibiza are usually able to get by without any Spanish or Catalan, as **English** is widely understood, especially in the resorts. In Formentera, the situation is slightly different: many people can speak a little English, but as most of their visitors are German the islanders tend to learn that language, and you may have some communication difficulties from time to time. If you

A FEW CATALAN PHRASES

When pronouncing place names, watch out especially for words with the letter *J* – it's not "Hondal" but "Jondal", as in English. Note also that *X* is almost always a "sh" sound – "Xarraca" is pronounced "sharrarca". The word for a hill, "puig", is a tricky one: it's pronounced "pootch".

Greetings and responses

Hello	*Hola*	Not at all/	*De res*
Goodbye	*Adéu*	You're welcome	
Good morning	*Bon dia*	Do you speak	*Parla*
Good afternoon/	*Bona*	English?	*anglès?*
night	*tarda/nit*	I (don't) speak	*(No) Parlo*
Yes	*Si*	Catalan	*Català*
No	*No*	My name is…	*Em dic…*
OK	*Val*	What's your	*Com es*
Please	*Per favor*	name?	*diu?*
Thank you	*Gràcies*	I am English	*Sóc*
See you later	*Fins*		*anglès(a)*
	després	Scottish	*escocès(a)*
Sorry	*Ho sento*	Australian	*australià/ana*
Excuse me	*Perdoni*	Canadian	*canadenc(a)*
How are you?	*Com va?*	American	*americà/ana*
I (don't)	*(No) Ho*	Irish	*irlandès(a)*
understand	*entenc*	Welsh	*gallès(a)*

If you want to learn more, try *Parla Català* (*Pia*), a good English–Catalan phrasebook, together with either the Collins or Routledge dictionary. For more serious students the excellent *Catalan in Three Months* (Stuart Poole, UK), a combined paperback and tape package, is recommended.

want to make an effort, it's probably best to stick to learning Spanish – and maybe try to pick up a few phrases of Catalan. You'll get a good reception if you at least try to communicate in one of these languages.

Getting by in Spanish

Once you get into it, Spanish is one of the easiest languages there is, with the rules of **pronunciation** pretty straightforward and strictly observed. In Ibiza and Formentera, the lisp-like qualities of mainland Castilian are not at all common – *cerveza* is usually pronounced "servesa", not "thervetha".

Unless there's an accent, words ending in *d*, *l*, *r*, and *z* are **stressed** on the last syllable; all others on the second last. All **vowels** are pure and short; combinations have predictable results.

C is soft before *E* and *I*, hard otherwise.

G works the same way – a guttural *H* sound (like the *ch* in loch) before *E* or *I*, and a hard *G* elsewhere – *gigante* becomes "higante".

H is always silent.

J the same sound as a guttural *G*: *jamón* is pronounced "hamon".

LL sounds like an English *Y*: *tortilla* is pronounced "tor-teeya".

N as in English unless it has a tilde (accent) over it, when it becomes *NY*: *mañana* sounds like "man-yarna".

V sounds a little more like *B*, *vino* becoming "beano".

X has an *S* sound before consonants, and a normal *X* sound before vowels.

Z is the same as *S*.

Phrasebooks, dictionaries and teaching yourself Spanish

Numerous **Spanish phrasebooks** are available, one of the most user-friendly being the *Rough Guide Spanish Phrasebook*. For teaching yourself the language, the BBC tape series *España Viva* is excellent. Cassells, Collins, Harrap and Langenscheidt all produce useful **dictionaries**; Berlitz publishes separate Spanish and Latin-American Spanish phrasebooks.

BASIC SPANISH WORDS AND PHRASES

Basics

Yes	*Sí*	Closed	*Cerrado/a*
No	*No*	With	*Con*
OK	*Vale*	Without	*Sin*
Please	*Por favor*	Good	*Bueno/a*
Thank you	*Gracias*	Bad	*Malo/a*
Where	*Dónde*	Big	*Gran(de)*
When	*Cuando*	Small	*Pequeño/a*
What	*Qué*	Cheap	*Barato/a*
How much	*Cuánto*	Expensive	*Caro/a*
Here	*Aquí*	Hot	*Caliente*
There	*Allí, Allá*	Cold	*Frío/a*
This	*Esto*	More	*Más*
That	*Eso*	Less	*Menos*
Now	*Ahora*	Today	*Hoy*
Then	*Más tarde*	Tomorrow	*Mañana*
Open	*Abierto/a*	Yesterday	*Ayer*

Greetings and responses

Hello	*Hola*	Good morning	*Buenos*
Goodbye	*Adiós*		*días*

Good afternoon/night	*Buenas tardes/noches*
See you later	*Hasta luego*
Sorry	*Lo siento/disculpéme*
Excuse me	*Con permiso/perdón*
How are you?	*¿Cómo está (usted)?*
I (don't) understand	*(No) entiendo*
Not at all/You're welcome	*De nada*
Do you speak English?	*¿Habla (usted) inglés?*
I (don't) speak Spanish/Catalan	*(No) Hablo Español*
My name is…	*Me llamo…*
What's your name?	*¿Como se llama usted?*
I am English	*Soy inglés(a)*
Scottish	*escocés(a)*
Australian	*australiano/a*
Canadian	*canadiense/a*
American	*americano/a*
Irish	*irlandés(a)*
Welsh	*galés(a)*

Hotels and transport

I want	*Quiero*
I'd like	*Quisiera*
Do you know…?	*¿Sabe…?*
I don't know	*No sé*
There is (is there?)	*(¿)Hay(?)*
Give me…	*Deme…*
Do you have…?	*¿Tiene…?*
…the time	*…la hora*
…a room	*…una habitación*
…with two beds/double bed	*…con dos camas/cama matrimonial*
…with shower/bath	*…con ducha/baño*
for one person	*para una persona*
(two people)	*(dos personas)*

for one night (one week)	*para una noche (una semana)*
It's fine, how much is it?	*Está bien, ¿cuánto es?*
It's too expensive	*Es demasiado caro*
Don't you have anything cheaper?	*¿No tiene algo más barato?*
Can one...?	*¿Se puede...?*
...camp (near) here?	*¿...acampar aqui (cerca)?*
It's not very far	*No es muy lejos*
How do I get to...?	*¿Por donde se va a...?*
Left	*Izquierda*
Right	*Derecha*
Straight on	*Todo recto*
Where is...?	*¿Dónde está...?*
...the bus station	*...la estación de autobuses*
...the bus stop	*...la parada*
...the nearest bank	*...el banco más cercano*
...the post office	*...el correo/la oficina de correos*
...the toilet	*...el baño/aseo/servicio*
Where does the bus to... leave from?	*¿De dónde sale el autobús para...?*
I'd like a (return) ticket to...	*Quisiera un billete (de ida y vuelta) para...*
What time does it leave (arrive in...)?	*¿A qué hora sale ? (llega a...)?*
What is there to eat?	*¿Qué hay para comer?*

Days of the week

Monday	*lunes*	Friday	*viernes*
Tuesday	*martes*	Saturday	*sábado*
Wednesday	*miércoles*	Sunday	*domingo*
Thursday	*jueves*		

BASIC SPANISH WORDS AND PHRASES

Numbers

1	*un/uno/una*	17	*diecisiete*
2	*dos*	18	*dieciocho*
3	*tres*	19	*diecinueve*
4	*cuatro*	20	*veinte*
5	*cinco*	30	*treinta*
6	*seis*	40	*cuarenta*
7	*siete*	50	*cincuenta*
8	*ocho*	60	*sesenta*
9	*nueve*	70	*setenta*
10	*diez*	80	*ochenta*
11	*once*	90	*noventa*
12	*doce*	100	*cien(to)*
13	*trece*	200	*doscientos*
14	*catorce*	500	*quinientos*
15	*quince*	1000	*mil*
16	*dieciseis*	2000	*dos mil*

Glossary

Ajuntament Town Hall.

Avinguda (Avgda) Avenue.

Baal Main Carthaginian deity, "the rider of the clouds", associated with the cult of child sacrifice.

Baluard Rampart or bastion.

Cala Cove.

Camí Road.

Campo Countryside.

Can or **C'an** House.

Capella Chapel.

Carrer (c/) Street.

Carreterra Highway.

Casament Ibizan farmhouse.

Castell Castle.

Chiringuito Beach café-bar, which usually serves snacks.

Chupito Shot of liquor.

Churrigueresque Fancifully ornate form of Baroque art named after the Spaniard José Churriguera (1650–1723) and his extended family, its leading exponents.

Correu Post office.

Cova Cave.

Ebusus Roman name for Ibiza Town.

Eivissa Catalan name for Ibiza, and Ibiza Town.

Eivissenc Catalan dialect spoken in the Pitiuses; it's known as "Ibicenco" in Castilian Spanish.

Església Church.

Far Lighthouse.

Finca Farmhouse.

Font Spring, fountain.

Hierbas Locally produced, sweet herb-soaked liqueur.

Ibosim Carthaginian name for Ibiza Town.

Illa Island.

Kiosko Beach bar or café.

Mercat Market.

Mirador Lookout.

Museu Museum.

Parada Bus stop.

Parc Park.

Passeig Avenue.

Plaça Square.

Pitiuses Southern Balearics: Ibiza, Formentera, Espalmador, Espardell, Tagomago and Conillera are the main islands.

Platja Beach.

Pou Well.

Puig Hill.

Punta Point.

Riu River.

Salines Salt pans.

Serra Mountain.

Torre Defence tower.

Torrent Seasonal stream, dried-up river bed.

Urbanización Housing estate.

Yebisah Arabic name for Ibiza.

Books

Historically, not a great deal has been written about Ibiza and Formentera in any language, but in the last decade a steady stream of literature has been published, especially about the club scene, with many more projects – most related to the clubbing scene – in the pipeline.

For all of the books listed here, we've given publishers in both the UK and US, in that order. If only one publisher is listed, or a title is published in Spain only, the country of publication is included. If you have difficulty finding any title, an excellent source for books about Spain – new, used and out of print – is Books on Spain, PO Box 207, Twickenham TW2 5BQ, UK ℡020/8898 7789 ⓦ*www. books-on-spain.com.*

Travel and guides

Hans Losse, *Ibiza and Formentera – A Countryside Guide* (Sunflower, UK). Excellent walkers' handbook, with 23 well-organized hikes, complete with accurate maps; plus cycle routes, picnic suggestions and photographs.

Paul Richardson, *Not Part of the Package – A Year in Ibiza* (Macmillian, UK o/p). By far the best introduction to the island, this is a compelling, witty look at Ibizan rural traditions and

4

history; the author also examines the impact of mass tourism, hippy heritage, club culture and the gay scene through interviews with some of the island's wildest, most influential and charismatic characters.

History, society and politics

Martin Davies and Philippe Derville, *Eivissa–Ibiza: A Hundred Years of Light and Shade* (Ediciones El Faro, Spain). A fascinating, immaculately researched study of twentieth-century Ibizan society and customs, with many rare photographs.

Robert Elms, *Spain* (Heinemann UK o/p). This penetrating look at modern Spain from a respected British journalist and broadcaster includes a chapter on Ibiza. Elms interviews a provocative collection of personalities, including the founders of the *Ku* club (now *Privilege*).

Ian Gibson, *Fire in the Blood – The New Spain* (Faber, UK). An erudite and highly readable portrait of contemporary Spain, this is a critical and passionately enthusiastic look at the country from an Irishman who has been resident in Madrid for over twenty years.

John Hooper, *The New Spaniards* (Penguin UK & US). Solid, but slightly dry, introduction to the country from an ex-*Guardian* correspondent. Worth buying just for his description of the hundred-plus ways of ordering a coffee.

Emily Kaufman, *A History Buff's Guide to Ibiza* (Tarita, Spain). An incisive, humorous and comprehensive summary of Ibizan history until the Catalan conquest, written by an *Ibiza Now* contributor and island resident.

Music and club culture

Wayne Anthony, *Class of 88 – The True Acid House Experience* (Virgin, UK). A rollercoaster tale of the rave years, written by the larger-than-life ex-Genesis and *Havin It* promoter.

Sean Bidder, *House Music* (Rough Guides UK & US). Definitive guide to the four-four rhythm, presented in mini-encyclopedic format.

Bill Brewster and Frank Broughton, *Last Night a DJ Saved My Life – The History of the Disk Jockey* (Headline, UK/Grove, US). Superb historical study, from the emergence of the DJ as a radio broadcaster in the early twentieth century to today's stadium-filling global superstars. Convincing accounts of the northern soul, disco and dancehall days and the importance of artists King Tubby, Larry Levan and Frankie Knuckles.

Jane Bussmann, *Once in a Lifetime* (Virgin, UK). Hilarious cut 'n'paste compilation of artwork, anecdotes and all-round tales of mental-mental mayhem from the rave years, with substantial Ibiza content.

Matthew Collin, *Altered State – The Story of Ecstasy Culture and Acid House* (Serpent's Tail, UK). A conclusive account of British club culture and all its mutant derivatives, including hardcore, jungle and the free party scene, with a brief description of the Ibiza clubbing scene of the late 80s.

Sheryl Garratt, *Adventures in Wonderland* (Headline, UK). Candid tale of party adventures and clubland history from the ex-editor of *The Face*, this is an insider's guide to the British acid-house revolution, from its Chicago and Ibizan roots.

William Shaw, *Losing It* (Bloomsbury, UK). Erudite account of the roots of the acid-house revolution and its emergence from the 1987 Ibiza club scene. The tale is recounted through interviews with all the major players and the young clubbers who couldn't leave the island.

Ben Turner, et al *Ibiza – Inspired Images from the Island of Dance* (Ebury Press UK & US). Lusciously illustrated coffee-table digest of the British–Ibizan clubbing experience, compiled by ex-*Muzik* magazine editor. Most of the writing is straight out of the "Ibiza is magic" school, but there are some

MUSIC AND CLUB CULTURE

provocative contributions from Colin Butts (see p.324) and Dave Fowler.

Wildlife and the environment

Hans Giffhorn, *Ibiza – An Undiscovered Paradise of Nature* (RGG, Germany). Limited, but fairly well-illustrated, publication dealing with the Ibizan environment, landscapes, flora and fauna, with a strong section on the island's wild flowers. The walk descriptions, however, are a bit vague and not terribly useful.

Joan Mayol, *Birds of the Balearic Islands* (Editorial Moll Mallorca, Spain). Reasonable, but far from comprehensive, introduction to the region's feathered fauna.

Miscellaneous

Wayne Anthony, *Spanish Highs – Sex, Drugs and Excess in Ibiza* (Virgin, UK). Anthony recounts his personal Ibizan highs and lows: industrial-scale drug consumption, cocaine psychosis, season-long benders and professional ducking and diving.

Colin Butts, *Is Harry on the Boat?* (Orion, UK/Trafalgar Square, US). Set in Sant Antoni, written by a former *2wenties* rep and currently being made into a sitcom, this blows the lid on the many faces of the holiday rep world: lewd sexual adventures, money scams and frauds, infighting and general all-round mayhem.

Elliot Paul, *Life and Death in a Spanish Town* (Greenwood UK & US). Sympathetic portrayal of Santa Eulària's transformation from an Eden-esque fishing village to troubled town plagued by the terror, murder and starvation of the Civil War.

Various, *The Cooking of Ibiza and Formentera* (Editorial Mediterrània Eivissa, Spain). Widely available in Ibizan book stores, this book has chapters on the historical influence on the cooking of the Pitiuses, the main ingredients and plenty of recipes.

INDEX

ROUGH GUIDES: Travel

ROUGH GUIDES: Mini Guides, Travel Specials and Phrasebooks

Miami
& the Florida Keys

MINI GUIDES
Antigua
Bangkok
Barbados
Big Island of Hawaii
Boston
Brussels
Budapest
Dublin
Edinburgh
Florence
Honolulu
Lisbon
London Restaurants
Madrid
Maui
Melbourne
New Orleans
St Lucia

Seattle
Sydney
Tokyo
Toronto

First-Time
Asia

TRAVEL SPECIALS
First-Time Asia
First-Time Europe
More Women Travel

PHRASEBOOKS
Czech
Dutch
Egyptian Arabic
European
French

German
Greek
Hindi & Urdu
Hungarian
Indonesian
Italian
Japanese
Mandarin
  Chinese
Mexican
  Spanish
Polish
Portuguese
Russian
Spanish
Swahili
Thai
Turkish
Vietnamese

Vietnamese

AVAILABLE AT ALL GOOD BOOKSHOPS

ROUGH GUIDES:
Reference and Music CDs

REFERENCE
Classical Music
Classical:
   100 Essential CDs
Drum'n'bass
House Music

World Music:
   100 Essential CDs
English Football
European Football
Internet
Millennium

Tango

World Music

Latin and North America, Caribbean,
India, Asia and Pacific

2

Jazz
Music USA
Opera
Opera:
   100 Essential CDs
Reggae
Rock
Rock:
   100 Essential CDs
Techno
World Music

ROUGH GUIDE
   MUSIC CDs
Music of the Andes
Australian
   Aboriginal
Brazilian Music
Cajun & Zydeco
Classic Jazz
Music of Colombia
Cuban Music
Eastern Europe
Music of Egypt
English Roots
   Music
Flamenco
India & Pakistan
Irish Music
Music of Japan
Kenya & Tanzania
Native American
North African
Music of Portugal

Reggae
Salsa
Scottish Music
South African
   Music
Music of Spain
Tango
Tex-Mex
West African Music
World Music
World Music Vol 2
Music of Zimbabwe

The Internet

AVAILABLE AT ALL GOOD BOOKSHOPS

Sorted

100
Essential
CDs

Eight titles,
one name

ROUGH
GUIDES

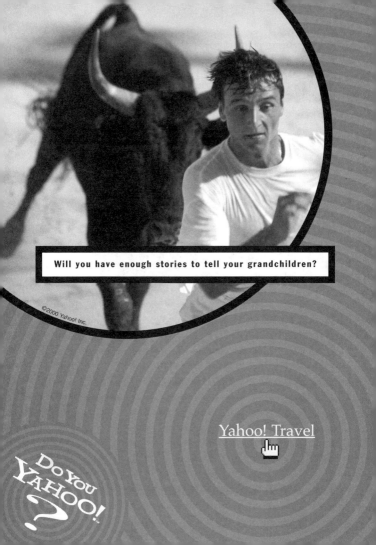

Will you have enough stories to tell your grandchildren?

©2000 Yahoo! Inc.

Yahoo! Travel

Do You
YAHOO!
?

Rough Guides
on the Web

www.travel.roughguides.com

We keep getting bigger and better! The Rough Guide to Travel Online
now covers more than 14,000 searchable locations. You're just a click
away from access to the most in-depth travel content, weekly
destination features, online reservation services, and an outspoken
community of fellow travelers. Whether you're looking for ideas for
your next holiday or you know exactly where you're going, join us online.

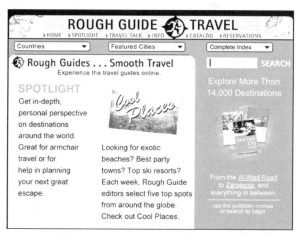

You can also find us on Yahoo!® Travel (http://travel.yahoo.com) and
Microsoft Expedia® UK (http://www.expediauk.com).

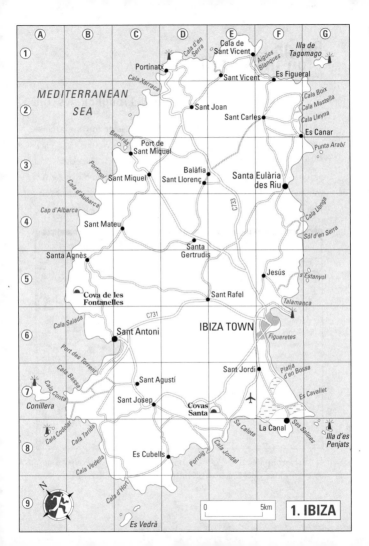

1. IBIZA

MEDITERRANEAN SEA

Illa de Tagomago

Cala d'en Serra
Cala de Sant Vicent
Aigües Blanques
Portinatx
Sant Vicent
Es Figueral
Cala Xarraca
Cala Boix
Cala Mastella
Cala Lleyna
Sant Joan
Sant Carles
Es Canar
Punta Arabí
Benirràs
Port de Sant Miquel
Portitxol
Sant Miquel
Balàfia
Sant Llorenç
Santa Eulària des Riu
Cala d'Aubarca
Cap d'Albarca
C733
Cala Llonga
Sant Mateu
Sòl d'en Serra
Santa Gertrudis
Santa Agnès
Jesús
s'Estanyol
Cova de les Fontanelles
Sant Rafel
Talamanca
Cala Salada
C731
IBIZA TOWN
Figueretes
Sant Antoni
Port des Torrent
Cala Bassa
Sant Agustí
Sant Jordi
Platja d'en Bossa
Conillera
Cala Conta
Sant Josep
Es Cavallet
Cala Codolar
Covas Santa
La Canal
Ses Salines
Illa d'es Penjats
Cala Tarida
Sa Caleta
Cala Vedella
Es Cubells
Porroig
Cala Jondal

N

Cala d'Hort

Es Vedrà

0   5km

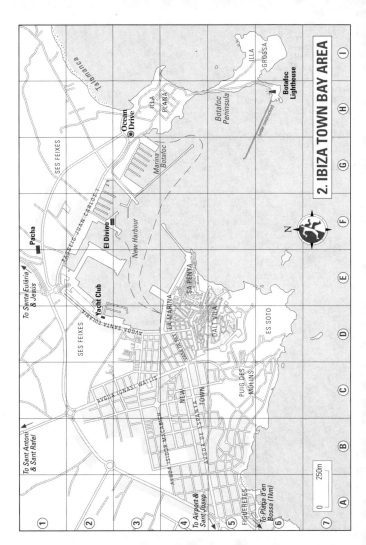

2. IBIZA TOWN BAY AREA

ISLA GROSSA

Botafoc Lighthouse

Botafoc Peninsula

ILLA PLANA

Ocean Drive

Talamanca

SES FEIXES

Marina Botafoc

New Harbour

PASSEIG JUAN CARLOS I

El Divino

Pacha

To Santa Eulària & Jesús

Yacht Club

AVGDA SANTA EULÀRIA

SES FEIXES

N

LA MARINA

SA PENYA

DALT VILA

ES SOTO

AVGDA IGNASI WALLIS

NEW TOWN

CARRER DE SES LLEVES

AVGDA ISIDOR MACABICH

AVGDA D'ESPANYA

PUIG DES MOLINS

To Sant Antoni & Sant Rafel

To Airport & Sant Josep

FIGUERETES

To Platja d'en Bossa (1km)

250m

0

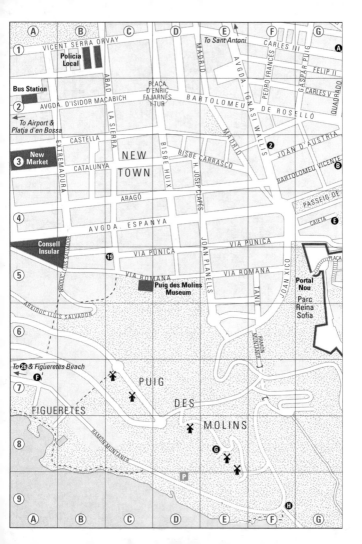

3. IBIZA TOWN

To Talamanca,
Jesús &
Santa Eulària

Formentera
terminal

0   100m

Dirt road

N

JOSEP MARIA

ANTONI JAUME

AVGDA SANTA EULARIA

Fisherman
Statue

Boat to
Plata d'en Bossa

Boats to
Talamanca &
El Divino

Estació
Marítima

RAMÓN

PASSEIG MARÍTIM

LLUÍS TUR I PALAU

Obelisk

VARA DE REY

AVGDA RAMON TUR

RIAMBAU

BISBE CARDONA

BISBE TORRES

COMTE ROSELLÓ

AZARA

ANNIBAL

CASTELAR

DE LA VIRGE

DE MONTGRÍ

ABEL
MATUTES

PERE SALA

PLAÇA
DES PARC

PLAÇA
ANTONI PALAU

LA MARINA

Església de
Sant Elm

PLAÇA DE LA
CONSTITUCIÓ

PLAÇA DE
SA FONT

PLAÇA
ANTONI
RIQUER

D'ENMIG
DE LA VERGE

Ferries to
Palma &
mainland

PASSEIG MARÍTIM

GARIJO

BARCELONA

FAÍLDA TUR

VIRGE

SA PENYA

FOSC

DEL RETIR

VISTA ALEGRE

PEDRERA

PLAÇA
DE SA RIBA

ES MURO

Sa Torre

ALADERN

SANTA CREU

PLAÇA
DE VILA

Porta de
ses Taules

Fish
Market

BISBE TORRES

MANUEL SORA

PIKON DE SA ROVA

DE LA SOC

SOL

SANT LLUIS

SANT JOSEP

SANT CARLES

CONQUISTA

JOAN ROMAN

PERE TUR

SAGRADA FAMILIA

SANT SALVADOR

GEN. BALANSAT

SANTA MARIA

DALT VILA

SANT CIRIAC

MAJOR

PONENT

PLAÇA DE
LA CATEDRAL

PLAÇA DE
ESPANYA

ES SOTO

P

BARS & CAFÉS
Angelo	23
Bar Zuka	20
Base Bar	14
Sa Botiga	2
Bulldog	1
Can Pou Bar	3
Capricho	17
Chill	19
Croissant Show	12
Dôme	23
GC	15
Monroe's	26
Montesol	16
Nación Tierra	16
Noctámbula	11
Rock Bar	13
Teatro Pereira	7
La Tierra	6

ACCOMMODATION
Hostal Bimbi	F
Hostal Mar Blau	G
Hostal La Marina	C
Hostal Parque	E
Hotel Apartamentos El Puerto	A
Apartamentos Roselló	H
Sol y Brisa	B
Casa de Huéspedes Vara de Rey	D

RESTAURANTS
El Bistro	24
La Brasa	10
Macao	21
La Muralla	25
Pasajeros	8
El Pirata	9
Sake Bar	22
Sa Torreta	18
Restaurant Victoria	5

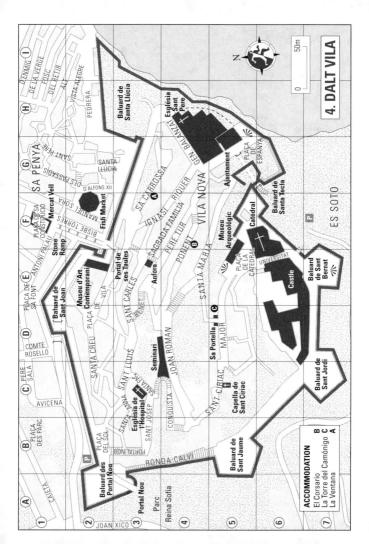

4. DALT VILA

N

0   50m

ACCOMMODATION
El Corsario   B
La Torre del Camónigo   C
La Ventana   A

Baluard de Santa Llúcia
Església Sant Pere
Plaça de Espanya
Ajuntament
Baluard de Santa Tecla
Catedral
ES SOTO
P
Museu Arqueològic
Castle
Baluard de Sant Bernat
UNIVERSITAT
PLAÇA DE LA CATEDRAL
Baluard de Sant Jordi
VILA NOVA
GEN BALANZAT
SANTA MARIA
PONENT
PERE TUR
SAGRADA FAMILIA
RIQUER
IGNASI
SA CARROSSA
Sa Portella
MAJOR
Capella de Sant Ciriac
SANT CIRIAC
JOAN ROMAN
CONQUISTA
Baluard de Sant Jaume
RONDA CALVI
Parc
Reina Sofía
Portal Nou
P
PLAÇA DEL SOL
PORTAL NOU
Baluard des Portal Nou
SANTA ANNA
SANT JOSEP
Església de l'Hospital
SANTA
SANT LLUIS
SANTA CREU
Seminari
SA CREU
PLAÇA DE VILA
Portal de ses Taules
Museu d'Art Contemporani
Baluard de Sant Joan
Stone Ramp
Mercat Vell
Fish Market
SANTA LLUCIA
SA PENYA
DES PASSADIS
D'ALFONS XII
MANUEL SORA
BISBE TORRES
PLAÇA SA CONSTITUCIÓ
ANTONI PALAU
PLAÇA DE SA FONT
COMTE ROSELLÓ
PERE SALA
AVICENA
PLAÇA DES PARC
CAIETA
JOAN XICO
DENMIG
DE LA VERGE
FOSC
DEL RETIR
ALT
VISTA-ALEGRE
PEDRERA
SANT PERE
Amfora
BENET

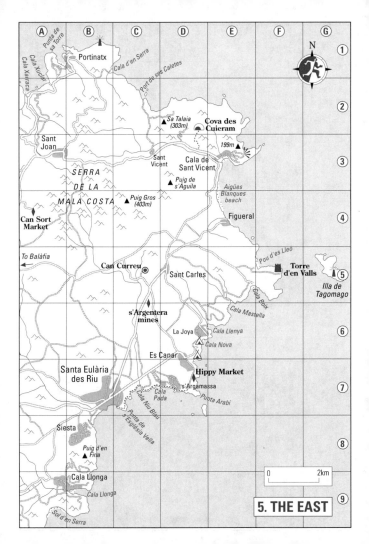

5. THE EAST

	A	B	C	D	E	F	G	

Punt de sa Torre

Cala Xuclar

Cala Xarraca

Portinatx

Cala d'en Serra

Port de ses Caletes

N

Sant Joan

SERRA

Sa Talaia
(303m)

DE LA

Cova des Cuieram

199m

MALA COSTA

Sant Vicent

Cala de Sant Vicent

Puig de s'Àguila

Aigües Blanques beach

Can Sort Market

Puig Gros
(403m)

Figueral

To Balàfia

Can Curreu

Sant Carles

Pou d'es Lleó

Torre d'en Valls

Illa de Tagomago

Cala Boix

s'Argentera mines

Cala Mastella

La Joya

Cala Llenya

Cala Nova

Es Canar

Santa Eulària des Riu

Hippy Market

s'Argamassa

Cala Pada

Punta Arabí

Cala Niu Blau

Punta de s'Església Vella

Siesta

Puig d'en Fita

Cala Llonga

Cala Llonga

Sol d'en Serra

0 — 2km

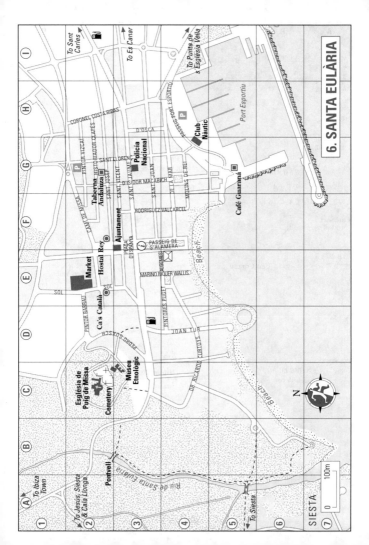

6. SANTA EULÀRIA

To Sant Carles

To Es Canar

To Punta de s'Església Vella

COLONEL COSTA RIBAS

D'OSCA

HISTORIADOR CLAPES

PINTOR VIZCAI

CAMI DE MISSA

Taberna Andaluza

SANT LLORENC

SANT VICENT

SANT JAUME

Policía Nacional

S. ISIDOR MACABICH

Club Nàutic

SANT JUAN

SANTA BICH

DE LA MAR

MOLINS DE REI

PASSEIG PORT ESPORTIU

Port Esportiu

RODRIGUEZ VALCARCEL

Ajuntament

Market

Hostal Rey

Ca's Català

PINTOR BARRAU

SOL

PASSEIG DE S'ALAMERA

PADAL DE SPANYA

Café Guaraná

Beach

MARINO RIQUER WALLIS

PINTORES PUIGET

JOAN TUR

DE RICARDO CURTOIS

PEDRO GUASCH

Església de Puig de Missa

Museu Etnològic

Cemetery

Beach

To Ibiza Town

To Jesús, Siesta & Cala Llonga

Riu de Santa Eulària

Pontvell

To Siesta

SIESTA

N

0   100m

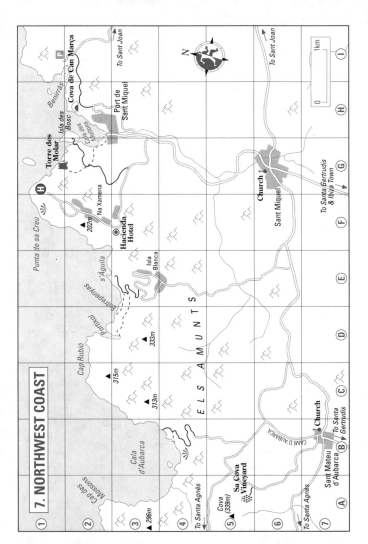

7. NORTHWEST COAST

Cap des Mossons

Cala d'Aubarca

296m

315m

313m

333m

Cap Rubió

Porthol

Balt'enyes

s'Águila

Punta de sa Creu

202m

Na Xamena

Hacienda Hotel

Isla Blanca

ELS AMUNTS

Torre des Molar

Isla des Bosc

Cala des Matons

Benirràs

Cova de Can Marçà

Port de Sant Miquel

To Sant Joan

To Sant Joan

Sant Miquel

Church †

To Santa Gertrudis & Ibiza Town

To Santa Agnès

Cova (339m)

Sa Cova Vineyard

Sant Mateu d'Aubarca

CAMI D'AUBARCA

Church †

To Santa Gertrudis

To Santa Agnès

N

0   1km

① ② ③ ④ ⑤ ⑥ ⑦

Ⓐ Ⓑ Ⓒ Ⓓ Ⓔ Ⓕ Ⓖ Ⓗ Ⓘ

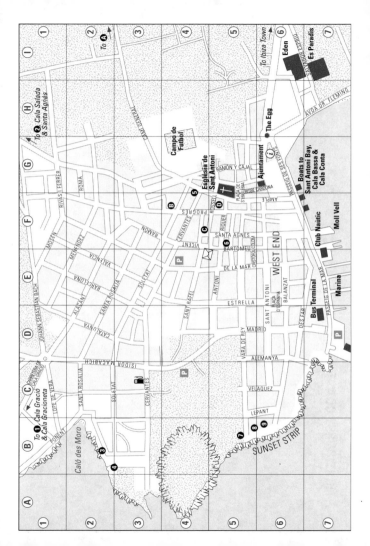

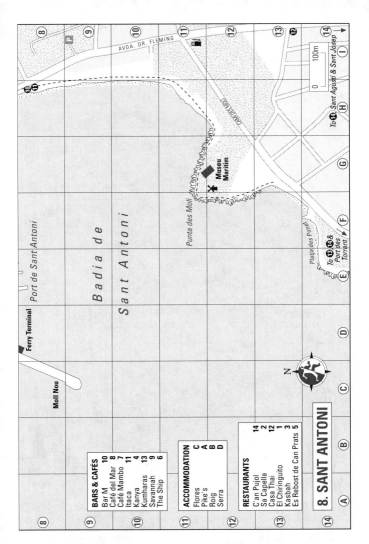

8. SANT ANTONI

BARS & CAFÉS
Bar M	10
Café del Mar	8
Café Mambo	7
Itaca	11
Kanya	4
Kumharas	13
Savannah	9
The Ship	6

ACCOMMODATION
Flores	C
Pike's	A
Roig	B
Serra	D

RESTAURANTS
C'an Pujol	14
Sa Capella	2
Casa Thai	12
El Chiringuito	1
Kasbah	3
Es Rebost de Can Prats	5

Ferry Terminal

Moll Nou

Port de Sant Antoni

Badia de Sant Antoni

AVDA. DR. FLEMING

Punta des Molí

Museu Marítim

Camí des Molí

To Sant Agustí & Sant Josep

To Port des Torrent

Platja des Pouet

0   100m

N

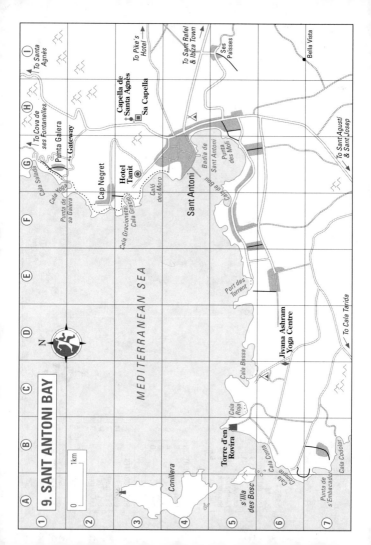

9. SANT ANTONI BAY

MEDITERRANEAN SEA

0   1km

N

To Santa Agnés

To Cova de ses Fontanelles

To Pike's Hotel

To Sant Rafel & Ibiza Town

Ses Paísses

Bella Vista

Capella de Santa Agnés
Sa Capella

Punta Galera
Gateway

Cala Salada
Cala Yoga
Punta de sa Galera

Cap Negret

Hotel Tanit

Cala Gracioneta
Cala Gració
Caló des Moro

Badia de Sant Antoni
Punta des Molí

Sant Antoni

Cala de Bou

To Sant Agustí & Sant Josep

Port des Torrent

Cala Bassa

Jivana Ashram Yoga Centre

To Cala Tarida

Cala Roja

Torre d'en Rovira

Cala Conta

Cala Comte

s'Illa des Bosc

Conillera

Punta de s'Embarcador

Cala Codolar

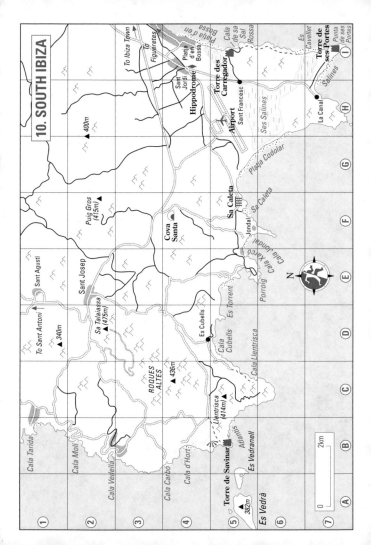

10. SOUTH IBIZA

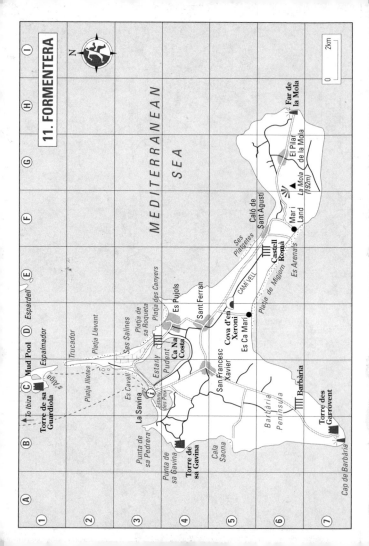

11. FORMENTERA

MEDITERRANEAN SEA

0 — 2km

A B C D E F G H I

1 2 3 4 5 6 7

To Ibiza
Torre de sa Guardiola
Mud Pool
Espardell
Espalmador
S'Alga
Trucador
Platja Illetes
Platja Llevant
Ses Salines
Platja de sa Roqueta
Platja des Canyers
Punta de sa Pedrera
Es Cavall
Estany Pudent
Ca Na Costa
Es Pujols
Sant Ferran
Ses Platgetes
Caló de Sant Agustí
Mar i Land
El Pilar de la Mola
Far de la Mola
Punta de sa Gavina
La Savina
Estany des Peix
San Francesc Xavier
Cova d'en Xeroni
Es Ca Marí
Platja de Migorn
CAMI VELL
Castell Romà
Es Arenals
La Mola (192m)
Torre de sa Gavina
Cala Saona
Barbària Peninsula
Barbària
Torre des Garrovent
Cap de Barbària